A Thief of Peirce

A Thief of Peirce

The Letters
of Kenneth Laine Ketner
and Walker Percy

Edited by Patrick H. Samway, S.J.

University Press of Mississippi   *Jackson*

"Hartshorne and the Basis of Peirce's Categories," by Kenneth Laine Ketner, in *Hartshorne, Process Philosophy, and Theology*, edited by Robert Kane and Stephen H. Phillips (Albany: State University of New York Press, 1989), pp. 135–49.

"Novel Science; or, How contemporary social science is not well and why literature and semeiotic provide a cure," by Kenneth Laine Ketner, in *Semiotica*, 93 (1993), pp. 33–59.

"Peirce's 'Most Lucid and Interesting Paper': An Introduction to Cenopythagoreanism," by Kenneth Laine Ketner, in *International Philosophical Quarterly*, 26 (December 1986), pp. 375–92.

"Pragmaticism is an Existentialism?" by Kenneth Laine Ketner, in *Frontiers in American Philosophy* (Volume 2), edited by Robert W. Burch (College Station: Texas A & M University Press, forthcoming in 1996).

"The Importance of Religion for Peirce," by Kenneth Laine Ketner, in *Gedankenzeichen: Festschrift für Klaus Oehler*, edited by Regina Claussen and Roland Daube-Schackat (Tübingen: Stauffenburg Verlag, 1988), pp. 267–71.

"Toward an Understanding of Peirce's Master Argument," by Kenneth Laine Ketner, in *Cruzeiro Semiotico* (Lisbon, Portugal), 8 (Janeiro 1988), pp. 57–66.

"Who Was Charles Sanders Peirce? And Does He Deserve Our Homage?" by Kenneth Laine Ketner, in *Krisis*, 1 (Summer 1983), pp. 10–18.

Library of Congress Cataloging-in-Publication Data

Ketner, Kenneth Laine.
    A thief of Peirce : the letters of Kenneth Laine Ketner and Walker
Percy / edited by Patrick H. Samway, S.J.
        p. cm.
    Includes bibliographical references and index.
    ISBN 0-87805-810-9 (cloth : alk. paper)
    1. Peirce, Charles S. (Charles Sanders), 1839–1914—Contributions
in semiotics. 2. Semiotics. 3. Ketner, Kenneth Laine—
Correspondence. 4. Percy, Walker, 1916- —Correspondence.
I. Percy, Walker, 1916- . II. Samway, Patrick H. III. Title.
P85.P38K47 1995
121'.68—dc20
                                                            95-14835
                                                            CIP

British Library Cataloging-in-Publication data available

To
Mrs. Mary Bernice Percy
Berti and Kenny Ketner
Ben and Nadine Forkner

Contents

Introduction

The correspondence between Kenneth Laine Ketner, the Charles Sanders Peirce Professor at Texas Tech University in Lubbock and a recognized scholar in the field of Peirce studies, and Walker Percy, author of six novels, three books of non-fiction, and winner of the 1962 National Book Award for *The Moviegoer*, has its origins in a modest fan letter. In February 1984, Ketner sent Percy a short note indicating his admiration for Percy's writings; he included a packet of essays he had written on various aspects of Peircean semiotic ("semeiotic" was the spelling that Peirce used, though "semiotic" is commonly used by Peirce scholars today). From there the correspondence grew gradually over the years, as Percy explained to Ketner his interest in semiotic, and Ketner, in turn, shared with Percy his insights into the labyrinthine world of Peirce's thought. As the bibliography and second appendix to this volume indicate, Ketner has long been engaged in interpreting Peirce's works, as well as editing Peirce's manuscripts and typescripts, including *Reasoning and the Logic of Things* (Harvard University Press, 1992), Peirce's Cambridge Conferences Lectures of 1898. Above all, Ketner wanted to provide Percy with sufficient information about Peirce's philosophy so that Percy could continue to proceed constructively with his criticism of the medical-scientific community and his interpretation of its agenda by focusing primarily on the Peircean concepts of the irreducibility of triadic relations to dyadic relations and the ontological status of the interpretant. Before long, as the letters flowed back and forth, each considered the other an epistolary friend.

One compliment that Ketner paid to Percy was most appreciated:

Ketner called Percy a "Cenophythagorean," that is, a new American Pythagoreas who, in this case, attempts to make a breakthrough in uniting philosophy, literature, and semiotic. In fact, *Percy as Cenophythagorean* could well have been used as the title of this volume of letters. Instead *A Thief of Peirce* was chosen since it reflects Percy's own stance vis-à-vis Peirce, as expressed in his letter to Ketner, dated February 27, 1989: "As you well know, I am not a student of Peirce. I am a thief of Peirce. I take from him what I want and let the rest go—most of it. I am only interested in CSP [Charles Sanders Peirce] insofar as I understand his attack on nominalism and his rehabilitation of Scholastic realism." Though Percy articulated his agenda concisely in these few sentences, he failed to mention the 30-plus years he spent reading in and out of Peirce's works, a passion (the word is used without exaggeration) that culminated in the 18th Annual Jefferson Lecture, entitled "The Fateful Rift: The San Andreas Fault in the Modern Mind," delivered at the invitation of the National Endowment for the Humanities in Washington, D.C., on May 3, 1989. An important unpublished draft of that lecture, critiqued by Professor Ketner, is included in this volume.

Percy's interest in Peirce can be traced back in all probability to the period just after his honeymoon in 1947, when he and his wife Mary Bernice ("Bunt") moved from Tennessee to a small rented house on Calhoun Street in New Orleans that was owned by Julius Friend, one of the editors of *The Double-Dealer*, a noted New Orleans literary journal published from January 1921 to May 1926. Over the years, Friend collected many books, not a few of which had been sent to the journal for review; these books remained in the house when the Percys arrived. Friend gave the Percys an inscribed copy ("To Bunt and Walker Percy, my friends, Julius Friend") of a 1936 book entitled *The Unlimited Community: A Study of the Possibility of Social Science* that he had written with James K. Feibleman, as well as two other books by himself and Feibleman: *Science and the Spirit of Man: A New Ordering of Experience* (1933) and *What Science Really Means* (1937), the latter a book that Percy referred to in his essays "Culture: The Antinomy of the Scientific Method" and "Semiotic and a Theory of Knowledge." In reading through *The Unlimited Community*, Percy would have discovered, if he had not done so before, the name of Peirce:

The first break with the nominalistic tradition came definitely with the work of Charles Sanders Peirce. It is difficult to believe that Peirce is the first man thoroughly to understand that scientific method involves science in a realism and not in a nominalism. He succeeded in reconciling medieval realism with scientific empiricism. He saw that the modern European philosophy from Descartes onward has consisted almost entirely in drawing inferences from the basically false nominalistic postulate. The low estate into which the study of logic had fallen because of this disparagement of reason seemed to him the great crime of philosophy, and he pointed out that the development of logic alone, and not the development of psychology, was the key to the understanding of anything. But Peirce was a lone voice in the howling wilderness of late nineteenth-century irrationalism; he was not appreciated during his lifetime, and has hardly been properly recognized since. The full consequences of his thinking have not had their effect on philosophy.

Percy was not alone in picking up the challenge contained in the last sentence of this paragraph. And if he needed any further information about the philosophical thought of Peirce, he had only to consult Feibleman's book, *An Introduction to Peirce's Philosophy, Interpreted as a System* (1946). The exposure to the thought of Friend and Feibleman most likely helped Percy, particularly as a beginning novelist, to compare further the thought of American philosophers with that of their European counterparts.

Feibleman was perhaps the one person in New Orleans at that time who involved himself professionally and publicly in the relationship between philosophy and literature. In 1947, Feibleman chaired the Philosophy Department at Tulane University and was an officer of the Charles Peirce Society. His discussion of literature as expressed in "The Decline of Literary Chaos" in the October–December 1946 issue of *The Sewanee Review* explains how an artist is apt to deal with the interplay of certain philosophical ideas, specifically uniformity, regularity, law, and system, while not excluding chaos, spontaneity, abundance, variety, contradiction, chance, and repetition. An artist, in Feibleman's mind, can show, as a scientist often does, the order that exists in apparently confused and chaotic existence. Though Percy never had a formal course in philosophy, he sought out people who could engage him intellectually. Feibleman, on the other hand, was not a disinterested philosopher looking over the fence at the literary world; much more in tune with fiction than other philosophers of his day (and an admirer of William Alexander Percy's poetry), he eventually married Shirley Ann Grau, the New Orleanian novelist.

While working on an unpublished novel entitled *The Gramercy Winner*, Percy wrote a review of Susanne Langer's *Feeling and Form* (1953), entitled "Symbol as Need," for the autumn 1954 issue of *Thought*. To prepare for this essay, Percy read Langer's earlier *Philosophy in a New Key* and traced the progress of her thought from her first book to the second, noting that Langer's new key in philosophy "is the universal symbolic function of the human mind." Writing with critical vigor and energy, Percy found in Langer the philosophical companion he had been seeking for a long time: "*Feeling and Form* is written with all the power and contagious excitement of a first-class mind exercising a valuable new insight. In brief, it is an application to art of a general thesis that the peculiarly human response is that of symbolic transformation. The communication of meaning, positivists to the contrary, is not limited to the discursive symbol, word and proposition; the art symbol conveys its own appropriate meaning, a meaning inaccessible to the discursive form." Percy was most attracted to the notion that each art form symbolizes not a series of abstract thoughts but the felt life of the artist, though he was somewhat surprised Langer did not validate her thesis by citing either Jacques Maritain's *Art and Scholasticism* or *Creative Intuition in Art and Poetry*, or, for that matter, St. Thomas Aquinas himself. In all likelihood, Percy would have been pleased that Langer mentioned Charles Sanders Peirce in passing and Ernst Cassirer in more detail. This essay proved to be the "open sesame" for Percy into the academic world of semiotic.

As explained by Professor Ketner in one of the essays in the second appendix to this volume, Peirce did not lead the life of a typical scholar of his day. Born on September 10, 1839, in Cambridge, Massachusetts, to Sarah and Benjamin Peirce, young Charles grew up in an academic household; his father was professor of mathematics and astronomy at Harvard. After graduating from Harvard in 1859, Charles worked for the U.S. Coast Survey in Cambridge, Maine, Washington, D.C., and Louisiana, an employment secured with the help of his father, who also served as the Survey's consulting geometer. Charles's early achievements were not without considerable merit; as a 25-year-old scholar, he gave the Lowell Lectures at Harvard, and later, during 1867, his work at the Harvard Observatory culminated in *Photometric Researches*, a pioneering treatise that mapped the Milky Way. In April 1872, Benjamin Peirce, now superintendent of the Survey, appointed Charles acting assistant in charge of pendulum experiments (gravimetry) for the Survey. After resigning his assistantship at the Harvard Observatory, Charles, accompanied by his wife Harriet Melusina ("Zina"), moved to the nation's capital, where he spent most of his time researching geodesy and gravimetrics. Unfortunately, three years later, as Zina and Charles traveled to Europe, they were experiencing serious marital difficulties, and not long after that Zina decided to leave her husband. For Charles, it was a low point in his life, even though he was a candidate both for the directorship of the Harvard Observatory and a professorship in logic at Johns Hopkins University in Baltimore, Maryland.

When Charles returned to Cambridge, his professional activities were hampered at every turn by President Charles Eliot of Harvard. During this time, Charles began seeing the mysterious Juliette, known also as Madame Pourtalai or Madame Froissy, who eventually became his wife in April 1883. Beginning with the academic year 1879–80, Charles taught for five years at Johns Hopkins as a lecturer in logic; he was dismissed from his university post because of his romantic involvement with Juliette prior to their marriage. In April 1887, Charles and Juliette moved to Milford, Pennsylvania, where Charles spent most of his time reading and writing philosophy, living off an inheritance from his mother. A year later, President Grover Cleveland appointed Peirce to the Assay Commission, though Peirce continued working for the Coast Survey until his forced resignation in 1891, which brought to an end a valuable association of more than 30 years that had earned him an international reputation in science.

From then on, until his death in 1914, Peirce never found the financial stability nor the intellectual environment he desired, and he often experienced great poverty and deprivation. In his latter years, he wrote reviews for *The Nation* to support himself and Juliette and became involved, at one point, in an ill-fated venture to produce a hydroelectric plant near Massena, New York. Yet, his legacy to the world of philosophy was enormous and can best be summarized in his own words: "[I intend] to make a philosophy like that of Aristotle, that is to say, to outline a theory so comprehensive that, for a long time to come, the entire work of human reason, in philosophy of every school and kind, in mathematics, in psychology, in physical science, in history, in sociology, and in whatever other department there may be, shall appear as the filling up of its details." For Percy, as he explains in an unpublished essay, "Peirce and Modern Semiotic," housed in the Southern Historical Collection at the University of North Carolina at Chapel Hill, it is only by returning to the logic of Peirce's philosophy that one can counterbalance the confusion caused by those modern semioticians who unite symbol and signal behavior through the univocal application of a stimulus-response language.

The introductory note to Percy's essay, "Semiotic and a Theory of Knowledge," published in the May 1957 issue of *The Modern Schoolman*, mentions that Percy intended to publish a book on semiotic to be called *Symbol and Existence: A Study in Meaning*. This essay reveals an amazing amount of erudition about semiotic on Percy's part. Among the authors cited by Percy is Peirce, whose "Logic as Semiotic: The Theory of Signs" and essays from the seventh volume of his *Collected Papers* had proved most helpful. Philosophers of science, this essay begins, normally think that any particular science creates greater syntheses and unanimity of thought, but they will find just the opposite—"an inveterate division of subject matters." Aware of the history of semiotic and certain schools of philosophy, Percy did not want to engage in a negative analysis of logical positivism or behaviorism, but instead try to show that a "true 'semiotic' " might prove to be vastly important for metaphysics. In particular, he diagrammed a Peircean view of the relationships among a sign, object (or *designatum*), and interpretant in an interpreter. In doing so, he pointed to the Cartesian notions of *res extensa* and *res cogitans*, a dichotomy that became increasingly important to him because he felt that a connection between the two polarities was missing, that is, an analysis of denotation and the mysterious process of naming. Percy believed that a creative writer's task is to select names and words so accurately that they go beyond evoking a dramatic sense of probability to re-presenting the real.

Percy's interest in semiotic, however, was based not just on the reading he had done, but on the felt difficulties he was having in his own living room, kitchen, and backyard with his deaf daughter Ann, who, when he published his essay in *The Modern Schoolman*, was not yet three years old. Percy's interaction with Ann reminded him constantly of the importance of speech and human communication. It is not difficult to understand why Percy in "Semiotic and a Theory of Knowledge" often asked basic questions, such as, "Why is it, we begin to wonder, the semioticists refuse to deal with symbolization, excepting only as it is governed by semantic rules?" Through lived experience, Percy felt the need to explore the Helen Keller paradigm, by stressing his belief that words were more than just signs, and specifically that the word "water" denoted and meant the substance water: "*The irreducible condition of every act of symbolization is the rendering intelligible; this is to say, the formulation of experience for a real or an implied someone else.*" Every sign-event, as Peirce and Percy believed, created moments of endless intelligible possibility.

Walker Percy often enfolded a Peircean sensibility into his fiction, as diverse as portraying an enigmatic, penitential black man with ashes on his forehead exiting a Catholic church on Ash Wednesday in *The Moviegoer*, to the creation of Allison Huger's schizophrenic speech patterns that enflesh new metaphors of love in *The Second Coming* (not dissimilar to the private code created by Anna in *Lancelot*), to the depiction of Father Simon Rinaldo Smith, a type of Simeon the Stylite character in *The Thanatos Syndrome*, who locates fires high up in a tower through a process of triangulation. As Father Smith tells Doctor Thomas More about the atrocities he witnessed in Germany in the 1930s, he succinctly comments about evil in the modern world: "We've got it wrong about horror. It doesn't come naturally but takes some effort." Father Smith knows from his experience that one locates destructive "brushfires or God by signs and coordinates." And just as the novel is about to conclude, it hints at a new beginning: Father Smith comes down from his tower and starts a hospice for AIDS patients, while Doctor More, somewhat of a doubter, serves on occasion Father Smith's Tridentine liturgy. For Percy, as for Peirce, signs are capable of helping us form new ideas and new habits as we move into the future.

In another example, this time taken from *Lancelot*, Lancelot Lamar, a patient in the Center for Aberrant Behavior in New Orleans, looks out of his window to see not only a corner of Lafayette Cemetery, but a slice of the levee and a short stretch of Annunciation Street. Yet, if he leans into the embrasure and cranes his neck as far left as possible, he can also see part of a sign around the corner. With the utmost effort, he can make out the following letters:

Free &

Ma

B

Lance can only guess at what the sign actually says: "Free & Easy Mac's Bowling" or "Free & Accepted Masons' Bar"—neither of which makes sense now or later in the course of the novel. What is important, however, is that Lance is trying to interpret the signs in his life, where one possibility leads to another and another. Likewise, Lance cannot interpret with any degree of accuracy the videotape that purportedly captures his wife's infidelity with Robert Merlin; and Lance's attempt to decipher what Merlin is thought to have said on film turns an effort of exegesis into one of terribly funny eisegesis, which provides, at the same time, a marvelously under-handed commentary on semantics and critical theory.

Percy never put aside his desire to write a book on Peirce and the theory of language. In a letter written on February 3, 1971 to his close friend Shelby Foote, Percy thought he would be able to write just such a book:

> I still think it would be as important as I told you. I would even say that it is revolutionary: that 100 years from now it could well be known as the Peirce-Percy theory of meaning (not Pierce but Peirce and so pronounced Perce-Percy). No kidding. I'm not even being vain. It just so happens that this old fellow, Charles Peirce, a U.S. philosopher very few layman ever heard of (by contrast, say, with William James, who got his idea of pragmatism from Peirce), who couldn't get along with fellow-professors and universities and ended up living out in the woods in Pennsylvania with his wife and literally went hungry—a curmudgeon Yankee philosopher—that this guy laid it out a hundred years ago, exactly what language is all about and what the behaviorists and professors have got all wrong ever since—laid it out, albeit in a very

obscure idiosyncratic style. I propose to take his insight, put it in modern behavioral terms plus a few items of my own, and unhorse an entire generation of behaviorists and grammarians.

(It is interesting to note that Ketner independently arrived at a similar version of the Peirce-Percy theory of meaning.) Yet, given the pressures of seeing *Love in the Ruins* through the press and of dealing with the let-down that usually accompanied the completion of a novel, Percy put the book aside. That year, he had to content himself by writing an article on the subject, entitled "Toward a Triadic Theory of Meaning," published in the February 1972 issue of *Psychiatry: Journal for the Study of Interpersonal Processes*, in which he contends that "although Peirce is recognized as the founder of semiotic, the theory of signs, modern behavioral scientists have not been made aware of the radical character of his ideas about language. I also suspect that the state of the behavioral science vis-à-vis language is currently in such low spirits, not to say default, that Peirce's time may have come." The Peirce project was not entirely abandoned; it transformed itself into a volume of 15 essays on language theory written by Percy entitled *The Message in the Bottle: How Queer Man Is, How Queer Language Is, and What One Has to Do with the Other*. Though these essays were previously published in such diverse journals as *The Southern Review, Forum, The Sewanee Review, Partisan Review, Katallagete, Thought, Psychiatry, The New Scholasticism, The Modern Schoolman, The Journal of Philosophy*, and *Philosophy and Phenomenological Research*, the last essay, "A Theory of Language," is original to this collection. Like several of the essays in the "Science, Language, Literature" section of *Signposts in a Strange Land*, these essays clearly manifest Percy's continued drive to explore and communicate Peircean semiotic. Percy once told me, as we sat in the quiet of his living room overlooking the Bogue Falaya in Covington, Louisiana, that, if he had a preference, he wanted to be remembered more as a semiotician than a novelist.

Not only did Percy read Peirce's works and critical essays about him, but he attended, as did John N. Deely, Carolyn Eisele, Kenneth Ketner, and other distinguished Peirce scholars, the First Annual Conference of the Semiotic Society of America in Atlanta, Georgia, in September 1976. (At that time, Ketner was not yet aware of Percy's writings on semiotic.) At the conference, Percy mingled, listened intently to the wide variety of talks, and tuned into the public conversation concerning the Peirce agenda; this conference experience ratcheted up Percy's energies, and on February 8, 1977, he wrote again to Foote that he wanted to start a long-term project in which he would demonstrate that the Peirce-Percy semiotic is true, though he had not actually found at this point the topic upon which to center his semiotic theory: "What I dream of is something neat and elegant and so convincing of itself that one can write it in the same offhand style as Einstein's relativity article (almost a throwaway style. Here it is, fellows, in case you're interested)." Three years later, he audited a course at the Summer Institute for Semiotics and Structural Studies at Victoria College of the University of Toronto from Visiting Professor Thomas A. Sebeok, an internationally renowned expert on semiotic. As a number of the letters in the first appendix to this volume indicate, Percy became friends with Sebeok and his wife Jean Umiker-Sebeok. Sebeok's course treated a variety of authors, including Ferdinand de Saussure and Roman Jakobson, and thus did not focus exclusively on Peirce. David Savan, professor of philosophy at the University of Toronto and author of *An Introduction to C.S. Peirce's Semiotics* (1976), was responsible for lecturing on Peirce. In discussions after class and over lunch, Sebeok noticed that Percy had become interested in Jakob von Uexküll, a German biologist and biosemiotician, as well as in the Thomistic orientation of semiotics, a dimension of Peirce's thought that also interested John Deely, who was responsible, in consultation with Ralph Austin Powell, for the interpretative arrangement of the bilingual edition of *Tractatus de Signis: The Semiotic of John Poinsot* (1985)—a work that Percy read, at least in large measure, and greatly admired.

During the 1980s, Percy deferred his dream to write his book on semiotic. In another letter to Foote, dated January 28, 1980, he noted, "You would not believe the main source of my distress these days. I would be perfectly happy to be let alone for the rest of my life because I know what I want to think about and write about: semiotics, which is very important though you may not think so—and which nobody knows anything about, or very little." As Percy entered the finishing stages of writing *The Thanatos Syndrome*, published in April 1987, he found that he was finally ready to begin work on the book on Peirce and semiotic, and he looked to Ketner as a mentor and guide—a Hermes who could lead him through the mine-fields of signs and symbols to the Elysian Fields of Peircean linguistic theory, where Percy, as a trained pathologist, could address comprehensively Kierkegaard's tenet that the sciences have not one word to say about what it is to be born a man or woman, to live, and to die.

When Ken Ketner saw Walker Percy face to face for the first time in Gompers Park in Washington, D.C., on May 4, 1989, he found that his friend looked wan, and it was only later that he learned that Walker had been diagnosed with cancer of the prostate. In fact, Walker had little over a year to live. This volume provides a record of their friendship, of Walker's persistence in articulating his desire to learn about Peirce's theory, and of Ken's affectionately meticulous commentary on semiotic (at times expressed with touches of down-home humor) as he provided intellectual stimulation and counsel. Ken sometimes included essays that he had written and published, which he thought would give Walker a more detailed explanation of semiotic than could easily be summarized in friendly letters. As is clear from this correspondence, moreover, Ken had wanted for a long time to meet with Walker in order to discuss at length the Peirce texts that would help Walker in his big semiotic project, since, deep down, Ken had profited from Walker's wisdom and felt a great sense of gratitude toward Walker—a need to repay in kind what he had received.

Ketner's essays, as well as the correspondence of Percy with other Peirce scholars, have been included in the two appendices in this volume in order to give as rounded a picture as possible of Percy's correspondence concerning Peirce. I would like to thank Robert W. Burch, Robert C. Collins, S.J., John F. Desmond, Diana Gonzalez, Arthur Stewart, Daniel T. Wackerman, Christine Wertheim, the Institute for Studies in Pragmaticism at Texas Tech University in Lubbock, the Shelby Foote and Walker Percy collections in the Southern Historical Collection at the University of North Carolina in Chapel Hill, and especially Mrs. Mary Bernice Townsend Percy for assisting in various ways in the publication of this volume. I am also grateful to Mark Stricherz for helping with the preparation of the index.

Patrick H. Samway, S.J.

Books by Walker Percy

NOVELS

The Moviegoer (New York: Knopf, 1961)
The Last Gentleman (New York: Farrar, Straus & Giroux, 1966)
Love in the Ruins (New York: Farrar, Straus & Giroux, 1971)
Lancelot (New York: Farrar, Straus & Giroux, 1977)
The Second Coming (New York: Farrar, Straus & Giroux, 1980)
The Thanatos Syndrome (New York: Farrar, Straus & Giroux, 1987)

NON-FICTION

The Message in the Bottle (New York: Farrar, Straus & Giroux, 1975)
Lost in the Cosmos (New York: Farrar, Straus & Giroux, 1983)
Signposts in a Strange Land, edited by Patrick H. Samway, S.J. (New York: Farrar, Straus & Giroux, 1991).

Five Basic Reference Works on Peirce

Annotated Catalogue of the Papers of Charles S. Peirce, by Richard R. Robin (Amherst: University of Massachusetts Press, 1967)

Collected Papers of Charles Sanders Peirce, edited by Charles Hartshorne and Paul Weiss (Volumes 1–6) and Arthur Burks (Volumes 7–8) (Cambridge: Harvard University Press, 1931–1958)

A Comprehensive Bibliography of the Published Works of Charles Sanders Peirce with a Bibliography of Secondary Studies (second edition, revised), edited by Kenneth Laine Ketner with the assistance of Arthur Franklin Stewart and Claude V. Bridges (Bowling Green, Ohio: Philosophy Documentation Center, Bowling Green State University, 1986)

The New Elements of Mathematics, by Charles Sanders Peirce, edited by Carolyn Eisele (The Hague: Mouton de Gruyter, 1976)

"The Peirce Papers: A Supplementary Catalogue," by Richard R. Robin, from *Transactions of the Charles S. Peirce Society*, 7 (Winter 1971).

A Thief of Peirce
Letters

꙳

February 26, 1984

Prof. [Kenneth Laine] Ketner,

Thanks for your treasure trove on CSP [Charles Sanders Peirce].[1]
When I get into it, I'd like to respond.

Sincerely,

Walker Percy [s]

꙳

August 8, 1984

Dear Dr. Ketner,

I take pleasure in being called a Cenophythagorean.[2] I've been called
worse. It is extremely pleasurable to see you quote CSP on the phaneron,
as to "totality of all that is before or on your mind—" and the notion of
phaneroscopy as a method of examination of same, and the idea of valency
of elements in the phaneron as a key to a classification system. I arrived at
the phaneron through a different route, my idea of the "world" of the
symbol-user (triadic) as opposed to the "environment" of the organism
(dyadic).

But you can help me. Unfortunately for me: Where CSP is very good
about giving *examples* in his classical discussion of the difference between
indexical signs and symbols, dyadicity and triadicity, such examples are not
forthcoming in his writings on diagrammatic thought and existential
graphs. You seem to set much store by these as a means of exploring the
valency or valencies of the phaneron. When CSP concentrates on logical
diagrams and leaves out examples of relevance in our perception in the
phaneron, frankly he loses me. You seem to be onto something I am missing. Tell me, give me a hint, how I can connect up these very formal, logical

diagrams of valencies with the data of experience, which is what interests me as an amateur-behavioral psychologist and novelist.

Thanks for citing me in your paper. I will certainly send your institute my only two non-fiction "semiotic" books.

Sincerely,

Walker Percy [s]

P.S.: Sometimes I could genuflect before CSP for his genius and for seeing, before his time and *before our time still,* the difference between dyadicity and triadicity.

Othertimes I could kick his ass for his deliberate withdrawal into logical games. W P

&

August 22, 1984

Dear Dr. Percy,

Thanks for your fine letter of 8 August. If you are an amateur, then I am Darwin's missing link.

I inclose a few extracts from the CSP manuscripts, plus one of my recent Institute Newsletters.[3] I forget if I have already sent you one. I have found a fairly common pattern in Peirce's writing. His letters and the earlier drafts of his books and articles are often much more explanatory than the final published article or whatever. This is probably due to multiple factors. He often was urged to cut his published pieces by editors, hence he ended up with an essay that had been abstracted to death. He also seemed to have wanted to be thought scholarly and academic, so even on his own, he would remove parts he regarded as simpler. One can often read several drafts and a finished paper, understanding the whole by working up through the drafts. Ditto for letters to James, Royce, or whomever. Also, a factor in misunderstanding Peirce is what I have called the mythical versus the real CSP (in article I got into *Krisis*. Did I send you a copy?).[4] There is an erroneous received version of what P [Peirce] is supposed to be like among a number of academic philosophy and intellectual history types. The received P is not the real one. I have recently been trying to put together a book of P texts taken mostly from the more informal kind, where he does explain himself better.[5] I inclose a few samples. The man that emerges from this exercise is vastly different from the received one.

I have often to suppress that urge to kick P's butt. There are more reasons than the one you mentioned. Often he will get to a crucial point in an explanation, then lapse into an autobiographical streak, or a diatribe, or etc. But I have found that he can be deciphered, and I feel I am making good progress in that regard. I would very much like to share any ideas or findings or examples with you about P. He had, by the way, a kind of personal life story that would itself make quite a novel. Moreover, he had a certain jerky or bastardly side of his character quite sufficient to match the part of it that we do indeed sometimes want to bow before (like the Zen master who bows before an archer who finally released his arrow in the proper way—remember Eugen Herrigel's book *Zen in the Art of Archery)*—we aren't genuflecting to the man but to the divine that we have seen somewhere in his neighborhood. Anyway, there was an anti-genuflecting side to P. His life could provide you with novel-fodder.

I will be glad to carry on a correspondence if that will help you. I'm sure I would benefit. But I would enjoy an opportunity to have a two-person informal seminar some time. Would you care to consider conversing in that way? I will have a sabbatical in the spring semester of '85, and could perhaps come over to your neck of the woods, or maybe we could meet in this area somehow. I'm open to your wishes or suggestions.

Aside from your Cenopythagoreanism, I admire the quality of your work which I would describe as the spirit of a surgeon's mind. Surgeons aren't afraid to look into the guts of things without blinking. I try to be that kind of philosopher, and your recent letter confirms my notion that you don't blink.

Warmest greetings,

Ken [s]

Ken Ketner [t]

September 2, 1984

Dear Ken,

Many thanks for the valuable material on old CSP. It was illuminating. It was the first time I had understood what he meant by his phaneron, phaneroscopy. I had more or less equated it with phenomenology and so was not especially interested. But now I see its strong sign dimension (valence $= 3$), which is exciting to me and what I define as the "world" of the sign-user, as opposed to the "environment." I said: The world of the sign-user is the world of signs—and as usual it seems that CSP said it first.

Same for "existential graphs." Thanks.

To tell the truth, I've never seen much use in CSP's "Firstness," except to make the system more elegant.

How do you think CSP would have answered these questions: (1) How does the sign-user go about living in his phaneron? (2) How would you investigate it? He gives a fascinating hint in "Lecture 1" when he contrasts the virtues and sins of humans with the lives of "lower animals."[6]

His remarks on religion both fascinating and strange; fascinating: Scientists as believers in God whether they know it or not, because they pursue truth; strange; His amalgam of East and West in "BuddhiChristianity" [see *CP* 1.673]. I wonder which "rascally clerics" he was after.

Many thanks again for your trouble.

Sincerely,

Walker [s]

P.S.: I notice that some current semioticists are getting interested in medieval semioticists, e.g., John of St. Thomas, Duns Scotus, some hundred years after CSP. W P

❧

September 21, 1984

Dear Walker,

Yours of 2 September received with much pleasure. Yes, phaneroscopy is quite important for the "world of a sign-user." It may be especially important because it is a way to investigate, to observe, to achieve correct hypotheses, about that world. Thus my analogy between the telescope as the scope of astronomy, and phaneroscopy as the scope of the science of the "world of the sign-user." I am trying in my next writing projects to first understand and then try to explain to others some more of the details of this strange observational science of phaneroscopy. What I have already done vis-à-vis trying to understand what he means by math and math methods (diagrammatic methods) is part of the story obviously, but recently I have come upon some talk of a method of "reasoning with continuity" in P's manuscripts, and I think that will play a role in the final word. It is clear that the following is also important: Consider what say a geometer does. A geometer says to fellow geometers "Consider an arbitrary triangle," and then draws not an arbitrary triangle on the blackboard, but an actual, specific, nonarbitrary triangle. So what the hell is this "arbitrary triangle"? The triangle that is existentially drawn is a token (in P's terminology), or better, the geometers understand it as a token. And by staring at this token, they are attempting to see the type (something in your "world of the sign-user," not something of the world of the "environment"). The way in which they are "seeing" the type is by dropping out of their consciousness (or better, ?understanding?), that is "preciding" out (via "precissive" abstraction) accidents having nothing to do with the "arbitrary" triangle, which is the type. Also involved in this (and here is where the continuity business comes in) is the assumption on the part of the geometers that this token is related to the type, not as part to whole, or instance to general, but as partial system is to larger system. And somehow P thinks (and I don't yet grasp this) that this relation of small system to bigger system strongly involves continuity. So the move from token to type, an essential part of mathematical method, and hence going to be an essential part of the method of phaneroscopy, is to grasp the relations that compose a bigger system by grasping part of the system in the token, then hypothesizing and testing that hypothesis by seeing if the consequences of the hypothesis are fulfilled within the larger system. The hypothesis gets confirmed if we have the "eureka" click. It is not just a matter of psychological experience, however. For we test the hypothesis in other settings, show its consistency with previously tested ones, etc. (We don't let the click be decisive or final). And (here is a neat one) why is the click a good indicator? P's answer is that our minds are continuous with the cosmic mind (we are tokens to its type); otherwise he says, we could not explain our ability to do science.

You are one of the best question askers on the planet, and the right question is pearl indeed. I can't answer the two questions you posed—how does a sign-user go about living in his phaneron? How would you investigate it (i.e., the phaneron)? I can give some ideas, however, but very preliminary. A good thing to notice is that the phaneron is "whatever is before our minds in any sense whatever" but what P wants to investigate in the phaneron is only its indecomposable elements. That helps a lot. And, he presumes that the indecomposable elements will be culturally universal, in all phanera, presumably even those of crazies (and if that is correct, I can see a line of research that psychiatry might pursue using CSP as a guide—e.g., How do we get in touch with the mind of a crazy and how do we help to bring him back? By using the indecomposables that both he and us have as a point of initial contact, a base from which to establish communication). Most persons don't know they have a phaneron, or that there are indecomposables therein. But if such a person through phaneroscopy studied themselves, wouldn't they be undertaking the ancient Buddhistic-Socratic-Christian (or better Jesus, the Palestinian Buddha) injunction to "Know yourself"? What does "know yourself" mean? I think it might mean, discover what kind of thing a self, or any self, is and how it works. For a long time I have held as quite likely the thesis that social science will not be possible until we can know what ontologically a self is. And it seems to me that the mystical tradition is able to answer this question. Something like a Zen *satori* is needed before we see what a self is, what an ego is, and we see that by momentarily actually leaving our ego, entering a state of "nothing," then returning to our ego, but now with something new, a new place (the nothing) from which to commence what we are now doing as egos, and as T.S. Eliot said (in "Little Gidding" in *The Four Quartets*) returning and knowing the place for the first time. As long as we are involved in being egos, we can't see the forest for the trees (like a fish in water not aware of the water because it is busy breathing it) (or like health, which you didn't know you had until you are lacking it for a while).

Do you know of Simone Weil? A remarkable story? In case you don't (which is unlikely) here is a citation: *The Simone Weil Reader*, edited George A. Panichas, David McKay Company, New York, New York, 1977. Anyway, I think her story is related to your two blockbuster questions, along the lines of my *satori* ramblings. I find it difficult to express the line of thought I mention above. Another reference that has helped me a lot is Herbert Fingarette's *The Self in Transformation*, particularly the last half (Basic Books, also was in paper = now OP, but probably in a decent library).

Your question is so good, that it virtually amounts to the ancient principal question of philosophy "How shall I live my life?" = "How does a sign-user go about living in his phaneron?" But putting it your way gives us a shot at answering it.

A passage from CSP that might contact our present discussion: The doctrine of Frank Abbot in *Scientific Theism*, which P is reviewing here in *The Nation*, February 11, 1886, seems to be that the relations are reproduced, without being embodied in any diagram, as "concepts of relations, dropping out of consideration the things related":

> The knowledge of relations depends [Abbot said] upon a special perceptive use of the understanding. This view, although it is not adequately set forth, is the center of all that is original in the book, and is sure to excite a fruitful discussion of the question of our mode of discernment of relations. Of all the sciences—at least of those whose reality no one disputes—mathematics is the one which deals with relations in the abstractest form, and it never deals with them except as embodied in a diagram or construction, geometrical or algebraical. The mathematical study of a construction consists in experimenting with it; after a number of such experiments, their separate results suddenly become united in one rule, and our immediate consciousness of this rule is our discernment of the relation. It is strong secondary sensation, like the sense

of beauty. To call it a perception may perhaps be understood as implying that to discern each special relation requires a special faculty, or determination of our nature. But it should not be overlooked that we come to it by a process analogous to induction.

That is, I take it that no special faculty need be posited because the ordinary processes of logic—abduction (coming up with a hypothesis), deduction, and induction—suffice to make the above function, to make the above intelligible.

I send you some more of my junk.[7]

Loyally,

Ken [s]

Ken Ketner [t]

ॐ

March 16, 1986

Dear Walker,

Yeah, I know I send you too much junk, but you're a big boy and sovereign, and will keep or throw away as you will.

I'm reading the inclosed at the Texas A & M Philosophy Department colloquium on the afternoon of 7 April.[8] Y'all come or if not, refute me by mail, or can it, or who knows what.

My original point in the inclosed is, I think, that there is a strong connection between everyday consciousness, mathematics, and novels—all three are model-making and model-manipulating activities. Manipulation in this case means to explore the model, find new relations in it, then seek relations in reality-under-study that are analogous to new-found-relations-in-model.

I'm beginning to get a strong whiff that for Charles Sanders Peirce a sign (representation, signifier) is a model of its object to an interpretant. "So what," you say. Well what if the interpretant is just $=$ to a receiver's successful manipulation of the transmitted model in view of general laws or habits:

MODEL

Receiver, interpreter of model:

(1) Icon-receiver manipulates model in terms of comparing properties between model and object.

(2) Index-receiver manipulates model in terms of causal laws, yacht hull model, architect's building, scale models, etc.

(3) Symbol. Model is a model of object simply because model will be so interpreted in that way by virtue of a habit of interpretation this receiver and similar receivers have. This habit thus is not a token habit (i.e., a specific habit of a specific person), but is a habit type, a general (recall your Helen Keller example—the word she got is not a word token, but a word type, a general). Now this habit type is an interpretant. It danged sure ain't an interpreter (person, person's specific habit); an interpretant is a general habit type.

Try it this way. Descartes wrote to Father Mersenne. In his letter he said: "Dear Father Mersenne: Mind-body interaction takes place in the pineal gland. Yours, René." Mersenne replied: "Dear René Descartes: What you proposed for interaction is logically impossible. As ever, Father Mersenne." Now what we have here are two interpreters, persons, acting and functioning as interpreters. However, now both René and Father Mersenne are dead. There is, in their case, no more interpreter. Neither can interpret the other due to mortification. Yet their signs (models, signifiers) survive, and the powers of these signs survive. Their signs still have the power to activate the general habit-type, even though they, as individual interpreters, are dead. Those signs would still have that power even if we were all dead and gone. So it is the general habit-type that makes interpretation go. The interpreter is just the material cause. Hence interpreters are secondary, interpretants (the general habit-types) are primary.

"But where do these habit-types live, exist, stay, or reside," says a skeptic. Why they are what make up the intelligible cosmos, and their sum total (vast) = God.

Is that not good sound Thomism (at least the part about the intelligible universe—St. Thomas would personify God a bit more)?

Descartes' damage, whether intentional or not, is to have made individuals logically primitive. "The opposite alternative is a horrid Buddhism," you say. Very well, screw the Buddhists. But what about the saints? What about the Christian mystics? Aren't the Christian mystics saying the same in regard to the sense of individuality we possess, that it is an illusion, and that the basic thing is a kind of society? Doesn't Walker Percy say the same (that individual is an illusion) in *The Message in the Bottle*, pp. 189–214?

Now if society is basic, if relations are basic, their interpretant is basic and interpreter (ego) is derivative. Both interpretant and interpreter are real; the former is primitive, latter derivative.

Out of steam. I hope for more later if I can conquer this damned flu bug. It's got me down.

Derivatively yours,

Ketner [s]

❧

April 11, 1987

Dear Ken Ketner,

Many thanks for your interesting paper. I appreciate your mentioning my name, though I'm not sure I really made an independent discovery of Cenopythagoreanism.

Actually I came at it first through Susanne Langer and Ernst Cassirer before landing on Peirce, the truly great, if sometimes mysterious, one. And if I understand you and him correctly when he speaks of the "inspection of the valency of the elements of the phaneron," it is true enough—though I admit I am much less interested in his "medads," "monads," "tetrads," etc., than in what I believe to be the seminal distinction between dyads and triads or Secondness and Thirdness—seminal because it is precisely there that so much of present-day psychology and semiotics stumbles.

Truthfully I am much less interested and certainly less competent in the area of Peirce's great interest in semiotic as formal logic, his existential graphs and so on. What does interest me is the use of semiotic, i.e., a natural science of signs, in a biological approach to human and subhuman animal behavior. I know you think my triangle, sign-referent-interpretant is not an accurate presentation of Peirce's valencies, but I find it most useful in demonstrating the irreducibility of "triadic behavior," or as Peirce would say: No combination of dyads can make a triad.

But what I need to ask you, since you are a Peirce scholar and I'm not, is how I can find some clarification of what he usually calls the "interpretant." He is ambiguous about it. For example in one place he'll say that the sign or the representamen creates its interpretant in the mind of the receiver of the sign, where it stands for its "object." This sounds fairly deterministic, indeed not much different from what the old behaviorists would call the "engram" in the brain, a neuronal pattern, created by the reception of a sensory stimulus toward the end of affecting the behavior of an organism toward an object. This, of course, is purely and simply "dyadic" behavior— chimps responding to banana by making sign, etc.

But then he will speak, in his theory of speech acts, very clearly about an *assertion*, whether the assertion of a proposition or the assertion of the relation between an indexical symbol and its referent—like Helen Keller asserting *water* (the sign in her hand) "is" water (the stuff running over her hand.

In fact, he even defines such an assertion as a "pheme" an "illocutionary" act.

My source of confusion and my question to Peirce and, short of Peirce, to you, is: What is the "interpretant"? Is he talking about a physiological brain-state? Or does he mean something like the transcendental ego, or mind or an "I"? Why in the hell doesn't he make himself clear on this? Clearly if a sentence is asserted in a speech act, a pheme, there must be an "asserter." I have, in fact, referred to it variously as "asserter," "coupler" (of the symbol and referent in the triangle).

Perhaps you could refer me to texts, CSP's, yours, someone's, who could help me out.

My own feeling is that what I could call Peirce's "triadic" theory is of seminal importance as a formal schema for making sense of that distinctive human behavior which involves the use of symbols (sentences, literature, art, etc.) and that it has not even begun to be explored—despite all the lip service to CSP by present-day semioticists—nor by literary theorists—nor by psychiatrists.

What I would like to do when I get rid of all the nonsense connected with "promoting" the last novel I wrote, is to settle down and spend my declining years trying to make a little sense of CSP's "triadic theory."

Any help would be appreciated and meanwhile many thanks for your letter and papers.

Sincerely,

Walker [s]

⁊℔

May 9, 1987

Dear Ken,

Many thanks for the imperial gift of the three CSP books.⁹ I looked through, but didn't see much on semiotics.

Am waiting for you or CSP to tell me what an interpretant is. Draw me a picture.

Best,

Walker [s]

September 17, 1987

Dear Walker,

I hope you will forgive this mechanical way of writing. Semester is howling along, and I am trying to compress where I can. I should have entitled the inclosed essay "Waltzing toward the interpretant," or "Snuggling up to the interpretant."[10] I started it with your request in mind. If I am reasonably correct in what I outline, I think I am about half way to the interpretant. But being well half way could perhaps be a worthy thing. Anyhow, I send it along to you hoping that you might find something useful in it. I'm going to continue to pursue the interpretant, my word on it as an Okie gentleman.

Recently I have been reading some from that book of conversations with WP [Walker Percy]. In one of those you reported on the extraordinary phenomenon of people out of the blue writing you in the most personal ways. I can surely say that after reading your novels, especially *The Thanatos Syndrome*, I have felt the same urge. Maybe I have repressed it, for it is in the Okie gentleman's code to leave one's fellow creatures alone (usually). My guess is that you would find such sudden personal outpourings a bit against your upbringing. But I suspect this is a record of a genuine, almost scientific (broad sense) phenomenon. Perhaps it is intensified in the end of the age as you talk about that. But probably it is to be found in any good novel in most ages. And perhaps that has to do with what I was trying to get out in the last part of "novel science." A novel can be a tremendous tool of analysis, both in the sense Freud meant it, and in the sense I mean it (explaining less well knowns with better knowns). And how does a novel do that (and yours are particularly strong at this)? The novelist constructs a triadic world, a relational world, which literally unfolds in the mind of a reader as a mental diagram, a picture. The novelist sets up certain relationships as the background, assumed, taken for granted parts of the fictional world. Then parallels between the fictional world and the personal world now inhabited by the reader are drawn forth or are encouraged for creation. Next, the known relations of the fictional world point to some unknown relation in the fictional world. The new fictional relation now points to a possible parallel relation in the reader's personal world. Thereby, the reader gains self-knowledge. And since the themes of your novels are universal ones, philosophical, religious, social ones even, one new relation discovered at that level in a reader and BY a reader, can be a whammy. No wonder people want to thank you. Behold—the reason I call you a psychiatrist, even though you "just write novels."

Relatively yours,

Ken [s]

Ketner [t]

P.S.: I hope you don't object to my use of your sentence as a motto. If you do, just let me know and I can cancel it. K

ॐ

September 22, 1987

Dear Ken,

Yours received just as I'm fixing to head for Maine for a couple of weeks.[11] So I'll take it with me in the fond expectation you're going to tell me in Maine what an interpretant is. Seems like you might even have drawn some picture of it.

Meanwhile, thanks so much for your letter.

Sincerely,

Walker [s]

October 20, 1987

Dear Ken,

Many, many thanks. For all the good things. The articles, letter, and the *Transactions of the Charles Peirce Society*.

Am most touched by your reference to me in the published version of "Identifying Peirce's 'Most Interesting and Lucid Paper': An Introduction to Cenopythagoreanism," e.g., to the first few pages of *The Message in the Bottle*.

Yes, you are quite right in your "triadic" analysis of the work of the novelist.

And yes, you are also right: I have been a Cenopythagorean all along without knowing it.

Have also found valuable the *Transactions*, especially Jarret Brock's paper (Volume 17), "An Introduction to Peirce's Theory of Speech Acts." Especially his addressing CSP's "theory of assertion"—the act of assertion having seemed to me perhaps the most dramatic example of here-and-now everyday Thirdness. As in the case of "interpretant" and "interpreter," here, too, in the matter of sentences and the act of assertion of a sentence (*parole* rather than *langue*), CSP, great as he was, had the almost maddening way of beating around the bush and not getting down to it. Maybe it is the influence of the 19th-century German philosophers, so regnant at the time.

Yes certainly, I'll send you any books of mine you want. By me and/or about me. Name them and tell me how to inscribe them and they're yours (I mean, are they for you or the library?) [Walker Percy subsequently sent Professor Ketner a copy of *The Thanatos Syndrome* with the inscription: "For Ken Ketner, Best wishes and thanks from a fellow Cenopythagorean. Walker. 11/5/87"]

But that is not why I write. I write for some scholarly assistance. There ain't no scholars or libraries hereabouts (an advantage in some ways but not in this case).

I need to locate a couple of books—if they exist.

Here's my situation. I'm thinking about writing a book, perhaps entitled *Thirdness* (Can't call it *The Delta Factor*). The thesis is that CSP's Thirdness, triadicity, properly understood and properly applied, can go a long way in pointing some right directions in the current mess in which the social sciences find themselves. Or, as Thomas Kuhn puts it in his *The Structure of Scientific Revolutions* (Chicago: University of Chicago Press, 1977), the traditional scientific paradigm (Cartesian and Newtonian), which has been so extraordinarily successful in the physical, chemical, and biological sciences, has proved quite as spectacularly unsuccessful in the so-called social sciences, i.e., the sciences of man *qua* man. As Kuhn expresses it in his own mild way: "Today research in parts of philosophy, psychology, linguistics and even art history, all converge to suggest that the traditional paradigm is somehow askew" (p. 121).

True enough. Of course, what Kuhn does not know (here at least) is that there may be a paradigm which could do the job, Peirce's triadic theory—applied correctly—and I mean quite as rigorously and scientifically as Newtonian mechanics.

Very well. You and I probably agree on that.

Here's what I need. I'm sure there've been books written in the last few years documenting and deploring the chaos in the social sciences. For example, I've just been reading an article on the current state of "psychotherapy" in which the author claims to have identified 400 "brands of talk therapy." Similar incoherence in linguistics and sociology.

Know any books on the subject, i.e., about the sorry state of all these disciplines, any or one or all, as compared, say, with modern physics and chemistry? I seem to recall seeing reviews of such books, but don't know how to lay hands on them. I'm not talking about hysterical, right-wing attacks on social scientists as being "atheistic" and suchlike, but serious studies of what Kuhn speaks of. The "somehow askew"?

Give me a title or two. Or refer me to somebody.

Meanwhile name your books and I'll send 'em along.

Would you believe that *Lost in the Cosmos*, which I hardly wrote to be a best-seller, now outsells all the novels? Is the country making a secret turn toward Cenopythagoreanism?

Sincerely,

Walker [s]

Ken: This appears to be p. 2 of a letter which must have mystified you.

W P

*

❦

October 24, 1987

Dear Walker,

Page 2 of your valued letter reached me just after I had sent off a post card wondering if there was a p. 2.

Hot damn! Nothing could be better news than your offer to inscribe a set of your books to me. They would be one of my most valued possessions—a family heirloom to hand to my son. I have read all the novels (except *Lancelot*) and the two nonfiction books (except some parts of *The Message in the Bottle*) and *Conversations With Walker Percy* (a well-made book, with the gem being your self-interview).

Perhaps here is some more feedback for the science of novel writing (the first and basic triadic science?): I tried to start *Lancelot* two or three times a few months ago. I got blocked up, couldn't start it. I wanted to read it, but something stopped me. Now that I have read *Conversations With Walker Percy*, maybe I have some ideas with which to get going in it.

The news about top sales for *Lost in the Cosmos* is indeed an interesting datum. Perhaps that encourages you even more to start the "Thirdness" project you mentioned. That sounds like an exciting prospect. I would be deeply pleased to help you on that in any way. And in regard to your request for some books documenting the constipation of the social sciences, I will begin a search next week. Meanwhile, I am sending along with this letter a package of some things that occur to me right away. Some of these I happen to have on hand, and some I can only mention by title. Those I have I will send. You can keep them as long as you wish, or quickly scan them, and if they are no good, send them back. Eventually I would like to have them back, but there is no deadline. By the way, if there are out of print books you need, let me know and I will look in our library, or use our interlibrary loan and send you a xerox. As I read *Conversations With Walker*

Percy, I learned that your family has a book store in Covington, so perhaps you don't need assistance with items that are currently in print. But in case you do, there is a book-a-holic hotline one can call any hour to order current items: 1-800-255-2665 (Book Call, 59 Elm Street, New Canaan, Connecticut). I hope you understand, Walker, that I take assisting you very seriously, so don't hesitate to ask.

In my course on philosophy of the social sciences this semester, I am using two books that could be of some help to you. The first, Peter T. Manicas's *A History and Philosophy of the Social Sciences* (London: Basil Blackwell, 1987), is a history written from a realist (Peircean) perspective, a book in which the author overtly has an axe to grind. Some parts of it might be on target with the theme you mentioned. The second, by Eugene Rochberg-Halton, *Meaning and Modernity: Social Theory in the Pragmatic Attitude* (Chicago: University of Chicago Press, 1986), is semeiotic at work in social theorizing. His Part 2 is a brilliant exposé of some bad contemporary misuse of CSP among some semioticists. I find his chapter on CSP and Charles Morris to be well done and important. The theme you want is to be found in some places in the book. If you can't get either of these two, I can arrange to send them to you from our book store.

Philosophy is nowadays in a very screwed up state. There are a number of pieces about that. I'm sending along a copy of *Post-Analytic Philosophy*, edited by John Rajchman and Cornel West. I think the last piece by Cornel West is a good summary of what is wrong. Richard Rorty's piece is interesting. Arthur Danto's essay about philosophy and literature is right on target. Rorty's recent book, *The Mirror of Nature*, is also a lament for the end of philosophy. I am also a big fan of Hilary Putnam's work. His little book on realism in logic is a gem, and is nontechnical.

Is theology a social science? I suspect that it is, or that those who work in it think of it in that way. Anyway, it is a disaster zone. One of my favorite works which tends to show that is Elaine Pagels's *The Gnostic Gospels*, copy inclosed. The way you wrote *Lost in the Cosmos* has led me to speculate whether you might not have a few Gnostic genes (not the Gnostics portrayed in the patristic anti-heresy tracts, but the real Gnostics, as portrayed by themselves, as Pagels outlines, the guys who made self-knowledge paramount in religion, and who were perhaps the first "bad Catholics," so bad that they were scourged).

Don't forget old CSP. He is a harbinger of your cry that the age has gone sour, that sciences are cracked. His "Doctrine of Necessity Examined" is a classic anti-mechanical treatise (*CP* 6.35ff.). It could be profitably read alongside his "Evolutionary Love" (*CP* 6.287ff.). You're talking to the head man when it comes to providing CSP items for your projects. I suggest you peruse the CSP *Comprehensive Bibliography* I recently sent you, select any things you want, then just tell me what they are, and I can duplicate them from the Institute files. Ditto on CSP manuscripts. If you don't have a copy of Richard R. Robin's *Annotated Catalogue of the Charles S. Peirce Papers* (Amherst: University of Massachusetts Press, 1967, still in print I think), or if you can't order one, let me know and I will get a copy for you.

You are absolutely correct that CSP often slid off the topic as he wrote. But he stays in place often enough so that one can dig the whole thing out from here and there. You should just about now be receiving a copy of my Peirce section in Stuhr, *Classical American Philosophy*. I put those CSP readings together with your complaint in mind, trying to get "on target" stuff and then splice it together in his general outline, thus eliminating the pesky digressions. I sent that by slow boat, so it might not have arrived yet. You might, by the way, find Royce as portrayed in that book of readings to be an interesting figure. Royce was CSP's only real and successful disciple.

I'm also sending along a typescript of my latest CSP project on CSP's 1898 Cambridge Conferences. (I have recently sent it off to Harvard University Press, who expressed interest in the project—I hope my mojo is working.) I became fascinated with his remarks which are listed in the *Collected Papers* as "Detached Ideas on Vitally Important Topics," which the *CP* editors chopped up pretty badly. As I tried to pursue obtaining the whole skinny on those manuscripts, one thing led to another, and behold—the whole story in this typescript, which is a fairly long story. This is an extra one, so use it as long as you wish, but eventually return it. Copy any or all of it if you wish. Should you decide to read around in it, I might suggest first reading my introduction, then skip to Part 2 at p. 406—end, then the eight lectures in Part 1. I find the "Detached" manuscript in Part 2, and the first lecture in Part 1 to be pretty wise stuff, reminiscent of themes you have developed in your novels. There is a good deal of high metaphysics in this. Some parts of that interest me, but not as much as the aforesaid themes which are quite like Emerson, whom CSP knew in his youth—you are a lot like Emerson, too, in a medical kind of way. Emerson's "Divinity School" address knocked the theologians of his time on their ears, for he said, "Why are you using old revelations and old religious experiences from centuries gone by? Why not get your own?" As you might have guessed by now, I think theology is bad and religion is good, and that theology is not religion. Religion is "right instinct, right emotion." Instinct is subconscious; digesting food is subconscious; digesting Christ in the Eucharist is a form of prayer for getting directly into one's bloodstream right instinct and emotion (the Christ principle which the Eucharist—one wants to say here "symbolizes," but remembering that the symbol is the man, one should say—is). Religion is damned difficult to comprehend without Thirdness. Is there a connection between the decline of true religion (or conversely the victory of theology over religion) in our time and the temporary victory of nominalism (CSP's catchword for anti-realism, anti-Thirdness-ism) over triadic things? A person who is locked in nominalism can't be religious.

I did the following experiment in my upper-division philosophy of social science class the other day. I put 10 paper clips in one box and another 10 in an identical box. I held up the two boxes, and told the students what was in them, "10 identical paper clips in each of the identical boxes, and no other object in either box." I then asked the students if the contents of both boxes were the same. They knew it was a trick, but in the end they had to say, "contents are the same." But they weren't the same, for in one box were 10 loose clips and in the other was a chain of paper clips. In other words, the second box had in it 10 clips plus a relation. That they could not even think of the relation as a possible item of content shows in a small way how nominalistic our age is. But we buy and sell relations—computer software. A blank computer disk costs less than a dollar, but put some relations between magnetic particles on that disk, and you can sell it for a lot of money as software. Ditto with a blank ream of paper and somebody's novel. One of P's most insightful remarks about the reality of relations is on p. 73 of the first of my volumes on CSP's contributions to *The Nation*. If you read that, or *CP* 2.227, you will begin to see that all the talk by CSP about mathematics is not really about technical mathematics. It is more about the spirit of mathematics, which is perhaps the purest and simplest instance of the world of Thirdness. I hoped that would emerge in my anthologizing for Stuhr and in some of my essays.

You want to get together someday for a face-to-face brainstorm about how to instigate the triadic paradigm, which we do agree could be rigorous and scientific but not deterministic? I think that only writing about it might not suffice to get it instantiated in culture, although it would help a lot. Perhaps what is needed is a working instance of the theory—something that produces (nondeterministically) results. I have often wondered if a Peircean based psychiatry might not be the place to start. Or, put it this away, WP's novels are almost a "working model" of a science of Thirdness. But people don't usually know that such is what is happening to them when they read one of them. It gets categorized as "a good time," or "interesting," or "art," or in the many high-class literary theory ways that some of your interviewers did on you in *Conversations With Walker Percy* (Southern writer, folktales on the front porch, North/South, Faulkner/Percy, etc.). Your self-interview in effect says "get off that track." But determinism is a tough addiction to break (Sartre). Maybe that is an idea for a crucial experiment in a "neo-tritology" crusade—develop a modified lapsometer that will knock "patients" into realizing that they are free beings and always have been. It's a hard awakening, for then one becomes responsible. But under my weak attempts at humor I can say that there are strong parallels between some of Sartre and CSP such that your general idea could perhaps take root there. Sartre envisioned an existentialist therapy. Did anything ever come of it? If not, marrying him to some of CSP's ideas might be worth a try and might produce success.[12]

With warmest greetings,

Ken [s]

Ken Ketner [t]

ॐ

November 5, 1987

Dear Ken,

Thanks for all the goodies. I hardly know where to start, so I'll start with a question of my most major concern and over the years the most fretful in CSP's philosophy. You've heard it before.

First, CSP is as infuriating a writer as he is brilliant. As you say, he has this rotten habit of sliding off the point, a sure sign of bad writing. He is almost as bad a writer as John Poinsot (John of St. Thomas), who was equally if not more brilliant and John Deely writing about John Poinsot. I wish these goddam semioticists has taken a course in ordinary writing—or had read Hemingway.

So. There's this business of the interpretant. In some places CSP seems to describe the interpretant in terms quite congenial to a behaviorist's or a neurologist's description of a change in a brain pattern—an "engram"—as a consequence of a stimulus. Thus: "It (the sign) creates in the mind of that person an equivalent sign . . . which I call the interpretant of that first sign. . . . The sign stands for something, its object."

Now B.F. Skinner would have no trouble at all with that.

In other places, he uses the word "interpreter" apparently as more or less synonymous with interpretant—implying, of course, that it is in some sense or other an agent performing an act, as indeed it would have to be if it combines sign with referent.

Does he shy away from saying so for fear of endorsing a Cartesian dualism because, once one admits to an agent performing an act, one is stuck in some sense or other with mind or soul or such. Of course, the neurologist Eccles makes no bones about it. Yes, there's such a thing, entity at least, which he even locates in Brodmann 44.

What to make of this? CSP a cop-out or not?

Am enjoying your "Consequences of Mathematics" and am up to existential graphs and You-are-a-good-girl logics.

Here's a passing question for you. Take bottom p. 136: "Let us pretend to assert anything we write down on the blackboard."[13] I follow what follows but I would like to back up to the pretend. That is to say, I have no trouble at all with what you and CSP say about assertions and assertions within assertions. What I want to know is, what is an assertion? We all know the difference between writing a sentence on a blackboard without paying much attention or reading it aloud paying even less attention or uttering the same sentence as a social manner of nonspeak. ("My, you are a nice girl," uttered to your best friend's brat in the company of your best friend.)

And there is an actual assertion, uttering a sentence and "meaning" it—or as CSP would say, putting yourself on the line like testifying in court under oath.

Okay. But what I wanted CSP to tell me or draw for me is not an existential graph or a trivalent node, but a picture of the *sort* of thing which is happening in the brain of the speaker. And I am not talking about the latest in the neurology and electrochemistry of the synapses. I am talking about this sort of thing. Of course, I believe that there is no escaping some sort of non-chemical, non-electrical agent, call it mind, soul, whatever you like.

Our problem, of course, is whether that lands us back in Descartes' old dualism, the mind-body split, the only progress being that instead of locating the mind in the pineal gland, now we can locate it in the Brodmann language area.

I write this only to advertise my own dilemma.

Okay, I'll return your books and manuscript presently.

Re the Nag Hammadi stuff: Interesting, but I cannot help but express a mild surprise. Which is to say, I don't see how a Peircean scholar can go for this ancient gnosis which seems not to require a semeiosis, that is to say, a transaction in signs between people, an intersubjectivity, a realism to the degree that the transaction is taken to be about something which, to some degree, can be known and talked about. Whereas all this gnosis requires is oneself.

I guess I find myself on the side of the Apostle and my friend, Flannery O'Connor. Paul said (to fuse two passages): If Christ is not God himself entered into history and if He did not in fact die and was resurrected from the dead, then our teaching is in vain and we're back in our sins.

Flannery (answering an Anglican): If the Eucharist (the bread and the wine) is nothing more than a symbol of Christ, I say to hell with it.

Thanks again for the good stuff (can understand your writings better than CSP or Deely or Poinsot—though I believe the last was onto something big and I am slugging away at it). Will be returning your books and some of mine—the ones I can lay my hands on.

If you want to do me a favor, find whatever you can on the Russian formalist, Viktor Schlovskij (spelled variously) whom I keep reading references to and who seems to be onto something. I have no library here but the Covington Public Library.

Cordially,

Walker [s]

November 19, 1987

Dear Ken,

Thanks for all the good things including your papers and the Manicas book. Looks interesting. I'll return it, maybe with triple stars (or some Xes—I make an X when I think the guy has gone wrong).

I know you're a premier CSP scholar, but I can't say I envy you, having to read all that stuff (plus another several million words, I understand, in manuscript). My main complaint against CSP; he didn't take a lesson from William James whose pragmatism after all is so well expressed. Which is only to say that WJ is a very good writer and CSP a very bad one.

You didn't answer the question about CSP which bothers me most. His greatness I concede, of course, and for me it mainly consists in his great distinction between dyads and triads, Secondness, and Thirdness. It is gospel to me. But what does he mean by this often-quoted statement, "The sign addresses somebody . . . creates in the mind of that person . . . the *interpretant*. The sign also stands for something, its *object*," etc.

Please tell me why this isn't a fancy form of Skinnerism! Stimulus (leads to) conditioned brain (leads to) response.

What I'm asking you is where does CSP speak of the triadic event as an *act*, performed by an agent. After all, if a sentence is asserted, there must be an asserter.

I know that CSP does in places speak of an "interpreter," but does he ever really address this problem? You're the only CSP expert I know, so I ask strictly for information and a reference or two. Please have pity on a poor novelist.

All best,

Walker [s]

🦎

November 26, 1987

Dear Walker,

Thanks for your two recent highly valued letters, the next to last of which I partially answered by sending *A History and Philosophy of the Social Sciences* by Peter Manicas, and the last of which I try to answer now, thus trying to redeem my marker which you have held for a while: My Choctaw word of honor to try to give a decent account of the interpretant and why it ain't Skinnerian a-tall.

I'm about halfway there with the paper I sent you a month or so ago ("Toward an Understanding of Peirce's Master Argument"), which you apparently read in Maine (what a great setting for a little metaphysics). I want to call that one to your mind at this point. The reason is that little trivalent node is something that just about everybody misses when they read Peirce. And that little sucker is terribly basic. It's no magical icon, but just a pictorial way of stating what is primitive, meaning that this we don't explain, but it is in turn used to explain other things.

I'm back in front of my trusty word processor. So I will proceed to think with my silicon.

Now I have heard you say (well, read you say) that you take these triads as basic, as primitive. But I have my doubts about whether you do. And I can't de-Skinnerize CSP for you until we have a mutual agreement about the old node, or at least find out where we stand, what each of us really thinks.

Here is my evidence for what I read that you said. You have the following chart on p. 96 of *Lost in the Cosmos* (the paperback version is all that I have found—was there a hardback? Can I buy hardbacks of your books from Kumquat Inc.?). (By the way, I'm including a description of my course in semeiotic for spring '88 semester—I'm going to try to flesh out the theory of novel science.)

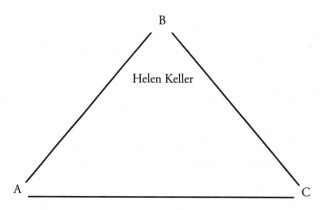

Signifier (*signifiant*):
W-A-T-E-R spelled in her hand by Miss Sullivan

Referent (*signifié*):
perceived liquid flowing over other hand

Below that figure on p. 96 in *Lost in the Cosmos* you stated, "Relations *AB*, *BC*, *AC* cannot be explained as dyadic interactions. This is a triadic event."

My problem with this is that *AB is* a dyadic relation, as is *BC* and *AC*. You seem to be saying, then, that a triadic relation (the whole diagram?) can be made up by a combination of three dyadic relations. CSP has arguments and considerations all over the place aimed at showing that such cannot be done. (Whether he is right in those arguments is another matter, but at this point I strongly suspect that he is correct, but I'm working on it.) I give some of those considerations as to why a triad can't be made up from dyads in my Master Argument essay. And you say the same thing in many places. But on p. 96 of *Lost in the Cosmos* WP seems to be saying that all you need to get a genuine triad is three appropriately placed (or appropriately combined) dyads.

Here's another way to express the same thing. I take it that your diagram is expressing the following sentence: "W-A-T-E-R is understood by HK [Helen Keller] as meaning the fluid stuff in her other hand." Now that is a triadic relation, the form of which (the rheme for which, CSP would say) is: _____ is understood by _____ as meaning _____. A successful understanding of that kind (of the kind that rhematic sentence describes) as it would actually occur is a process that CSP calls semeiosis (sign action, action of a sign). That rheme is triadic, with three relates. But that relation cannot be composed (made up from, put together using only) from just dyadic relations, as your diagram suggests. Thus the following three dyads do not make a triad: HK *feels* the code sequence WATER (your *AB*); HK *feels* fluid in other hand (your *BC*); Code for WATER in one hand *and* fluid in other hand (your *AC*). This had the rhematic form: __1__ feels __2__ , __3__ feels __4__ , __5__ and __6__ . Counting the number of blank spots in this rheme we have 6. All your diagram does is to join these in the following way: 1 and 3 are identical (i.e., HK), 2 and 5 are identical (i.e., the code sequence WATER), and 4 and 6 are identical (i.e., fluid). Furthermore, "identical with" is also a dyadic relation (which is what you are using to join things up here). So what you get in your triangle is this:

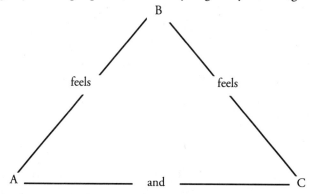

That is a bunch of dyadic relations joined to make a daisy chain. Where is the triad in such a chain? There ain't one. You say there is, but I can't see that what you draw and what you say are identical. I believe what you say, but not what you draw.

On the other hand, when CSP drew the naughty node, he wanted what he said and what he drew to coincide, and he is saying with such a drawing, "Here is a triad, which is fundamentally a triad, not made up of anything else, is basically, ontologically, nonreductively a triadic relation, which can't be dissected, reduced, boiled down, nor fat rendered therefrom." Why did it take me a long time to grasp that? It sounds so simple. Probably I didn't because our culture is so damned causal. Here I call up WP's profound analyses of our dying age as found in *The Message in the Bottle*, which has manipulation of nature, technology, etc., etc., as its basic mode of thinking, which is fundamentally a dyadic thought style, which says "When facing a problem, seek the causes." The best example of that which occurs to me is that now in Texas the leaders are saying, "We can end our economic downturn by cultivating high tech." Nuts. So if I was enculturated in such a society, little wonder that it took me so long to grasp that simple fact—I had to change one of my most fundamental (and hence subconscious until recently) modes of interpreting. Such is a kind of conversion experience, one of the little mysteries of philosophic life (but also one of its pleasures).

Another piece of the evidence that WP may have dyadic tendencies is that in the note on p. 87 of the paperback in *Lost in the Cosmos* I see not three technical terms used to discuss triadic sign relations (as CSP has), but two: ". . . Saussure's valuable dissection of the sign into its two elements, *signifier* (*signifiant*) and *signified* (*signifié*)." This makes the sign to be a dyadic relation. Where is the third relate? A triadic relation has to have three relates, not only two.

On the other hand, as you continue in *Lost in the Cosmos*, pp. 97ff. (indeed most of the book), everything sounds right to a triadic ear. So I am puzzled.

Back to the three-legged snake. —— Now this is a miniscule *system*. In a way, the nodes (the relates, the noun entities) are *aspects* of the system. And they shift in meaning or significance as the system (the triad) is viewed from different logical angles. If you look at it one way, say as a person would who wants to convey a meaning to someone else, then the focus or attention paid by the sender to a triad chosen to convey a message will lead the sender to emphasize particular aspects of the triad in order successfully to get understood. A mediator, say in the Cuban prison riots in Oakdale, Louisiana, will see the facets of the triad in a somewhat different way, something like how to link two ends via a medium. Ditto for a "pure receiver" as one might conceive Robinson Crusoe to be when he saw that odd other footprint, and sought to discover some things about it (or like a physician trying to discover what is wrong with rearward presenters in Feliciana in *The Thanatos Syndrome*).

The fundamental thing in CSP's semeiotic is triadic relational forms. True, he often shifts his terminology, and sometimes his terminology is tough to comprehend because he is doing his best to create a scientific (chemistry-like) terminology for semeiotic. The way in which chemical or medical terminology functions is exactly what he had in mind for semeiotic terminology (he didn't quite finish the job, however, at least not in one single work). In chemistry "sulfuric" calls to mind the numbers for proportions in a particular compound or formula, different from "sulphurous," which to the initiated calls to mind another characteristic aspect or formula. Or to consider medicine, when a surgeon talks about a _____-ectomy or a _____-plasty, no matter what organ is in the blank, a knowledgeable person knows that it is either a "cut it" or a "stretch it" operation. Likewise in semeiotic P wanted a patterned set of terms that would call to the mind of the experienced phanerochemist (an alternate word for phaneroscopy, which is an alternate word for phenomenology, which is an alternate word for how the logic of relations can be mapped onto the world) the way in which a particular kind of semeiosis is compounded.

By the way, for a long time, I have thought that CSP's ideas would be likely to help out in psychiatry, or be useful there. A lot of your writing has tended to confirm that for me. Did you study psychiatry, or are you a natural?

People often talk of sign relations in working with CSP. Probably the best approach is to think of semeiosis as being the basic phenomenon. As I stated in my little "Master Argument" essay, P distinguished between the action of semeiosis and that of dynamic or dyadic action. Here is one fundamental confusion that troubles a number of persons. Some folks want to think of the sign as the thing that carries the message in a triadic communicative activity. Suppose a redneck gives Tom More the bird. That frontal presentation of the interstitial digit is the message bearer (sign) of the message sent by the redneck to More, the receiver. But in this narrow sense of sign, to talk of a sign relation may seem strained to some folks. Someone might say, it's just a gesture—where's the relation? On the other hand, CSP sometimes uses sign in a broader sense, something like: A sign is the entire triadic relation whereby Something is represented by Something to Something. This second formulation is the best way in general to think of sign or theory of signs, in CSP's sense. The first one really is about the same as the second, if you think it through.

Here is another little conversion experience I had. A second enculturation we have laid upon us is the notion that the world is made up of two kinds of stuff, matter and mind. Descartes is our culture's master in this regard. As the saying goes, Descartes saved science by stripping off mind from body, and giving mind to religion and body to science—a kind of King Solomon resolution of the dispute. One sees this everywhere—physical sciences vs. social sciences emblazoned across the catalog of almost every university and college in the world, all the dying age factors you have mentioned, etc. If CSP had done nothing else in his career but write the three articles (a set) "Questions Concerning Certain Faculties Claimed for Man," "Some Consequences of Four Incapacities," and "Grounds of Validity of the Laws of Logic," he would still be famous, for those articles blow Descartes out of the water.[14] The problem is, the culture doesn't know that yet, and relatively few scholars do. What did P put in place of the old comfortable body/mind dual-stuff ontology? For P, the basic stuff of the cosmos is relation. Now that is weird. Too weird ever to be accepted, even though it might be true? To quote Fats Waller, "One never know, do one?" Is it true? If it is, will it replace the cultural knee-jerk dependence on Cartesianism? We shall see. (After all, WP, the other Cenopythagorean, is briskly selling a book that appears to argue, when it gets past dyadic diagrams of triangles, that the cosmos is a bunch of relations and worlds and like.) Such a doctrine that the basic stuff is relation is a form of philosophical idealism. CSP is an idealist—an objective idealist. Idealism can resolve René's old mind/body problem with no mention of the pineal gland or any other wiggling organ. It does it basically by saying that there is no body—it's all mind. As CSP said, matter is just effete mind, too weak, too hide-bound with habit to be vigorous interpreting mind.[15] Matter, in other words, is just a certain kind of relational pattern or system (as is everything, says the Cenopythagorean). The impact of all this on science is terrific, but its impact upon religion might be even more terrific, for spirit (being just another kind of relational pattern) can readily thereby be seen to be real (Martin Buber or Simone Weil or St. John of the Cross or WP in some of the moods in his novels), as real as matter. (Real, of course, for CSP, means "those properties something has no matter what we hope or desire or wish those properties to be.") Are you still with me? We are driving a 1939 Chevy Six convertible with bald tires on a dirt road in a deep rut three miles from town and it's starting to rain.

The next item to consider is that individuals are not basic. They are derivative. Yes, you are WP and I am KLK, but these beings that we are are not fundamental, which is to say that you and I are to be explained or understood in terms of something else. The usual strategy in everyday speech is to take individuals as fundamental and to explain things in terms of individuals. Thus our culture thinks of a society as a collection of individuals—individuals are basic, and they explain the nature of the group. In CSP's approach, an individual is a convenient abbreviation for something that is more basic, a particular web of semeioses, a rather complicated one actually, and one that is changing all the time. I am not the same person I was a few years ago. All the relations that constitute me at some given moment are changing, sometimes slowly, sometimes quickly. I have a kind of identity in that the emerging relations have (usually) a prior set of relations to refer back to (but sometimes even that is absent or marginal, as in your electroshocked heroine in *The Second Coming*—her semeioses were almost nil). This is the meaning of P's remark that "man is a sign," which could be best understood as "human beings are, ontologically speaking, semeioses."[16]

An individual, then in CSP's sense, is a hypostatic abstraction, the kind of abstraction that makes the intellectual move from "Opium puts people to sleep" (description of a process and its result in process language or activity language) to "Opium has a dormitive power" (substantive language, used I think in our language habits as a way of saying that we have conducted a survey of the processes and they function that way—that is, the move from process talk to substantive talk is our linguistic marker for saying that an inquiry has been conducted into this process, say of opiates, and the substantive talk asserts that the process has that result and you can depend on it, and you can use the result of that process as input into some future activities). The whole subject of hypostatic abstraction is very important in CSP's work, and it is little studied, even by Peirceans. It is a rampant move in math, being the way in which we change the process of a moving dot into the substantive "line," or how we change a laterally moving line into the substantive "plane," or how we change a series of "processual" experiences someone might have at Turner Falls near my home town of Davis into "Southern Oklahoma culture," or how we turn our own personal flowing processual relational beings into "me" and "you." It is also the way in which the actual reality of a semeiosis (a triadic and nonreducible relational process) is changed into substantives like sign, or object, or interpretant according to the interests we have at the moment ("Keep the bacon warm mamma, for I'm gettin' close to home tonight!").

Now for Walker's supposedly crypto-Skinnerian quote from CSP. In what text did it originate? I got to look it up. Time out.

Here is one place that sounds like your quotation (*CP* 2.303) [CSP's definition of "sign" in James Mark Baldwin's *Dictionary of Philosophy and Psychology* (1902), Volume 2, p. 527, reprinted in *CP* 2.303]: "Anything which determines something else (its *interpretant*) to refer to an object to which itself refers (its *object*) in the same way, the interpretant becoming in turn a sign, and so on *ad infinitum*." (Another one from *CP* 1.541, from the Lowell Lectures of 1903): "A REPRESENTAMEN is a subject of a triadic relation TO a second, called its OBJECT, FOR a third, called its INTERPRETANT, this triadic relation being such that the REPRESENTAMEN determines its interpretant to stand in the same triadic relation to the same object for some interpretant."

This seems to be the kind of thing you have in mind. I suspect that the word that is bothering you the most is "determine." It did me for a long time when I first started reading CSP. P, being (or better, trying to be) the consummate philosophical terminologist, thought he had an obligation to older philosophers, especially the medieval logicians, to keep their terminology, which he regarded as admirable. Since all is semeiosis, even in science, any procedure that will ruin or discolor previously established terminology was viewed with alarm by CSP. He thought it a part of the ethics of science that a term once created by a qualified scientist should be used as the originator designated unless there was some over-riding new reason to change matters. Here he had in mind the practice of biologists who let the discoverer of a species name it.

So you can bet your bippy that CSP used "determine" with full presence of mind. But what does (did) it mean? Our first impression of it (mine certainly was) is to think of it on a causal (dyadic) model. In a note entitled "What Is Meant by 'Determined'," in *The Journal of Speculative Philosophy* for 1868 (see p. 4 in my *Comprehensive Bibliography*—I can send you a xerox of the whole article if you want), I take him to be saying that "determine" means "to make the less definite more definite," or one could say it this way, "to fix (pin down, specify, get clear on) something to be this or thus." So the concept is like Sherlock saying to Watson, "Did you determine the victim's name?" That means: We know there was a victim (something vague), but can we make our vague conception of this victim more definite (less vague), for instance, by getting the victim's name? There is no causal undertone in this sense of determine, as there is in "cultural determinism," the notion that all our actions are caused (determined, predetermined, predestinated) through the social physics of our culture, as Comte or Marx or Freud thought.

So let us paraphrase these passages, modifying "determine." I'll also put in some other paraphrased or inserted items which will tend to show how I interpret these passages:

> [A sign is] anything which [makes something else—the interpretant of the sign—less indefinite] . . . [so that the interpretant can better refer] to an object to which itself [the sign, in the sense of the representing medium or message] refers (its *object* [the sign's object] in the same way, the interpretant becoming in turn a sign, and so on *ad infinitum*.

> A REPRESENTAMEN is a subject of a triadic relation TO a second, called its OBJECT, for a third, called its INTERPRETANT, this triadic relation

being such that the REPRESENTAMEN [specifies, makes less indefinite] its interpretant to stand in the same triadic relation to the same object for some interpretant.

The idea is, I think, that the interpretant explains the object through the sign. Or one could say that the interpretant refers to the object through the sign (representamen). If one reads "determines" in the causal sense, one gets the feeling that there is a cause emanating from the object, passing through the sign (message, medium) to the interpretant, making the interpretant be a particular thing, which no matter what it is, would be the end result of a dyadic causal chain. That is not what CSP meant. If anything, the action is coming from the reverse direction: The interpretant through the sign (message, medium) explains or makes more definite the object. That is, CSP's theory of signs could almost equivalently be called the theory of interpretation (interpreting always being seen as a triadic relation). The final interpretant is another concept of CSP's that is often missed. Here "final" doesn't mean "last"; it means "final causal," as in Aristotle. The final interpretant is just reality, and P's idea is that reality is drawing a fair-minded scientist to it in a telic (final) manner. (P loved to quote "Truth dashed to earth will rise again.")

The three relates of the triadic representation relation in the most general sense for CSP are object (could be a thing, or could be a concept, in general it is the relate which the whole representation relation is *about*), the representamen (the message bearer, the medium), and the interpretant (that which interprets, understands). What is the interpretant, then? That question, in effect, makes the interpretant of a previous sign relation the object of a new sign relation. So the answer to the question, what is the interpretant, is that it is but another triadic representation relation, the object of which is our old interpretant, with a new sign and a second inter-pretant—What is interpretant 2? And so on, *ad infinitum*, although this is an *infinitum* that stops when we stop asking questions, so it is not a nasty *infinitum*. As CSP said, we stop inquiry when doubt ceases and we have a stable belief. We start it up again when we have a new doubt (when we need to make a new interpretation).

"But what is the object?" says someone. Is there a logically first object?

There is a similar *ad infinitum* on this end as well. The alpha and omega are infinities. There is no first object. We can always ask for more interpretation about what underlies any given object. In other words, there is never a last interpretation on either end (on the object end, or on the interpretant end). Same thing for the middle of the triadic relation, the middle relate, the representamen. Tom More gets the bird. Was that bird flashed in an Italian style or was it the Arkansas manner? When we run out of money to conduct the inquiry, or we get tired, or we feel satisfied, or whatever, we will stop interpreting (asking questions). See how this works out with nodes (notice we never break out of triads):

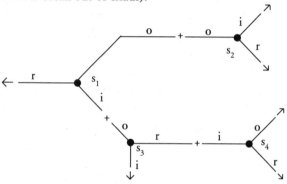

Many permutations are possible; this is but a snapshot of a potentially infinite network. What about the interpreter? Since neither you nor I as individuals are fundamental, and since triadic semeioses are what are fundamental, interpreter is just a convenient name we use when the interpretant is a web of triads that is also a living person. All interpreters are interpretants, but not all interpretants are interpreters. So a human person could be either an interpreter or an interpretant. CSP preferred the latter term, but on a number of occasions said he had despaired of making his more abstract notion of interpretant understood, so as a "sop to Cerebus" (so he said) he used "interpreter."[17]

"Does CSP prove all this?" people ask. No, not in the math sense of proofs as understood today. He argued for it. But the thing to remember in this regard is that he offered it as explanatory hypothesis, to be confirmed, modified, or disconfirmed. The thing I have been concentrating on is just getting his hypothesis out in the form he might have wanted it.

You seem to be saying CSP was a bad writer. I think in one sense he was. He often would stray. But in another sense he was a fine writer. Some of his prose is among the best I have read in English. If you want a sample or two let me know. He had such a troubled life history that he was often distracted. Also, he was jerky from time to time, like the character in *The Second Coming* who fell down, P had a kind of catatonia once in while, probably partly genetic (his papa had it as I recall) but also probably activated by his work habits through which he abused his body fiercely. There are manuscripts in which as one reads his time and date records, he is just awake and working for 48 hours or so at a whack, while also not eating much or well. He needed a genius agent, a manager. He had one for a while in the years when his father was alive, but after Ben passed away, he had no manager, so his personal traits took him in and out of the dumper. Still the closer one reads and studies him, the more one has to admire his resilience and his sense of duty in which he tries to get his thoughts out somehow because he senses he is onto something vital for humanity. Be patient with him, for as with anyone who has a new idea, it is a struggle to get it expressed, for it is new.

Now maybe you see why I was reluctant. For to answer your wonderful question about the interpretant is in effect to ask for CSP's whole system of science (see my chapter on CSP in John J. Stuhr's anthology in *Classical American Philosophy* I recently sent). The above is but a weak sketch, full of gaps and inadequacies. But I believe the inadequacies are mine, not P's. It is all there (for the most part) in his works, and we are getting it out as time passes. Meanwhile, your own somewhat similar work is terribly important, for you are addressing our culture in powerful ways with your novels and through your essays. Don't stop. Maybe you can appreciate why I want to help you if I can.

I still think that it would be worthwhile to meet to discuss these and other questions. I'm going to the American Philosophical Association meetings in NYC during 26–31 December 1987, in case you might be back East then (bad time to travel, but the phil pros must meet during Christmas—ugh). Or I will be off duty at the University from about 15 December through 15 January. Would be pleased to drive over to Covington, shack up in Motel 6, and have a couple of beers with you as desired; or you could come to Lubbock on the sly (your privacy protected) and visit the Institute collection in our library, chat a little, stay in my guest room, and relax, as you wish. I don't want to be at all pushy in suggesting this, and no offense taken if your destiny takes you otherwise.

Your loyal correspondent,

Ken [s]

Ken Ketner [t]

&

December 1, 1987

Dear Ken,

Am still overwhelmed by your letter, your taking the time and trouble to answer the questions of the most amateur of all Cenopythagoreans.

Needless to say, I have not yet digested your letter. And also needless, I do not pretend that I will ever get hold of the technical-philosophical-Peircean argument advanced in some places.

What I will do is simply respond more or less off the top of my head and *ad libitum*.

A good place to start is our native Cartesianism, which, as you suggest, we have inherited as scientists along with the American Way of Life. So first, if it is true that CSP "blew Descartes out of the water," I'd like you to put me onto the set of articles wherein he did this: "Questions Concerning Certain Faculties Claimed for Man," etc. I've got the 8-volume *Collected Papers*, so give me a reference therein. If anybody has routed Descartes, I'd like to witness it (and wish him, the router, well). But I doubt it.

That is to say, if you don't mind my saying it: As I read CSP's tortuous exposition of the interpretant, and yours as equally exciting exegesis of it, the thought kept coming to me: Aren't these two guys doing an extraordinarily talented and even heroic job to escape the Cartesian trap—like Houdini bound and gagged and locked in a cage and thrown into ninety feet of water. Houdini does get out, but do CSP and KLK? Well maybe they do, but I'll have to read close and again to make sure.

Okay, I'll take CSP's word for it that he only used "interpreter" as a sop to Cerebus. But that does not remove the difficulty.

The difficulty is that though neither you nor CSP like to use "interpreter"—presumably because it invokes some such notions as "subject" or "mind," in a word is too Cartesian. I agree, but here's the trouble:

When you and P are not speaking of interpretant in a somewhat casual-sounding "determined" context, you say things like this: "The interpretant explains the object through the sign" or ". . . the interpretant is that which interprets, understands," etc.

In sentences like these, "interpretant" is the subject of verbs like "explains," "understands," "interprets."

Very well. But there is an unresolved ambiguity here. I can say the sentence, "The rhesus monkey responded to the sound of the bell by salivating." We both understand the sentence and the event described without ambiguity. The rhesus may be the subject of the verb "responded" but we understand very well that the rhesus in the event described is an element, albeit complex, in a causal chain: sound of bell, sound waves, excitation of auditory receptors, impulse in the auditory nerve, other S-R events in CNS neurones, motor or glandular response, etc.

But, in the case of the sentences about the interpretant, what are we to make of the status of the subject of the sentence if it is not a similar complex entity in a similar causal chain?

What is the alternative to being so understood except to be understood as some manner of agent or actor—or mind?

I realize that you're doing your best to answer this question and to provide a tertium quid with yours and CSP's three-legged snake, the tertiary node, the minuscule system.

My difficulty is that I can't be sure you (and CSP) are not doing a bit of conjuring, pulling the coin out of the baby's ear, by swapping back and forth between logical categories and "real" categories.

It seems to me the only common ground we can be sure of—a place to start, however, faulty, in fact doomed it may be—is the Cartesianism we're stuck with.

My method is to start with the Cartesian stance of our natural "science"—which is well and good as far as it goes—who questions the validity of "mind" studying "matter" for the past three hundred years since the scientific revolution, in the physical, chemical, astronomical and biological sciences?—and then see how the objective Cartesian method gets into trouble. In fact, it is almost a commonplace since Kuhn to admit that the classical paradigms of science—matter in interaction, energy exchanges, field forces, S-R interactions and such—fail when the object of the science is man, man *qua* man, i.e., the social sciences.

So why not retain the objective method—man looking at a natural phenomenon toward the end of making sense of it by some productive and verifiable paradigm—and apply to those man-*qua*-man behaviors which are simple enough and accessible enough to get hold of?

One can use Helen and the water and the word "water." But perhaps even better are the classical two-word sentences of an infant just acquiring language—like *stove hot* or *dog bad* or *daddy home*, which I suppose can be fairly called sentences or rhemes.

Maybe it's my medical training—yes, I was headed for either psychiatry or pathology until the mycobacterium bit me—but my ingrained method is to look at the patient, the rhesus, and make a diagnosis, a guess really, at what is going on inside the organism. One does this, of course, by constructing a model, drawing a mental picture, and then seeing whether the model works. Thus one sees certain symptoms, takes a guess, makes a model of say a dyadic dysfunction of the Langerhans islets in the pancreas, i.e., diabetes, then runs tests, etc., to "verify" the diagnosis.

So, instead of arguing with you whether the Helen triangle is a congeries of dyads, *AB*, *BC*, and *AC* dyadic events, I'd rather pose for you the methodological problem. Clearly Helen's own account is that of a breakthrough event. Now we would have no trouble at all in understanding Helen's previous signing—or rather signaling, behavior according to classical biological models. Which is to say: When Miss Sullivan signs to Helen (making a mark in her hand) to go get some cake and Helen "understands" and runs to the kitchen to fetch the cake, you and I can draw a dyadic picture of what happens, a series of events connected by arrows: a pattern of stimulation of the sensory receptors in Helen's hand, afferent nerve impulse, sensory-motor brain events, afferent nerve impulse, response (learned), behavior (Helen fetching cake).

But I defy anyone, Skinner included, to draw me any such picture or even the roughest schema, of even the sort of thing that happens within Helen when it dawns on her that water (spelled out) "means" the water flowing over the other hand. She puts the two together. And does so thereafter with her naming and her rhemes.

I'm sure we agree so far: That it is at this point that Helen (and the rhemic infant) become semiotic creatures as well as being good responding organisms.

My difficulty with CSP is this. While I can agree with him about his interpretant, it does not seem to go beyond the passive accretion of meaning, connotations, associations, and such which occur with any received sign—sign "cat" is invested with all the familiar sensory-gestalts of catness, furriness, etc., on its way to denoting this individual cat. As such, I don't see it differing much from Saussure's sign, a signifier hooking up not with the actual object but with the signified, the perceived object.

Which is only to say that once you admit the triad, the rheme, the naming act, the understanding of a name given, etc., there is no escaping—the interpreter, the actor, the understander, the namer, the coupler.

Which is finally to say: We may indeed deplore Descartes' crude dualism, the *res cogitans/res extensa*, and propose an alternative semeiosis as sophisticated as you please (actually I prefer the tetrad which is really two triads interfaced, a model which allows for the various variables of intersubjectivity, misunderstandings, etc.), there is no escaping, no sleight of hand, no logicizing, by which one can escape the residual actor, interpreter call it whatever you please—"I," "utterer," "mind," whatever.

In fact, what I would like to do is, instead of explaining away mind, exorcizing the Cartesian ghost in the machinery, rather to give the utterer his proper place in the semiotic. If you can't altogether exorcize the ghost, you can at least see how he's hooked up to the machinery. In a word, what we need is a phaneroscopy of the ghost. Which is what I mean by "a semiotic of the self" with its variables like modes of re-entry, etc.

In passing: It bothers me a little to hear you call CSP an idealist—which has bad echoes of Kant, Hegel *und so weiter*. Wouldn't one be justified in calling him a philosophical realist in the sense that he believed there was something out there, whether he chose to call it matter or not, about which something could be known? I will not quarrel with him or you about "matter"—call it effete mind if you like or anything you like—but if there is not a something out there which we can guess about, abduct about, to a degree confirm each other about—then what is CSP going to so much trouble about? Surely—and here's the tetradic model—he's telling me something about something else, using words, rhemes, reams of rhemes, to set before me for my edification a state of affairs.

Well, enough—I haven't even digested your letter, which I'll be working on. But I was turned on enough to write prematurely.

What it comes down to for me, where I'm at right now, is this. I am less interested in the precise nature and status of CSP's little triadic node than in seeing what would happen if one came up with a halfway decent semiotic model which would legitimize a phaneroscopy of a semiotic self— and see what would happen if one applied the model to the almost total incoherence of present-day "social science"—including linguistics and psychology-psychiatry.

One could start with Freud who was a genius and who did an absolutely mad thing. Psychoanalytic theory is a brilliant and lunatic misappropriating of the dyadic model and slapping on the mind, conscious, and unconscious. The ultimate triumph and folly of Cartesianism—swiping the model of the *res extensa* and sticking it, where else but—on the *res cogitans*! stretching mind-stuff onto the rack of body-stuff. And it seemed to work! Or rather, and worst of all—we thought it worked. In fact, to a degree it does. But what a nutty business: The ghost in the machinery laying hold of itself and applying to itself the mechanics of the machinery.

I might write a book about it. Best for now.

Walker [s]

December 5, 1987

Dear Walker,

Now we are even—I have a big letter from you which I must take some time to digest. Meanwhile, a few quick responses to you that won't take any time, and might be of some use. As my old teacher, Herb Fingarette used to say, those who respond are respons-ible. By the way, I don't see myself as "answering your questions." If I only could! I don't have the answers, just some ideas of my own, one of which is the strong conviction that CSP is ahead of me on this path, and that his public voice has been stifled by a strange sequence of events (his message can't come through—corruption in the public interpretant—that reminds me, the possessor of *The Thanatos Syndrome* was Comeaux, not the drinkers of ionized water, right?). One aspect of the strange set of events is that much of the time Peirce thought like a medieval Roman Catholic, if you will forgive me. I don't hold that against him at all—it's one of his strengths. But, what is the attitude of many (if not most) of our co-civilizationists about such "extreme realist" modes of thought? Before I forget, your tetradic picture on p. 97 in the hardback edition of *Lost in the Cosmos* seems right, but how about trying it this way:

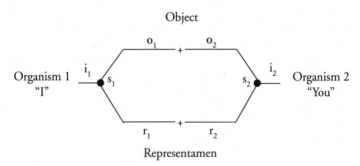

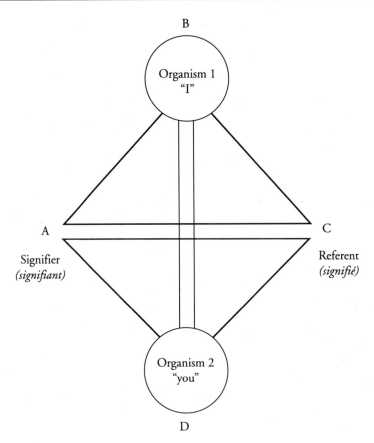

Relation AC—your giving a name to a class of objects to make a sign, and my understanding or misunderstanding of such a naming—cannot be understood as a dyadic interaction.

Relation BD—the I-you intersubjectivity of an exchange of signs—cannot be understood as a dyadic interaction.

These are two conjoined triadic events which always happen in any exchange of signs, whether in talk, looking at a painting, reading a novel, or listening to music. It allows for such peculiar properties of triadic events as understanding, misunderstanding, truth-telling, lying.

[Organisms 1 and 2 assume that o_1 equals o_2 and that r_1 equals r_2. In this diagram, o = object, r = representamen, i = interpretant, s_1 and s_2 are sign relations (signs).] And your making a tetrad out of two triads is good Percy-an doctrine, that Peirceans could accept.

CSP whups up on Descartes in "Questions Concerning Certain Faculties Claimed for Man," *CP* 5.213–63. Immediately following it in that same volume are "Some Consequences of Four Incapacities" and "Grounds of Validity of the Laws of Logic: Further Consequences of Four Incapacities." These three articles form a unitary whole. They should be considered as a three-chapter book. P wrote very closely in these articles. By that I mean he packed a lot into each sentence. His method of composing was to write a whole article, then be told by an editor that it had to be condensed, then write it again from scratch, typically taking out some explanation needed. This is one reason one has to get into his correspondence and manuscripts to get the whole message. Since he was so damned poor most of the time, he had to keep editors pleased.

The *CP* is rather badly edited. It's OK for published papers, which these three are. But if in the head note for some article in *CP* the editors say "from a manuscript so-and-so," proceed with great caution. Another thing they did was to break up unified series of published papers into different volumes of *CP*. Luckily the "Questions" series is an exception.

The "Questions" series was written by CSP after being challenged by William Torrey Harris, leader of the St. Louis Hegelians and founder of *The Journal of Speculative Philosophy*. Harris had asked CSP how, on P's philosophy, the laws of logic could be anything less than unintelligible. P replied with the "Questions" series, and in the bargain wiped out Descartes too (I think).

I have always thought that a couple of other articles make a good continuation of "Questions. . . ." These are in Volume 6 of *CP*. Some editions of *CP* bind Volumes 5 and 6 together, others were bound with each volume in its own set of boards. Anyway, in Volume 6, I warmly recommend "The Doctrine of Necessity Examined" (*CP* 6.35ff.), "Man's Glassy Essence" (*CP* 6.238ff.) and "Evolutionary Love" (*CP* 6.287ff.). The section on religion in *CP* Volume 6 is prone to misleading one again due to the way it is edited, and the fact that Paul Weiss had his head on wrong on that topic. But, the material printed on pp. 340 through 355 is reasonably reliable, and a nice introduction to P's thoughts about religion, which he sharply distinguished from Theory of Religion (Theology, Philosophy of Religion . . .). That is, he thought that clerics who offer their flocks theory (theology, etc.), when living religion was what was needed, were offering them stones instead of bread.

I got to stop so I can put up some Christmas lights on housefront trees, then study your esteemed letter. Wife and 7-year-old son decorated the indoor tree, and informed me that my duties were external.

I still say we need to meet somehow and discuss all this. Doing it by letter is perhaps not the best physical medium. My impression is that we are awfully close on a couple of very basic points, but kept off by accidents of our communicational medium. Scientists need a community, and there ain't too many Cenopythagoreans per square mile in the USA. Why not seminar for short while? What do you say? How about a sit down? If you want to do it, you tell me how and where. If you don't just say "No." You say we haven't been properly introduced? Hows about we count both of us in the same edition (42nd) of *Who's Who in America* as a sufficient introduction?

Ken [s]

❧

December 14, 1987

Dear Professors Putnam and Ketner,

I deeply appreciate your invitation to speak to the Peirce society.[18]
Fact is, I'm working on a book, and have had to give up such commitments, however pleasant.
Thank you again. It is indeed an honor.

Sincerely,

Walker Percy [s]

P.S.: Thanks, Ken, but I quit the lecture circuit sometime ago. Don't you know what happens when novelists fool around with philosophers? They turn into something French.

Sincerely,

Walker [s]

☙

December 21, 1987

Ken,

Many many thanks for the Manicas and the Rochberg-Halton books.[19] Both go to heart of matter: Manicas to the incoherence of the social sciences, R.-H. to the semiotics. I'll xerox a couple of places and return them to you, since they are clearly hand-used. I know, because you mark up a book the way I do, even using Xes.

My ambition to use CSP's semiotic to develop a coherent anthropology (i.e., combine Manicas and R.-H.). But here is where CSP let us down. He plays the shell game with interpretant. In one place he says this: "The symbol is connected with the object by virtue of the idea of the symbol, using mind without which no connection would exist." Also "interpreting mind." Then he's into "interpretant" being determined by sign, etc. "Interpreter" and "mind" seem to have disappeared.

How would CSP reply to Descartes if latter said to him in heaven (or maybe purgatory): With all your fancy semiotic, you're still stuck, as you should be, with a mind, my *res cogitans*?

All best to you and yours for Xmas.

Walker [s]

※

[n.d., approximately late January 1988]

Dear Ken,

Check one:[20]

___ Do have Max H. Fisch
_X_ Don't have Fisch
___ other

Ken. Just back from Rome and am not sure what I've got, but all I can find is dust jacket of Fisch edited by Ketner.

All best,

Walker [s]

※

January [February] 5, 1988 [Apparently January is an incorrect date. Since the letter was postmarked February 6, 1988, it is reasonable to presume the letter was written on February 5, 1988.]

Dear Ken,

Many thanks for "The Importance of Religion for Peirce."[21] I'm glad you put it together because it's hard to figure him. Still is. I gather by "religion" he means something either synonymous with Reason, a Reasonable Universe—or a sort of pantheism, as you suggest.

One caveat: Orthodoxy is not formula, as you and CSP suggest. It is, of course, *ortho* (right), *doxa* (opinion), e.g., what Christians believe to be a true statement. One can dispute it, but it is still a "truth-claim" sentence.

E.g., It is orthodox to believe these two statements: 1) God entered into a unique covenant with the Jews, 2) God was uniquely incarnated as a man in history, Jesus Christ. To deny this, as in Arianism, that J.C. was only a good man, the best, is unorthodox.

You and CSP may not believe this, but at least admit that it is not a *formula* but something worse = a true or false sentence.

WP [s]

⁂

February 8, 1988

Nobel Committee of the Swedish Academy
Kallargrand 4
S-111 29 Stockholm, Sweden

Dear Friends,

I would like to suggest someone as a possible recipient of the Nobel Prize in Literature. I am a professor of philosophy at Texas Tech University, one of the five major public universities in Texas. I have recently received an information package from the Swedish Embassy in Washington. I am not sure if you would consider me as a "qualified person" (p. 26, of the pamphlet *Alfred Nobel and the Nobel Prizes*), one who may submit a nomination to you directly. If I am in that category, I would like to make a nomination. Any information you could send about how to go about doing that would be very welcome.

On the other hand, if I cannot according to the rules make a nomination directly, please tell me to whom I could write to suggest that a particular person be nominated by someone who is a qualified nominator.

With cordial greetings,

Kenneth L. Ketner [s]

Kenneth Laine Ketner [t]
Charles Sanders Peirce Professor of Philosophy
Texas Tech University

꙳

Sunday [March 6, 1988]

Dear Ken,

Your Peirce-Percy course sounds fine.[22] Yes, I'd love to see a student's paper.

Sorry, but I didn't receive *Classical American Philosophy*. But don't replace. I'll get it and look up pp. 234–45. Meanwhile draw me a picture of an interpretant. (I can draw you a picture of the interpreter.)

All best,

Walker [s]

꙳

March 18, 1988

Dear Ken,

Just a word to acknowledge your letter and "Novel Science."[23] I think you've got something there, in your modeling. Have only just read it through quickly (in car, at post office), so I'll ponder it.

Needless to say, I am somewhat awed to be hyphenated with CSP in the "Peirce-Percy conjecture," but I'll take it.

I need a word. What would you call the entity which asserts an assertion, interprets an interpretant, receives and understands a name (like Helen Keller), constructs a model, etc.? There are dozens of names, none any good—e.g., interpreter, namer, soul, spirit, self, consciousness, person, etc.** I am thinking of writing something smart-alecky, presently entitled *Contra Gentiles*. Thesis: The great superstition now is not religion as generally held, but science or scientism, i.e, the real fuck-up of applying "dyadic" science to human behavior. Incidentally many thanks for Manicas whom I'm just about to jump on.

All best,

Walker [s]

**Am tending to *person.*

ᕇᐤ

April 14, 1988

Dear Walker,

I read "Novel Science" at Texas A & M a few days ago. Quantitatively I hadn't much of an audience, only six. But qualitatively, it couldn't be better. Ph.D.'s and one M.D. who wants to be a Ph. too. (By the way the latter doctor was Harry Lipscomb, a fellow admirer of WP, HL being apparently, as I was later told, a pretty famous doctor.) Altogether, these six kept me hopping in the question session. The general reception seemed positive.

The semeiotic class here took an interesting turn the other day. I had brought them to the cliff edge so they could see the fair fruitful plain of Thirdness, universal (cosmic) intelligibility; that the dyadic experts of our day lacked same; that we should now acknowledge the importance of Thirdness and intelligibility and understanding (this being the main point of WP's and CSP's semeiotic) in all our cognitive efforts, especially social science. And guess what? They revolted. They wanted to crawl back into the old expertly built dyadic crystal womb! They wanted to continue to feel bad in a good environment. What kind of syndrome is that? Now what do I do? Make 'em walk home thru a swamp? Prescribe for me Doctor. The cure is in sight but there has been a relapse. HA! a *re-lapse!* Double HA!

I inclose the finished form of "Peirce and Turing" for your archive. You had an early rough version. I'm trying to show that Alan Turing's results confirm CSP's Thirdness, etc. Also confirms the Peirce-Percy Conjecture. But at the time I wrote it, I hadn't discovered WP. We Choctaw Taoists are slow, but I like to think steady in the long run.

Friendliest greetings,

Ken [s]

&

April 28, 1988

Dear Walker,

I'm still stalking the interpretant. Your criticism of it is profound, and one of the major reasons why, as said at the outset, it is a bitch. But I still have hope that with proper diagnosis and surgery it can be cured. I struggle toward a healthy definition of interpretant.

Sooo, here is a recent item from my work here, a transcription of CSP's letter to Papini, one of the originally bustling Italian pragmatist school (which Mussolini literally killed off).[24] I hope you will forgive my commenting in the margins as a brief way of dialoguing with you.

Ketner [s]

&

January [April] 30, 1988 [Inaccurate January date. The letter was most likely written on April 30, 1988; according to postmark on the envelope, it was mailed on May 2, 1988.]

Dear Ken,

I'd have answered earlier but they threw me down and took out my prostate.[25] Seems to be working out, but it laid me out in good style. I don't recommend it, but I understand Choctaw Taoists don't need it.

Was quite fascinated by your account of the semiotic session. Folks, especially scientific folks, have no way of getting hold of Thirdness. My own prediction is that most educated folk are going to end up schizoid: Practicing "dyadic" science and Hindu New Age shamanism at the same time. Am working on "Peirce and Turing."

More later.

All best,

Walker [s]

🪷

May 12, 1988

Dear Walker,

Sorry to hear of your surgical encounter. Warmest wishes for a prompt recovery.

A couple months ago I told you about my Peirce-Percy semeiotic class. You expressed an interest in seeing what kind of student papers emerged from it. I told that to the students, and encouraged them to do their best. I inclose one paper from each, also included is a pair of visual blandishments. I used an old studio photographer's trick. Said "WP wears panty-hose" just before shuttering. I couldn't stop their laconic grinning the rest of the class time.

This was a good class. Most made an A, but there were a couple lower grades. Most were seniors. The best paper I thought was Masters' (architecture). Dougherty (also architecture) a close second, if not a tie. Hill (probably a med schooler) did a fine job on art. Fox (philosophy) has a good insight on CSP's common sense (which I think is his version of your "triadic world of man"). Huckins had his own interesting insight on Marx (political science). McIntyre (psychology) calls up the dreaded orientals and tries to place them in a good light (so did Merton the monk, remember, in his book on Zen), but WP will probably reject all such moves. Bannister (philosophy) attempts to generate some doubts about valency matters. Weiner (history) probes the corporate mind. Johnson (advertising) exposes the dyadic ad world. Bannister and Fox exercised their freedom during the photographic class (i.e., skipped class that day).

I'm proud of these folks. They seemed, each in their own way, to have broken through educational packaging. Cenopythagoreanism is indeed the coming thing.

Loyally yours,

Ketner [s]

P.S.: Please return papers eventually, so I can send same to students.

❧

May 18, 1988

Dear Ken,

Am reading your student's papers with much interest. How soon do you want 'em back?

They're a good looking crew. I bet it was fun teaching them.

All best,

Walker [s]

❧

May 20, 1988

Dear Ken,

These are remarkable papers. They're bright kids and you obviously turned them on.

I couldn't help but scribble a response on the back of each.

Congratulations on getting a piece of the NEH grant![26]

Surgery went OK. Gradually coming around.

All best,

Walker [s]

P.S.: Am pleased you pushed Percy onto them—a classy company.

ॐ

[Comments made by Walker Percy on papers written by students of Professor Kenneth Laine Ketner.]

(1) About the paper entitled "Common Sense" by Jerry Fox: "Interesting, but if CSP favors conservatism—common sense—tradition—heart over reason, wouldn't he have favored traditional geocentrism over Galileo's heliocentrism? You have given me a new approach."

(2) About the paper entitled "Peirce: Science and Art" by Laura M. Hill: "A very interesting comparison of the *public* nature of both the scientific and artistic triadic enterprise. A question for Laura, because I'm not sure of the answer myself: Assuming that a second scientist can verify the first scientist's experiment and hypothesis by reporting it—publicly—how does the reader of a good novel publicly verify the truth which he receives from the novelist? By shouting "Hooray! He's right! That's the way it is!""

(3) About the paper entitled "Semeiotic, Valency Equivalence, and Cenopythagoreanism" by Bryan Bannister: "A very clear and close reading. My only reservation: I don't see how Bannister thinks my 'triads' are decomposable to dyads. It is precisely the point that Helen Keller's dawning understanding of the 'word' water spelled in her hand meant the water flowing one to other hand is irreducibly triadic even though a chain of dyads is involved: Stimulation of sensory nerve by water (leads to) discharge of afferent nerve to brain (leads to) neural transactions in brain, etc. But no combination of these can yield Helen's great discovery."

(4) About the paper entitled "The Similarity of Peirce's Views on Religion and Those of Vedic Psychology" by Christen McIntyre: "Okay—I follow—

but I wonder what CSP would think of this since he was a philosophical realist—that is, he believed there was something out there which we, you and I, can learn something about and tell each other. Whereas the Vedic and Buddhist 'I' is oceanic, even illusory, disappearing into the *atman*, etc. A question for a CSP student (I'm asking because I don't know): What did CSP think of the Jewish-Christian claim: that God entered into a Covenant with a single tribe, entered history as a man—doctrines, of course, which horrify Buddhists, Vedists and Brahmanists? I hope Christen can steer me to a CSP passage."

(5) About the paper entitled "Marx and How He Relates to Semiotic" by John Huckins: "Thanks. I hadn't thought about Marx and semiotics before. Incidentally, I wonder what John would think of Marx's dialectic (Thesis [leads to] antithesis [leads to] synthesis) as a sort of dyadic model which Marx was trying to impose on triadic behavior. Note: Page 3 (1): Elsewhere I said (along with Kierkegaard) that the only way a man can know himself is with another, or others, under God."

(6) About the paper entitled "The Stimulus-Response Approach to Advertising" by Marvin Johnson: "Figure 2—Kid and G.I. Joe—is a lovely dyadic model, better than mine. Does Marvin mind if I steal it?"

(7) About the paper entitled "The Bringing of Common Sense to Architecture" by Travis Dougherty: "Right. I like Dougherty on the triadicity of shelter. An interesting semiotic investigation: A mistaken triadicity imputed to the Giza pyramid: constructed to cast a pointed shadow at equinox in a certain mythical place, making use of a series of dyads: light from star, refraction in atmosphere, etc. Then the weary Western traveler seeking shade and shelter and resting in shadow, thinking this was what the Giza pyramid had in mind all along."

(8) About the paper entitled "Physical Process and the Corporate Personality" by Rob Weiner: "A very nice analogy. What I would like to see Rob do is explore the differences between the pseudo-triadicity of a molecule and the more-or-less true triadicity of a church, e.g., church members responding to each other and to minister or priest or rabbi dyadically (I don't like his voice, her hat, but I'm drawn to this strange girl next to me in the

pew), compared with triadic elements, e.g., the churchgoer suddenly penetrating the drone of the preacher's voice, hearing what he says. 'Listen, I have some good news for you.' Maybe actually hearing it for the first time."

⁂

May 24, 1988

Dear Walker,

Your letter of 18 May and package and letter of 20 May arrived in the same mail yesterday. There was no rush on returning them. I see you kept Masters' piece. I thought it was the best—a kind of search record. Shall I tell him you liked it so well that you kept it?

Yes, they were a fine group. But I have felt all along that you were a co-teacher by triadic remote control. I think WE had a memorable set of students. Their course evaluations are the kind that makes putting up with all the crap of academic life worthwhile. *We* got remarks like (and I quote): "Probably the best class I've had at Tech— . . . .The most important formal learning I have had in 17 years"; "*Lost in the Cosmos* and *The Message in the Bottle* were excellent"; "Probably the best class I have taken at Texas Tech—I learned more about what it is to be a human"; "My favorite one of the semester, and probably of my whole career here at Tech—I learned much more about myself—These thoughts will continue with me for the rest of my life." Congratulations to you, Walker. You did that to these children. I just served as master of the tea ceremony for you and CSP.

I'll see that each child receives your marks on their papers. They will be thrilled.

Box Nabisco,

Ketner [s]

❧

May 29, 1988

Dear Ken,

Yes, for some reason, I did hold out David Masters' paper. Here it is. How about sending me something on this "Chaos" business?[27]

All best,

Walker [s]

About the paper entitled "How to Write a Philosophy Paper and Discover the Mystery of the Self in One Easy Lesson" by David Masters: "It's all very well to speak of God, religion, Christianity in connection with triadicity. Maybe you're right and maybe I agree with you. But one step at a time. If you're convinced of the irreducibility of the triad in a *scientific behavioral* study of man, where do you go from there? Somehow I feel you're in a good position to work on this."

❧

June 23, 1988

Dear Walker,

Yes, the chaos guys *think* they are determinists, but they are confirming Peirce's ideas, unknown to them. For one thing, their math is a process that *persons* must witness, experiment upon, do, etc. That brings our favorite number right into the heart of science. I'm going to have to write on it.

I inclose the paper I read at the Frontiers of American Philosophy Conference at Texas A & M.[28] Very fine, warm, humane conference. American philosophy is well at Texas A & M.

Loyally,

Ketner [s]

P.S.: Those students were deeply honored by your remarks.

❧

[n.d., though presumably after June 23, 1988]

Ken,

Thanks. I don't see that "Chaos Science" is any less dyadic than that of Newtonian Mechanics (see my small works, e.g., p. 316).

WP [s]

❧

July 1, 1988

Dear Ken,

Many, many thanks for "Pragmaticism is an Existentialism?"
Like everything you write, it was a matter of much interest. But the thesis: CSP's "interpretation" similarity to Sartre's "choice" may prove to me a revelation. At least it gives me much to think about.

All best and thank you.

Walker [s]

❧

August 15, 1988

Nobel Committee of the Swedish Academy
Kallargrand 4
S-III 29 Stockholm, Sweden

Dear Friends,

It is my pleasure to nominate Walker Percy, M.D., of Covington, Louisiana, for the Nobel Prize in Literature.

Dr. Percy has written six novels: *The Moviegoer* (New York: Alfred Knopf), *The Last Gentleman, Love in the Ruins, Lancelot, The Second Coming*, and *The Thanatos Syndrome* (the last five: New York: Farrar, Straus & Giroux). He has also published two non-fiction books, *The Message in the Bottle* (Farrar, Straus & Giroux), and *Lost in the Cosmos* (Farrar, Straus & Giroux).

I have read all his novels, some of them more than once. I intend to continue re-reading them over the years, for more treasures are to be found there. I won't attempt to discuss these works. But I do want to mention a few general things. I find, and others with whom I have compared notes agree, that the literary art of Walker Percy has some unusual and profound effects upon readers. After a certain point, one begins to feel that the author is somehow doing something extraordinarily fine for the reader, and that is a severe understatement. Although this phenomenon is general, is in the experience of many readers, I find that the only way to describe it is by speaking in the first person. After reading one of Percy's novels, I want to seek him out, to hug him, to thank him for the great artistic and curative experience I feel he gave me. I have read many things, from science to philosophy to literature. I am an avid reader in areas from technology to poetry. I read constantly because I am a student of civilization in general. I simply have never felt anything like this. It is amazing, and wonderful, and warmly human. I swear it sometimes makes me weep. I have not achieved an adequate understanding of this phenomenon. Maybe one should rest, and simply say that it is an instance of the power of great literature.

His novels are philosophical, in the sense that they put before us the great questions of human life. These works ask us to think about questions we have shoved aside, and they give us a magnificent literary format through which such issues can be accessible to thoughtful persons of virtually any background. The phrase "literary format" is perhaps too sterile, for Percy's writing is in itself beautiful—as I have mentioned above, sometimes intensely and almost unbearably so.

But Percy does not dogmatize, he does not indoctrinate. After providing a beautiful symposium, readers are carefully and gently, almost lovingly, weaned, left to themselves, given to their internal resources. It feels as if Percy were quietly urging, "Now you must take some steps, you must go forward; be brave dear reader, you can do it." I suspect Percy believes that this is the only possibility for each of us, and that his task is completed if through his art he can place us in the presence of these great questions knowing that our only hope for answers lies within our own deep personal resources. It is an interesting datum that this process a reader of Percy lives through does not produce arbitrary or solipsistic outcomes. That is, one might imagine that such a procedure would yield a wide range of ideas among readers. But there is a surprising similarity. My guess is that this similarity arises from the fact that human beings are very much alike at this instinctive level.

Dr. Percy's non-fiction works are also profound, but in a different way. I am a close student of the works of Charles Peirce, the founder of philosophical pragmatism, a man widely acknowledged to be the most original and versatile American intellect. Peirce was a great theoretician, the equal of Kant or Descartes. Peirce's best contribution was his semeiotic, an attempt to give an explanation of interpretation and intelligibility.

Percy's non-fiction is focused on the same kinds of issues. And I find that he often gives me new lessons, after thinking that I had worked out all the difficulties through my study of Peirce.

The fact that Dr. Percy has mastered both fiction and non-fiction prose, both literary art and literary science, is another reason he should be recognized as a Nobel Laureate in Literature. The main reason he should be so honored is simply that he is a profound teacher (a physician in the old sense) to our present civilization.

Stuart Wright has provided a careful account of Percy's publications in *Walker Percy, a Bibliography, 1930–1984* (London: Meckler Publishing, 1986). Robert Coles has written a fine intellectual biography: *Walker Percy: An American Search* (Boston: Atlantic Monthly Press/Little, Brown, 1978). There is a relatively large and growing body of secondary studies of Percy; a good summary is in *Understanding Walker Percy*, by Linda Hobson (Columbia: University of South Carolina Press, 1988).

I would be pleased to provide additional information or resources if you would let me know your wishes.

With friendliest greetings,

Kenneth L. Ketner [s]

Kenneth Laine Ketner [t]
Charles Sanders Peirce Professor of Philosophy
Texas Tech University
Lubbock, Texas

❧

August 21, 1988

Dear Ken,

Thanks for *The Lubbock Avalanche-Journal.*
You already know my feelings: If one does not grant a religious warrant for the sacredness of human life, one must consider the scientific grounds, i.e., that there is no essential difference between the human organism, genetically or hormonally, before and after birth. Thus, if you allow the destruction of the unborn for however good and private a reason, why not get rid of undesirable 1 year olds, or middle-aged subversive professors for that matter?

All best,

Walker [s]

p.s.: Just getting over a bout of fever and hope to get to work on *Contra Gentiles.* WP

August 25, 1988

Dear Walker,

Thanks for yours of 21 August. Sorry to hear you have hosted a bug. I have been writing, reading and office working this summer (no teaching), and now have to stop such sinning and get ready to teach next Monday. I'm through 1.8 volumes of Shelby Foote's trilogy on the Civil War. What's this talk of it being *like* the *Iliad?*—it's better!

I hope I didn't absentmindedly send you the wrong *The Lubbock Avalanche-Journal.* What a strange name for a paper in a flat place like this. What I may have accidently done was send you one with something about abortion in it (I have got you figured out on that one). I meant to send you the issue with a big report on our local extension of the Medjugorje phenomenon. It's been the talk of the town. Big crowds of faithful and curious out at St. John Neumann's parish church on the west side of town. It's a new church, built West Texas style in a semi-dugout fashion. Very energy efficient because the earth covers much of the walls. It also has five beautiful (to my old engineer's calibrated eyeball) electricity generating windmills. (I entered the study of philosophy by flunking out of electrical engineering—well, not exactly flunking, but getting bored out.) I wanted to send that issue to you in case you were curious how a small-town paper tried to report on the M phenomenon (I find that long Croatian word full of linguistic hairpin turns and tough to type, so I'll just write M). I remembered you had M from Yugoslavia in *The Thanatos Syndrome*, Part 4, Chapter 13.

I have no problems with miracles and apparitions of the Virgin: If there are such, then so be it. But if they are real, it seems to me to be no blasphemy to want to study them (which I do want to do), and to study the *nimbus* of surrounding phenomena especially, the *nimbi* of not-quite-miracles-but-we-thought-they-were (to use the Germanic way of solving the problem of being at a loss for the right word). Hell, if the behaviorists and nominalists are right, then our corresponding is a cotton-picking miracle. Or if you know of a Catholic who had an adverse reaction from a Protestant about the Assumption, that's mild compared to how a modern formal logician reacts to a doctrine like "the nonreducibility of triadic relations." They even use the same vocabulary in their denunciations.

The M case (I just saw the BBC documentary on it last night on our PBS) seems to have a number of factors in the "genuine" column: young children, no apparent axes to grind, no other apparent factors associated with human greed, egocentricity, pride, etc. The bishop of M took a fence straddling stance, which I admired: We shall study this, we don't know what to think at this point. No scientist could have done better, and on the whole, they would be likely to have done worse (recall some of the Stanford Researchers who pronounced that Uri Geller really could bend spoons). Interesting that young Bishop Michael Sheehan of Lubbock (a new diocese) took an identical stance.

Here, however, the parish involved is in big debt, the town fathers (whether Baptist, Church of Christ, or Mormon, or burned-out Ohioan insurance executives) were happy to see 10–20,000 folks come on 15 August, the feast of the Assumption, to see what would happen, or to get cured, or just to worship in what was thought to be a very spiritual surrounding. A couple of the volunteer nurses brought out to St. John Neumann's were from my nursing/philosophy class last year. They gave me an account of the 15th, said they literally had a few folks with hospital bracelets still on them, others not from hospitals equally as sick and barely ambulatory, all out in a burning hot and humid Lubbock afternoon. The "planners" for the event had arranged for a medical tent staffed with a doctor and some nurses. National guard volunteers in summer greens were apparently joyfully directing traffic; squads of city cops on hand for crowd control. Media folks everywhere doing live remotes from their vans direct to the stations across town. Newspaper articles twice a day. Folks saying that this is the first time they can remember a story from Lubbock being picked up in lots of major papers around the country, and how that would help our image. Interesting that the local ministers of the protesting type were pretty quiet about some of the things they usually harp on, such as the anti-Assumption stuff. They seemed to just politely register their disagreement. The parish prepared for this event by building special facilities, altar outdoors, etc., as if the Pope were coming to town. The Assumption day event had been preceded by a number of parishioners receiving messages, which they announced to the congregation, all in a rather organized manner, as opposed to the M case. The phenomena here in rosary sessions before the 15th seem to have been the usual kind of charismatic events—tongues, animal sounds, messages, healings. One memorable one was recorded by a TV crew: A woman stated that "Our Lady spoke in the voice of a wolf to her to show how she cried out for the people to come back to the church." She then proceeded to vocalize a fairly accurate wolf cry while kneeling up in front of the church near the altar. When I read about that, it struck me as ludicrous; but when I saw it on TV, I found it strangely moving.

The point I am trying to make is that the miracle in Lubbock, if there was one, seems to have been drowned by the umbra of miracles—all the surrounding phenomena which are rather predictable and rather human. Whereas the case in Yugoslavia seems to have been, at least initially before the extra baggage came along, just a miracle. The Lubbock event, also, strikes me as having been nearly consciously modelled on the M case in Yugoslavia.

What is a miracle? A supernatural happening? Or a natural event of importance that is not yet understood? I incline toward the latter, but I have an open mind on the subject. It would be a great pleasure to talk with heaven, in the direct way that is pictured in the old Biblical accounts or in the experiences of say the recent Catholic miracles (Lourdes, etc.). And, I am not an anti-Catholic, almost the opposite is true. I have a great deal of admiration for folks like St. Teresa of Avila, St. John of the Cross, your buddy Merton, etc. (e.g., some guy on the north shore of Pontchartrain whose name escapes me).

I guess I prefer the way of the Choctaw Taoist, for we feel that it is heaven to read a beautiful book, write to a friend, look upon nature. Or as our comrade Peirce said (I rephrase him slightly, but it's the same thought), "Open your heart, which is an observational organ, and you will have direct contact with God." In other words, humans have a natural religious capacity or ability, but because the species haven't been using it much in the past century or so, it has atrophied, but it can be put back into health by use, by flexing it. That means it must be a religious muscle, as opposed to a religious endocrine gland.

No need to take the time to respond to this. I just wanted to share with you the advent of Yugoslavia in Lubbock, Texas, of all places. No charge for the editorial evaluation.

Yours truly,

Ken [s]

Ketner [t]

๛

September 4, 1988

Dear Ken,

Many thanks for *The Lubbock Avalanche-Journal*.

Re the apparitions: I am as skeptical as the church. I remember talking to French doctors at Lourdes. They, skeptical as only the French can be, accepted the cures before the church did.

One tends to forget the much more scandalous proposition: That God chose the Jews and that a Jew was, is, God.

But please keep me informed about "apparitions." If she really shows up, please ask her to give me a hand with this bloody book which is about to do me in. Title: *Contra Gentiles*—or a kind of update of Aquinas's Scholastic treatment.

All best as always,

Walker [s]

꙳

September 14, 1988

Dear Walker,

I sent an offprint of this ["Toward an Understanding of Peirce's Master Argument"] to you, which was probably freer of typos than this article. Must have been set by a typesetter who is a card-carrying member of the Jack Acid Society. I also got no proof. I pasted on (or wrote in) a ton of corrections. How does this read if one substitutes "choice" and cognates for "interpretant" and cognates?

Ken [s]

꙳

September 15, 1988

Dear Ken,

Do you know anybody who can translate Russian to English? (I am thinking of your faculty friend who sent you—and me—the info on Viktor Schklovsky.) What I need to know is how he would translate the two famous opposed literary devices of Schklovsky. The words: *obnazhenie* and *ostranenie*. I suspect they mean defamiliarization and overfamiliarization, but don't know. How about a hand? Ain't no Russians here. I greatly prize "Pragmaticism is an Existentialism?."

All best,

Walker [s]

P.S.: The reason these Russian words are important to me is that they fit in well with my notion of the evolution/devolution of symbols, so that a thing/event can come to be cancelled by a symbol/word, hardened through over-familiarity into what Gabriel Marcel called a "simulacrum"—

same event/thing can be recovered in times of disaster or great poetry—simulacrum broken, *being* revealed as being, etc. Thanks, WP

❧

September 21, 1988

Dear Walker,

Glad to get your letter, and always more than happy to help you in any way.

I called Professor Peter Barta, our Russianist, today. He offers the following:

Obnazhenie

Pronounced something like "Ob na zhen ee aa." To bare, to uncover, to make naked, to reveal for what it is. Sound to me like "get intimate."

Ostranenie

"OOst ra nen ee aa." To make strange, unfamiliar, to alienate, to make the world less normal, to reveal artificiality. Barta suggests one compare Brecht's plays on this second word.

In general he suggests reading up in English-language books on literary theory in which there are sections on Russian Formalists, including Mikhail Bakhtin. He says such books are common.

That is the report. Do you want me to find you such a book? I bet we got same in our Library here. They recently counted, and we got 1.5 million titles. Ort to be some Rusky stuff in such a sample.

I'm totally at your service.

Y'r Obd't Sv't,

Ken [s]

Ketner [t]

October 12, 1988

Dear Walker,

Here is a draft of my essay "Hartshorne and the Basis of Peirce's Categories"—another attack on the reducers.[29] The first few pages will be familiar to you, but I launch into new ground on p. 5. I try to whup up on the set theorists, who I have discovered, are the guys who license all the other reducers. That is, since math lays at the bottom of much science today, even psychology (perhaps psychiatry has escaped it somewhat, but the psych guys are fully captured); and since many mathematicians take set theory as mother's milk, and since set theory is bodaciously reductionistic (as I think I show here), then voo ee la, as the French say, I think I have rolled back the big rock and found the ur-bug.

Hartshorne is probably the greatest living philosopher. And it is a great thrill that he lives in a humble house in Austin, Texas. He is still a real philosopher, wrestling with real problems, not just chopping nominalistic logic. So it was a real pleasure to respond to a call last summer to write something for a book honoring him to be put out by State University of New York Press. I'll ship you a copy of the book one of these days.

Bishop Sheehan here has quietly closed down the apparitions/messages phenomena out at St. John Neumann's Church. The press pretty well ignored that phase of the events. He has had a report from a committee of investigation that told him nuthin happened. Now if you get a message you got to ask the bishop before you can read it in church. That might be a slight over-reaction. Suppose your island guy got a message in a bottle, but couldn't read it without a form from the bishop.

I have to confess that all my plots to figure a way to meet you at a conference have failed. Now I got to play my hole card. If I were to get in my wife's sturdy little car and drive over to Covington one of these days, would it be possible to enjoy the pleasure of your conversation and company in some manner or form? I'm busting with things to discuss, and corresponding about philosophy and literature and such is like trying to drink a cherry phosphate through a broken paper straw. Besides I want to see your face and shake your hand, and particularly to thank you directly for what you gave me. (I'm referring to that mysterious phenomenon: Read Walker's books and fasten your seat belt, cause you gone on a ride, son.)

Warmest greetings,

Ken [s]

Ken Ketner [t]

ॐ

October 20, 1988

Dear Ken,

Many thanks for your papers on Charles Hartshorne and CSP, and on CSP's religion. I agree. He would hardly have called himself a Christian, though he was very reticent on the subject.

Would you have a copy of Ketner's "Identifying Peirce's 'Most Lucid and Interesting Paper' "—1987?

I am working on a lecture-article presently entitled "Science, Religion, and the Tertium Quid"—The *tertium quid* being CSP's triad being considered as an *event*, e.g., an 18-month-old naming for the first time, the assertion of any sentence. I undertake to prove that aspect of the triangle (variously called by CSP interpretant, interpreter, judger, mind, soul) is an entity which is both real and non-material. Too ambitious?

I'd like nothing better than to spend time with you. But right now I am going through Ochsner Clinic with an obscure complaint which they can't seem to track down. Will let you know when I identify it one way or another, terminal or otherwise.

All best,

Walker [s]

October 23, 1988

Dear Walker,

Yours of October 20 received with gratitude. I'm flattered you are interested in my "Identifying . . . " paper. I would have sent you a copy, but because it is so manuscriptually technical I thought you would be bored by it. Somebody has to grub through those manuscripts, and since Hartshorne and Weiss did it badly in their *Collected Papers*, and because I want to study what Peirce said (not what somebody erroneously said he said), I'm forced into the manuscript business. I hope to convince you in a moment that the business is paying off in an increased understanding of CSP. Anyhow, here is a copy of "Identifying . . . " in the form of a copy of the *Transactions of the CSP Society*, which doesn't send out offprints—just several copies of the issue in which your article appears. Do you subscribe to the *Transactions*? It's cheap, and has good articles on CSP.

I inclose another item, the big red thing. It is the first laser-printer draft of my edition of CSP's Cambridge Conferences Lectures of 1898. This is a big example of why I had to become a manuscript grubber. In the *Collected Papers* you can hardly find that CSP gave such a set of lectures. A few extracts are found here and there from some of the manuscripts that made up the lectures, and you are even encouraged to think that CSP gave a lecture series called "Detached Ideas on Vitally Important Topics" (he did not, he only thought he might, then things changed, as my intro shows). So the Cambridge Conferences Lectures lay buried. As I began to seek info about this and that topic within the general P manuscripts, I kept getting echoes of a lecture series I had not studied. I finally decided to try to track it down. As I did, this beauty emerged. I think it is the best popular introduction to CSP's late system that I have found. Hilary Putnam has agreed to write a preface for it, and I am negotiating with Harvard University Press about publishing it. If they don't take it, I'm sure I'll find someone else who will.

I hope you won't refuse me the honor of dedicating it to you (p. 4). I'm not kidding when I referred to that mysterious phenomenon "what happens after you read Walker's books." I understand I'm not the only effectee.

As you might/can tell from reading the introduction, CSP led an interesting life. You could write a novel on his life (matter of fact, wish you would).

Lecture 1 is a barn burner, a little masterpiece of rhetoric. He uses the phrase "Vitally Important" ironically, and he is reacting to James's *Will to Believe*. Lectures 2 and 3 are kinda technical. Four is a gem, about not blocking inquiry. The reductionist materialists or behaviorists should read it, for blocking inquiry is exactly what they do in pushing their anti-realism, their notion that everything can be explained by resort to environments, to use your fine terminology. The remaining ones are mixed in regard to technical issues. Overall the whole thing is relatively easy reading compared in some of his other writing. Lecture 3 is a good presentation of the categories, showing how they are related to diagrammatic thought (which one shouldn't thumb one's nose at, because it is the way to give Thirdness its due).

The article-in-progress you described sounds right on target. Doesn't sound too ambitious to me. I agree that interpreters, judgers, minds, and souls are entities that are *real*. They, however, do not exist; P's reality/existence distinction is one tailor-made for this kind of discussion. I would go on further to agree with CSP that the reality of minds is the highest kind of reality, and existences are the lowest kind.

Here's a little anecdote from a teacher's logbook. Bryan Bannister, a senior (graduate of the CSP class last semester) is helping me in the Institute now, on work-study. He is a psych major. He called my attention to the text *Physiology of Behavior* by Neil R. Carlson he is reading in Physiological Psychology this semester. The first few pages are a kind of mandatory introduction to the history of psych, how it "developed" out of philosophy (the rest of the book being guts and chemistry). It goes on for a few pages. I'll try to remember to package a copy of it when I send this stuff to you tomorrow morning. It is one of the most fanatical pieces of writing I have encountered in a long time. The only explanation he will accept is one involving causes. He is "not biased against non-material entities," but he doesn't know how to study them in a lab. And he thinks behavior is a proper thing to study (it being clear that by "behavior" he means "wiggle").

Now what really burned me about this guy is that he is teaching his crap to young citizens with this book, and doing so with the finest formaldehyded example of a closed mind I have encountered in some while (and I'm in the business!). He seems to think that he can simply postulate the foundations of his science.

Is he wrong? There are a lot of reasons to suggest that he is, and you know all or most of them. The one that struck me was his maintaining a "nonmaterial-entity-free" lab. That is a question-begger. I can just see the sign above the entrance to his lab: "No signs allowed."

One reason I was kinda pleased with my Hartshorne paper was that I got down to the mathematicians. They can't do their thing without signs either. So Brother Carlson won't have any math in his "n-e-f" lab, because math is precisely about nonmaterial entities. Carlson may stimulate (nonmaterially) me to write a book on his fallacies.

Hang tough in the clinic. Choctaw Taoists do pray—it is the easiest thing to do, yet profound. If you feel a funny encouraging little nonmaterial twinge, might be a Choctaw Taoist at work.

Ken [s]

Ketner [t]

ᘏ

October 26, 1988

Dear Ken,

Just to acknowledge all the goodies that just arrived in the mail. Will respond after poring.

What do you mean, a thing can be real but not existing?

What do you think of this as a title to Jefferson Lecture: "Science, Religion, and the Tertium Quid,"—the tertium quid being CSP's Δ. It is a novel reconciliation of "Science" and Judeo-Christianity based on CSP and which he probably wouldn't like.

WP [s]

P.S.: I'm floored by dedication.

☙

October 29, 1988

Dear Walker,

Glad to see from your card of 26 October that my package arrived OK. I'm not kidding about that "mysterious phenomenon": It's probably a nonlinear, nonenergic natural phenomenon, to quote something I read once. I'm tickled you won't object to my humble dedication. (Now I've got to get the darned thing published!) It's just my way of trying to send a nonlinear back to you in gratitude. That "mysterious phenomenon" is a topic (along with CSP stuff) that I hope to discuss with you over tea someday.

I have to confess my ignorance: I don't know about the institution of the Jefferson Lecture. If you are associated with such a tradition as lecturer, then it must be something worthwhile. Where and when will it be held? To be published? Could a Choctaw attend it?

I know virtually no Latin, other than fallacy names gotten from teaching freshman logic for a living since nineteen and aught sixty-four. I take it that Tertium Quid means something like Thirdness or Sign Relation in CSP's sense. If that's it, then you have a good title. There is no reason for religion and science to be in conflict, and they ought to be reconciled, and you are the guy who can do it. The essays and novels you write are extremely important for world culture, according to me; and this new one I'm sure would be yet another. Maybe you already figured out that I felt that way.

I've been studying CSP for a long time, and WP for a while too, and my impression in terms of my knowledge of CSP is that by and large he would applaud you. There are a few points about which he would wrangle with you, but the general drift is right up his alley. One reason he would appreciate your present effort is his almost lifelong quest to reconcile genuine religion with genuine science. The "philosophers" have pretty much overlooked that in CSP. (I think the "genuine" qualifier needs to be added, for there is a lot of bad science and bad religion—maybe the point ought to be that the essence of both are really close, maybe having only something like a mere verbal difference.) He called himself a Christian from time to time, but he surely acknowledged something like Kierkegaard's distinction between real Christian and Christian in the institutional sense. He was raised in a Unitarian family, loved William James's father, the Swedenborgian and read Swedenborg often, but later on converted to Episcopalianism, becoming a loyal member of the little Episcopal Church in Milford, Pennsylvania. CSP thought many of the institutional aspects of Christianity were defunct: He especially disliked the doctrine of papal infallibility, or any doctrine of infallibility for that matter; he would have equally disliked the idolatry of the Bible that one gets among the folks that subscribe to a "literal interpretation" of the same (there's a phrase that wears its sins on its sleeve, just like "military intelligence"); he thought theologians were terrible frauds, posing as scientists, but scared to death of any kind of experiment in their work (dogmatists, in the bad sense, in other words—dispensers of "truth" as opposed to seekers of the-truth-not-yet-known). So he loved and respected and revered Christ (in the sense of St. Paul or St. John), but disliked Christianity for the most part in the way I perceive (through reading you) that Kierkegaard did. CSP even had a kind of direct experience of Christ in the early 1890's (rather like St. Paul on the road), and after that, kept mentioning that such a direct experience was essential for genuine, mature, religion (in that like Simone Weil). I like to think that CSP was a follower of Jesus, not a Christian (meaning that he revered Jesus whom some call the Christ, but was repulsed not by the idea or institution of a church, but by what bad things that institution had become, at least in his day). I also happen to think, but can't yet fully document (I'm working on it), that P was strongly influenced by Buddha, and that he probably would draw a similar distinction there (follower of Buddha, but not a Buddhist).

The *Collected Papers of Charles S. Peirce*, the eight volumes you have, has some pretty good stuff on CSP and religion—look in Volume 6, all after p. 283. On the anti-theologian theme, see *CP* 6.1–5 (as this appears in *CP*, it is a chopped off version of an early draft of one of the Cambridge Conferences Lectures of 1898).

One of CSP's best essays is "A Neglected Argument for the Reality of God," *CP* 6.452–93. The problem with it, however, is that it requires (for full comprehension) decoding of a bunch of his special terms. So one has to read several other things in order to decrypt "Neg. Arg." His whole philosophy is at work in that little article; moreover, I happen to think that his whole career can be seen as an attempt to serve God via science and philosophy (I'm very careful to whom I say this, by the way), and that if so, this little article is the key to a lot of things in CSP.

You raised the question of CSP's reality/existence distinction. Notice in the "Neglected Argument" article, the argument that folks have neglected is one for the Reality of God, not the existence of God. Veddy imPertunt. The distinction goes something like this. The real is that which has the properties it has independently of any single person or group of persons who wish or hope or dream that it have those properties. The properties are not arbitrary, but are there to be discovered. For example, the contents of my dream last night was a figment, a nonreality, but that I had that dream with those contents is a reality. Secondly, all existing things are real—no sweat. But, there are some real things that don't exist. For instance, Tom More's Lapsometer, the stethoscope of the soul, is real, yet it doesn't exist (but that may be a matter of time, see the November 1988 issue of *Popular Science*, pp. 84–88, on magnetometering the brain). The Lapsometer of Thomas More has certain properties independently of anybody's wish or hope (even yours now that the book was published) as to what those properties are: Ditto Shakespeare's Hamlet, Twain's Huck, etc. Crudely put, you can kick existing things, and sometimes they kick you. But you can't kick real nonexistents such as your constitutional rights, or Aunt Susy's bank account, or the saltiness of as yet untasted salt.

Take your average everyday scientific law, say something of your choice from chemistry, or something of my choice from electrical engineering. Ohm's law sez in a complete DC circuit, $E = IR$: Voltage = Current times Resistance. Scientific law was the initial focus of CSP's realism, and he said that all scientists are unconscious realists. Now a scientific law doesn't exist, but is real, as opposed to the nominalists who say that a scientific law is but a handy collection of words indicating certain specific experiences. Behavioral psychologists are arch-nominalists in CSP's sense. Mind, says CSP, is real but it don't exist. P's critique of Descartes in a nutshell: Descartes was wrong when he said mind is some kind of thing, for mind is a reality, not an existence. Minds don't knock together like dyads, like billiard balls.

The famous materialist physiological psychologist, Sepp Dienarr, former resident of that village in upper Austria, Eseldorf, says, "Vell, because zer iss no opjekt zat iss a mindt, zen zer iss no mindt. Konzekvently, nonmaterial enteteze are verbitten in my labp." But that is just a ridiculous *non sequitur*. Dienarr's distinguished assistant lab director from Connecticut, an associate professor of material physiological psychology, in his corner of the great man's lab that is carefully quarantined against the presence of nonmaterial entities, says to his lovely lab-coated Californian graduate assistant as he habitually squeezes her butt, "Hand me the forceps sugar." And what happens to those forceps?—bing, they are shortly in his hand. He turns to his jealous junior colleague, a rather common kind of paranoid assistant professor from Chicago who hasn't had a graduate assistant for a while, and says with obvious enjoyment of his superiority, "Got that math report yet John?" In other words, nonmaterial entities everywhere, a plague of them. Jealousy, language, the chain of command, mathematics, employee's rights to a nonsexually oppressive work environment, a herd of nonmaterial entities. When is the last time our physiological psychologist stumbled over a statistical algorithm, or had a parallelogram of forces for lunch, or cut himself on a chi-square, or kicked a failing relationship? These entities simply don't exist, but they are realities that are integral parts of life in the lab. Walker Percy, grinning fiendishly, brandishing a copy of "The Delta Factor" like it was a charm against Dracula, bursts in the lab entrance screaming, "The lab is contaminated! Call the Ghostbusters!"

Signs are realities, not existences. True, signs are embodied in existing things. But the sign relation is not the thing in which it is embodied; the law is not its instance, not even the set of its known instances, for there is always the next instance, which means its instances are an infinite set. Also relations are realities, not existences. Existences are by and large matters of Secondness; Realities that are nonexistences are by and large matters of

Thirdness. So God is real, but doesn't exist: The cosmos is God's embodiment perhaps; God is the intelligibility of the universe, which sounds Spinozistic. But P goes further, to say that this cosmic intelligibility (law-likeness of the cosmos) is a personality of some kind, which leads some writers to call P a theist. If he is a theist, his kind is so different from the stock type that I think a new word is needed to avoid confusion. Pantheist is already taken (that ain't P's deal either). So what would you call it? I always thought George Lucas came close to P with "The Force." And CSP sure as hell ain't a Berkeleyan idealist, although he did like some aspects of Berkeley. In all this, CSP is quite close to that favorite institution of yours, the RC Church. That explains why many Catholic scholars have been interested in CSP. One big reason for their interest over the years is in my humble opinion the real/exist distinction, which upholds the reality of law, of relation. Another thing it upholds is the reality of spirit. Now ain't that Merton's position? Or what? It's also the position of Buddhists, and of Choctaw Taoists. It is also the clue to how to proceed toward further knowledge of the Percy nonlinear, nonenergic natural phenomenon thesis, seems to me (*The Message in the Bottle*, "The Delta Factor," p. 39).

Passages in *CP* on real/exist distinction = 6.453–55; 8.12; 8.153; 4.541 (note possible parallel between "existence" and causal environment, and then real nonexistent and world—WP's account of world in *Lost in the Cosmos* is a beaut), 1.328. None of these are exactly the passage I want to lay before you. The one I want is in the manuscript, and I'm typing this at home. I'll try to remember to send along a xerox copy from the manuscript file at the Library in a couple of days. The *CP* also often didn't publish the best stuff, and this must be a case of that.

Forgive me for foisting this on you. No need to answer. Just trying to help any old way I can. (But you're partly responsible, for your books gave me a psychic lube job, so now I run on like this.)

Loyally,

Ken [s]

Ketner [t]

❧

November 14, 1988

Dear Walker,

This one came as a thunderclap on a clear day.[30]

As I think about what to say, one thing is clear to me: I won't do it without your blessing.

On the other hand, I'm not sure I can do it—I'm still working on understanding you, after an initial burst of overconfidence on that point. And you might want someone else doing this sort of thing.

Damn, I feel so inadequate. Shrive me, Doctor.

Ken [s]

❧

November 17, 1988 .

Dear Ken,

I am delighted. You don't have to worry. Whether or not you "understand" me or disagree with me won't matter. If I were you, I'd do it only if I could have a good time. Very few semioticists approve of me—And I am the rankest amateur. I give my own peculiar, even idiosyncratic reading to CSP, especially since he was so vague about some things, e.g., "interpretant." Anyhow you know far more about it than this here poor novelist. What little I know is in *The Message in the Bottle* and the "intermezzo" part of *Lost in the Cosmos*. If you like, I'll send you a rough draft of my final version: "Science, Religion, and the Tertium Quid" (or "Science, Religion, and the Delta Factor").

Anyhow, only take it on if you can have fun with it. You can't offend me. I only make up stories.

Best,

Walker [s]

❧

December 8, 1988

Ken,

Here is something for your private edification. It is the first draft of the Jefferson Lecture and not to be circulated and certainly not published.

Any comments appreciated. Your letter to Jean Sebeok sounded good to me.

Best,

Walker [s]

❧

"Science, Religion, and the Tertium Quid"
Walker Percy

1   The title of these remarks is "Science, Religion, and the
2   Tertium Quid," but don't be alarmed. Tertium Quid means a little
3   thing lying around between two big things having a standoff, a
4   very important little thing, as it turns out, but one which has
5   been generally overlooked.

6   The tenor of these remarks is by and large discordant,
7   even negative, consisting as it does of attacks, controversy and
8   disrespect. It is not an attack on science in the name of
9   religion, nor an attack on religion in the name of science—both
10 of which attacks are invariably dreary. Least of all is it yet
11 another "reconciliation" of science and religion, the dreariest
12 business of all. No, what it is an attack on Science (with a
13 capital S), or what passes for science, an attack mounted in the
14 name of science.

15 As a matter of personal choice. I have always had a better
16 time attacking than defending.

17 What I wish not so much to attack as call attention to is
18 a strange incoherence in the sciences of man, that is, those

---

1 sciences which have man for their subject. What is extraordinary
2 is that the incoherence, striking though it is, has gone largely
3 unnoticed.

4 The only positive thing about these remarks is a brief
5 examination of the tertium quid, the overlooked little third
6 thing. The inspiration for both the attack and the little third
7 thing is the work of an American scientist and philosopher over a
8 hundred years ago.

9 No, it is not so much an attack as it is a nudging in the
10 ribs of a fellow bystander to take a look—do you see what I
11 see?—like the little boy who noticed that the emperor had no
12 clothes on and, more remarkably, that no one seemed to notice. In
13 this case though, it is not so much that the emperor is naked: no,
14 he is dressed to kill, except that his fly is open.

15 Let me begin with two statements of belief which have
16 informed men's minds in the Western world. Indeed it is
17 impossible to imagine Western man as other than as a composite of
18 the two beliefs in various proportions or as the ascendancy of the
19 one over the other.

20 When I say "men's minds in the Western world." I am
21 speaking of the educated denizen of a modern technological
22 society. I have in mind most academics, most professionals, most
23 of the students at the best colleges, including Catholic colleges,
24 most Presbyterians, show-biz types, in fact most educated
25 Christians and Jews—to say nothing of one-hundred percent of

1   educated atheists, agnostics and California Buddhists.
2   I will leave aside for the present the question whether
3   this educated denizen of the West is truly educated or not.
4   This person, this denizen, cannot in any case have failed
5   to be informed by these two beliefs, whether by actively rejecting
6   the one and accepting the other or by accepting both by a kind of
7   passive consumership without a second thought.

8   Yet it is difficult to imagine two statements which,
9   apparently at least, are more disparate, less reconcilable, not
10 to say contradictory.

11 To make matters more confusing, both beliefs appear to
12 many to have dead-ended. That is to say, to him, the average
13 educated denizen of the West, these two views, at least in the
14 popular understanding of them, appear to him insufficient,
15 irrelevant, or in some sense lacking as a guide for leading his
16 own life.

17 One sign of the dead end is the appearance all over the
18 place of cults and movements which owe more to the East than the
19 West, like the "New Age" religions with the increasing acceptance
20 among this very educated class of such exotic elements as
21 yoga, Sufism, Unity, conscious raising, human potential, ESP
22 —the various shamanisms which would have been regarded as loony
23 only a few years ago by this same denizen of the West, the very
24 class within which it is enjoying its greatest success.

25 The two traditional beliefs are familiar.

26 One has been called variously the "scientific,"

1   "objective," "secular humanist" and so on.

2   The other is the "religious."

3   I have put these words in quotes to indicate that they are
4   generally understood not by their dictionary definitions but by
5   their popular connotative meanings.

6   Thus the words "scientific," "objective," evoke certain
7   visions, certain avowals and repudiations. There is the cool
8   savant-technician who, sitting among his test tubes and computers,
9   understands the visible world before him by this or that formula
10 or abstraction, a world from which he himself is somehow curiously
11 exempted, who accepts only what he sees before him, and so
12 disavows most if not all the wisdom of the past.

13 The word "religion" wears its own connotative costume—
14 or should I say effluvium of odors? I can do not better than quote
15 the novelist Elizabeth Spencer from one of her stories. There is
16 "the smell of hymnbooks, Sunday school literature, the pulpit
17 Bible, the uncertain cleanliness of aging congregations, the
18 starch of little girls' dresses, the felt of the organ stops, the
19 smell of sunlight filtered by panes of stained glass discoloring
20 the musty maroon carpet." I can smell it now.

21 But allow me to give brief versions of the two statements
22 or belief—statements which the reader could as well make for
23 himself.

24 Here is the first or "scientific" statement.

25 The world is understood as an interaction and

PAGE 5

1   exchange of energy between various material
2   entities, the entities being either visible to
3   others or in other ways confirmable, the
4   interactions being quantifiable and expressible
5   by this or that formula of relations.

6 Man is an organism which has evolved from
7 lower organisms over the course of hundreds of
8 millions of years. It is possible to speak of
9 man as a "higher" organism in the sense that as
10 a consequence of his evolution, particularly of
11 his cerebral cortex, he has acquired the
12 capacity apparently unique, but again through
13 natural selection, to use signs, language and
14 other symbols, to form cultures, to develop
15 technology and to acquire more or less valid
16 information about himself and his environment.
17 Science is recognized as the most reliable
18 method both of acquiring knowledge and devising
19 technology, because it is based on public,
20 consensually validable information and on
21 verifiable (or falsifiable) theory.

22 Through the use of science, man has leanred [sic] a
23 great deal about himself and other organisms as
24 well as his environment, the cosmos, which is
25 unimaginably large, though not infinite,
26 containing billions of galaxies and no doubt

PAGE 6

1 other solar systems and planets on which other
2 forms of life may well exist.

3 The events which occur in any part of the
4 cosmos: within the human organism, in the
5 environment, the interactions between the two
6 and between two or more organisms—whether
7 chemical or physical reactions, electrical or
8 field forces—are recognized as natural
9 phenomena, i.e., not supernatural, and are

10 accordingly open to investigation by a publicly
11 verifiable science.

12 One is free of course to make one's own statement of what
13 science is about. I would only suppose that any such statement
14 would have the same tone. All such statements would, I think,
15 subscribe to Wittgenstein's famous motto: Whereof one does not
16 know, that is scientifically and empirically, one does not speak.
17 Because if one does speak, what one speaks is nonsense.

18 It should also be noticed here that the mysteries of
19 modern physics, the almost mystical behavior or misbehavior of
20 subatomic particles which refuse to be timed and placed, does not
21 weaken the force of the scientific statement. Because in the
22 large view, by statistics, particles behave quite as
23 deterministically as Hobbes's mechanics, one billiard ball hitting
24 another billiard ball.

25 It is difficult to imagine any educated denizen of the

PAGE 7

1 Western world who would not accept this statement in some form or
2 other, at least as far as it goes, does it not in fact almost go
3 without saying? If one tries to imagine a person who rejects the
4 scientific statement, who probably comes to mind is either an
5 ignorant person or perhaps an ideologue, say a Marxist bound by
6 the Hegel-Marx dialectic, or a "fundamentalist" christian [sic], or
7 perhaps a Western devotee of Eastern religion who believes that
8 the world explored by natural science is itself an illusion,
9 obscured by the veil of Maya, and hence not worth scientific
10 exploration. Reality, what one explores, is one's self. Brahma
11 himself is to be found within the *atman,* the self.

12 There remains, of course—despite the spectacular
13 triumph of natural science, the stubborn split between mind and
14 body, thought and matter, Descartes' famous division of the world

15 between the *res cogitans* and the *res extensa*. But would it not be
16 fair to say that it doesn't bother most of those who profess the
17 scientific credo, so triumphant is natural science and accordingly
18 so strong the conviction that all puzzles, even Descartes' dualism
19 will in the end yield up its mysteries to the scientific method?
20 But let me give you the second credo, a statement of
21 belief which, along with the scientific revolution, has so deeply
22 informed the very consciousness of Western man:

23 The entire cosmos, man included, was created
24 by God, an omniscient and omni-present spiritual
25 being, in no way identifiable with the cosmos or

---

1   the self save as creator to creature. Unlike
2   other creatures, however, man was created in
3   God's image, allowably through evolution though
4   it is by no means clear even to scientists how
5   evolution works. The expression, "in his
6   image," can be understood to mean, among other
7   things, that he, man, uniquely among creatures,
8   shares certain properties with God, such as a
9   degree of freedom, the capacity in a degree to
10 know, and the presence in his composition of a
11 non-material or spiritual element, the soul,
12 which is indestructible.

13 At an early time in his history, man, *Homo*
14 *sapiens sapiens*, lived in a period characterized
15 by a state of innocence, an openness to and
16 enjoyment of the cosmos and his fellow and by
17 his knowledge of and friendship with God.
18 At some juncture of man's history, there
19 occurred, again uniquely among the species, an
20 aboriginal misfortune amounting to a calamity of

21 such dimensions that all men suffered thereafter
22 a dislocation marked by an estrangement from his
23 fellows and the rest of creation, by a
24 consciousness of his own decline, suffering and
25 death, and by a capacity for misdeeds and malice
26 unlike the innocent depredations of other

PAGE 9

1 creatures, in a word: sin.

2 God, who loved man nevertheless, took the
3 following actions toward the end of rescuing man
4 from his predicament without infringing upon his
5 freedom:

6 One, according to most who profess this
7 credo, God, the creator of the entire cosmos.
8 entered into a covenant with an obscure Middle
9 Eastern tribe, promising a messiah who would
10 save man, i.e., in some sense deliver him from
11 his predicament.

12 Two, according to others God has in fact
13 already entered human history as a man, a member
14 of this same tribe, as this man and no other,
15 who not only bore a message from God to men, but
16 was himself God, who was not only not accepted
17 in his lifetime and his message ignored, but who
18 allowed himself to be executed as a criminal for
19 the salvation of other men. In order to be
20 saved, i.e., rescued from his predicament and
21 restored to his preternatural happiness, one has
22 only to believe this man and accept his message.

23 Three, still others believe not only the
24 above but that he, God, also founded a visible

25 institution, founded upon another man, a member
26 of the same tribe, through whose agency men are

PAGE 10

1 provided with a means of worshipping God and
2 receiving certain gifts from him, for example,
3 the Eucharist which, though having the
4 appearance of bread and wine, is believed to be
5 in a real, not symbolic sense, the body and
6 blood of the man-God himself.

7 Further, it is maintained that, unlike the
8 discoveries of natural science, the truths of
9 the Judeo-Christian religion cannot be arrived
10 at through thought, observation or
11 experimentation, however strenuous the effort or
12 gifted the thinker, but can only be known
13 through "hearing," that is by receiving the news
14 of these events from another person or source.
15 It seems fair to say, finally, that most
16 believing Jews and Christians believe the first
17 part of this statement, most Protestant
18 Christians but not Jews the first two parts, and
19 only Catholic Christians all three.

20 Both statements are necessarily over-simplified and
21 incomplete. For example, the first statement is a statement of
22 modern positive science and does not take into account such
23 postmodern developments as the almost subjective character of some
24 hypotheses in particle physics or of the relativism of the new
25 textual analysis.

PAGE 11

1 The religious statement omits Islam which, of course,
2 should be included along with Judaism and Christianity as one of

3 the "historic" religions, as in fact having historic claims in
4 common.

5 But for our purpose these omissions are not disabling.
6 Let me hasten to reassure you. In setting down these two
7 statements side-by-side so to speak, the last thing I have in mind
8 is to undertake some polemic or other, or an apologetic, in the
9 name of one against the other. We are all too familiar with and
10 weary of such attacks mounted from both camps. Accordingly and
11 for purposes of the present argument it does not matter much which
12 claim you set alongside the scientific statement. All three—
13 Jewish, Protestant, Catholic—are equally scandalous from a
14 certain scientific perspective. It is enough for the moment to
15 call attention to the paradox, that, on the one hand, it is
16 impossible to imagine Western civilization, indeed Western
17 consciousness itself, without both: without its Judeo-Christian
18 origins with the unique emphasis on the incursion of God into
19 history, a strictly linear and unrepeatable history; this on the
20 one hand; and on the other, the scientific revolution and the
21 scientific method with its view of singular events and things as
22 specimens of, exemplars of, certain classes and formulae.

23 And yet it is surely difficult to imagine any two
24 statements more disparate, not to say contradictory.

25 No, my purpose here is not to defend science against the

---

1 superstitions of some religions, nor to defend religion against
2 the dogmatic atheism of some scientists. It is rather to call
3 attention to a truly remarkable state of affairs, a curious
4 oversight and incoherence in the current sciences of man, and to
5 explore its consequences for both science and religion.

6 First I shall say a word about the oversight, call
7 attention to the naked emperor, then mention a possible remedy. I

8   am speaking of an insight-discovery first put forward by the great

9   American philosopher-logician-scientist, Charles Sanders Peirce,

10 over a hundred years ago, and which has been largely overlooked by

11 the sciences of man, both by scientific anthropologies and

12 religious anthropologies. You will look vain for even a

13 mention of it in standard works of psychology, sociology,

14 anthropology and linguistics. And yet it has, if true, the most

15 far reaching consequences for both the sciences of man and man's

16 theology.

17 But before talking about Charles Peirce's discovery, let

18 us take a Martian perspective and get out from under, as best one

19 can, the traditional dead weight of one or the other statement to

20 which we are all subject. To do so, to sharpen the contrast

21 between the two statements, let us first take note of certain

22 all-too-familiar declarations of victory of the one over the other

23 and certain "reconciliations" of the one with the other as being

24 unavailing or boring or both.

25 To begin with, it says nothing about the existence or

26 non-existence of God when the Gallup Poll reports that 98% of

---

PAGE 13

1 Americans believe in God.

2 Nor does it say anything about his existence or

3 non-existence if 98% of the graduates of M.I.T. do not believe in

4 God.

5 It says nothing against the claim of Christianity if Jimmy

6 Swaggart claims to be a Christian.

7 Nor is it an argument against Christianity if Mahatma

8 Gandhi, a saintly man, denied that God himself entered history as

9 one man, he and no other.

10 Nor will it do to say that since man is an encultured

11 creature, the tenets and myths of his culture are "true" for him

12 accordingly as his culture is viable, which is to say that the
13 religious credo is true for the believing Jew or Protestant or
14 Catholic in the same sense that belief that totemism and belief in
15 the *bwaga'u* or sorcerer is true and workable for Malinowski's
16 Trobriand Islanders.

17 Nor will it do to say that Judeo-Christian belief is
18 "true" only in the Jungian sense that it validates this or that
19 archetypal longing of the human psyche, perhaps the archetype of
20 the Suffering Son or the Eternal Mother.

21 For to say so is to use the word *true* analogically and to
22 surrender all genuine truth claims to the scientist. Let us agree
23 with the classical positive scientist that in the end the claims
24 of Judeo-Christianity must be either true or false.

25 Myths, after all, are stories which are not true.

26 Nor will it do to say, as many reasonable people do, that

PAGE 14

1 science treats the realm of facts, while religion lies in the
2 realm of faith, for it is hard to understand this separation
3 otherwise than as allowing faith in any proposition one chooses to
4 have faith in.

5 Nor will it do to call attention to the fact, true though
6 it might be, that with the decline in religious belief there has
7 occurred a noncomitant and spectacular rise in crime, drug use,
8 depression, suicide, family instability and so on—and so to
9 call for a return to the "values" of Judeo-Christianity. It is
10 not enough for a religion to have "values."
11 Nor is it an argument for or against Christianity if some
12 of the greatest rogues are preachers in the media and if the very
13 language of Christianity has undergone a devaluation over the
14 years. The very words of religion—God, Jesus, devil, sin,

15 salvation, Abraham's bosom, born again—have become, whether or
16 not they have referents, over-used and over-familiar, like the
17 worn-out furniture of grandmother's house.

18 Take the very words *religion* and *Christian*. Who wants to
19 go to a Christian bookstore?

20 But what about some more respectable defenses of the
21 second or religious statement? For example, the characterization
22 of religion by the great Danish philosopher Søren Kierkegaard as a
23 movement from reason to something else, as a "leap of faith"?
24 *Credo quia absurdum est.* I can only reply for myself that I
25 cannot believe an absurd proposition, let alone believe it because
26 it is absurd.

PAGE 15

1 But is there not a more compelling argument, underwritten
2 by science itself? I am speaking of what is known popularly and
3 vulgarly as Big Bang, the scientific evidence that the entire
4 cosmos had a beginning, that it came into being from nowhere and
5 nothing. Does not the existence of creation imply, indeed prove,
6 a creator. I can only reply that this hypothesis, while it may
7 have been confirmed and, for all I know, proved to be true by
8 natural science, does not appear to be compelling. I do not know
9 nor have I ever heard of anyone who, being apprised of the
10 discovery of the Big Bang and the creation of the cosmos from
11 nothing, has fallen to his knees in awe and worship of its
12 creator.

13 Finally and perhaps most impressively there is the
14 traditional contention that, after all, natural science arose, not
15 in the Buddhist East nor in the Islamic South nor anywhere else
16 but in the heart of the Catholic Christian West. For it was the
17 Incarnation, it is said, which conferred upon created being the
18 value, reality and significance sufficient to make it worthy of
19 study in itself.

20 Can anyone imagine a Buddhist in a lamasery or a Brahman
21 in India becoming curious about the properties of falling bodies
22 and dropping objects from a tower?

23 Yes, but didn't Galileo get in trouble with the Church
24 when he began to draw conclusions from his observations?

25 True, but does that prove anything other than that popes
26 can be as dumb as anybody else when it comes to science?

PAGE 16

1 The point is, so the argument runs, that what offends a
2 certain scientific temperament, both ancient and modern, is
3 attaching importance to what the Emperor Julian called the
4 *merikos*, that is, the *particular*. Julian, a Platonist of the
5 Fourth Century, was offended to the point of apostasy by the
6 Jewish and Christian claim that God entered history at a
7 particular time and place, by entering into a covenant with a
8 particular people, with them and no other, and as a single man, he
9 and no other.

10 The argument may be true enough, but it is not difficult
11 to imagine the response of most scientists as well as most
12 educated denizens of the Western world. Indifference or a shrug
13 of assent. So what? Does the argument have any interest other
14 than the historical? Suppose natural science did arise in the
15 heart of Catholic Europe. What matters now is that all
16 scientists, American, Indian and Japanese—and there are plenty
17 of them—study particulars, whether electrons, falling bodies or
18 galaxies, in order to arrive at generals. No significance can be
19 attached to a particular electron or a particular comet.

20 Then where does that leave us, if the so-called arguments
21 and reconciliations of science and religion can be disposed of?
22 What is the upshot?

23 There appears to be only one upshot. And hardly any
24 educated denizen I know, Christian, Jew, scientist, believer or
25 unbeliever, would disagree. And I am not telling you anything you

---

1   don't already know.

2   It is that the Judeo-Christian proposition is in serious
3   eclipse. I am speaking of the central belief in what a Jewish
4   theologian called God's incursion into history.

5   It is an eclipse not only among Jews but Christians as
6   well, that is, "secular" or nominal Christians. The orthodoxies.
7   whether Jewish or the mainline churches, Protestant and Catholic,
8   are not barely viable at best. The only flourishing "churches" I
9   know of, that is, sects which bear some relation, however
10 peculiar, to Christianity, are the Mormons and the Fundamentalists
11 and Evangelicals who are having huge success evangelizing the
12 world.

13 At any rate it is surely a commonplace that the
14 Judeo-Christian proposition, at least in the traditional orthodox
15 understanding of it, is in serious eclipse. Indeed it is usually
16 viewed by the denizen of these times as an anachronism. I do not
17 propose here to examine the possible causes of the eclipse,
18 whether it be science itself winning out because it should, or
19 scientism, or New Left dogmatics, or New Age nuttiness, or the
20 consequence merely of disinterest following upon the passive
21 consumption of the goods and services of technology—six hours
22 of TV daily.

23 In any case, the eclipse can hardly be doubted. Indeed so
24 nearly total does it appear to educated denizens of the West, that
25 alternative religions come inevitably to mind. I am thinking of
26 course of the great traditions of the East. And is it not in fact

1 the case that the tenets of Hinduism and Buddhism are far more
2 consonant with the scientific worldview than Judeo-Christianity?
3 For if the natural scientist, like the Emperor Julian, can attach
4 little importance to the *merikos*, the particulars considered in
5 themselves, let alone staking everything on a particular
6 person-event in history, neither does the Buddhist or the Brahman.
7 And what objection can the scientist have to the Eastern
8 preoccupation with self, with seeking the ultimate secret of the
9 cosmos by looking not out but in? The two, the scientist and the
10 *siddhi*-meditator, are plowing two different rows, but they do not
11 get in each other's way.

12 And of course this is what has happened. With the decline
13 of belief in the Judeo-Christian proposition among educated
14 denizens of the West, there has occurred almost in inverse
15 proportion an increase of interest in and adherence to various
16 Eastern beliefs and practices, sometimes in wonderful and exotic
17 variety.

18 I need not look beyond my own community in Louisiana
19 where, amid the Catholics and Baptists, theosophists have long
20 offered a respectable alternative. More recently there has
21 appeared along the bayous a more exotic Eastern hybrid. There a
22 group of very nice educated ladies hold "human potential programs"
23 which emphasize elements of both American Indian rites and
24 Buddhist philosophy. They periodically enter a small circular hut
25 constructed of willow branches covered by black plastic bags and
26 heated by hot stones. It is called a "sweat purification

1 ceremony." They sweat, chant, meditate, pray and discover the
2 inner self. Each hot stone is dedicated to a cause: world peace,
3 inner peace, personal growth, children, the hungry, the sad.

4 Who can object to such a ceremony? Who cannot applaud
5 these goals? I for one am glad to live in such a wondrous
6 fragmented society and in such times as this crazy, murderous,
7 warm-hearted century. How else could I write novels?
8 But before entering the sweat house, I have a penultimate
9 proposal for the foundering West—which is indeed the point of
10 these ramblings.

11 I propose, not another "reconciliation" of science and
12 religion, a boring and unprofitable enterprise. It is more
13 useful, I think, and certainly more fun to call your attention to
14 a remarkable incoherence, not to say stupidity, of modern science.
15 It comes to light whenever science addresses, not subatomic
16 particles or chimps or galaxies, but man himself, man *qua* man.

17 The dilemma is as familiar and embarrassing as a family
18 skeleton, a state of affairs which one has come to accept but not
19 talk about. This embarrassment is of course the mind/body split,
20 the Cartesian division of reality into the *res cogitans* and the
21 *res extensa* where natural science has been hung up for three
22 hundred years—ever since Descartes.

23 In a word, how do we get from the physical and biological
24 sciences to the socio-psychological sciences where all of a sudden
25 we encounter such strange entities as mind, ideas, thoughts,
26 consciousness, the unconscious, archetypes, role-takers? We

PAGE 20

1 don't. That is, we don't get from matter to mind by any
2 explainable route. We just jump the gap. And like any
3 embarrassing family affair, we don't talk about it.

4 What I wish to put before you in the next few minutes is
5 not my discovery—I wish it were—but that of Charles Sanders
6 Peirce, hit upon over a hundred years ago and ignored by natural
7 science ever since.

8 But why should such a discovery, wherever it was made,
9 matter to us in the present context? Because, for one thing, it
10 sheds light on some of the incoherences in modern science. Why is
11 it, for example, that two great scientists, Darwin and Freud, seem
12 to be talking about two different worlds which have nothing in
13 common: Darwin about goings on between beasts, Freud about
14 repressed thoughts inside the head of one beast? So it is more
15 useful, I submit, to attack Darwin and Freud, not for being too
16 "radical" and hence offensive to religion, but not radical enough
17 —and let religion take its chances.

1 Charles Peirce aimed among other things to give the death
2 blow for once and all to what he saw as the ancient discredited
3 dualism of Descartes who had bisected all of reality into matter,
4 *res extensa*, and mind stuff, *res cogitans*. To do this, he came up
5 with what he saw as modern scientific confirmation of the
6 ancient realism of Aristotle and the later realism of the medieval
7 schoolmen who saw mental entities like ideas as part of the same
8 reality as things and bodies—which realism of course had been
9 sundered first by the dualism of Descartes and then, in Peirce's
10 time, by the regnant and diverging materialism and idealism of the
11 Nineteenth Century, one of which set out to explain everything by
12 the doctrine of matter in motion, the other by various submersions
13 in Kantian subjectivity, such as Hegelian dialectical idealism.
14 One put everything in one box, the box of things, the other in the
15 mind box. But the nagging question remained: what does one have
16 to do with the other?

17 Peirce subscribed to a realism which recognized a
18 continuum of real objects. The world we see and study by science
19 is real. The amoeba we study, the flower, the other person, even
20 the electron, is really out there. But equally real are the ideas
21 and hypotheses by which we know and talk about them.

1 But still, how to get from one to the other, from matter
2 to mind? Peirce found one way: by focusing on the familiar place
3 where the two intersect: language. Language, the observable
4 behavior of a speaking and listening human, is the obvious place
5 where ideas find expression in words and words evoke ideas.

6 Peirce came at this intersection of mind and matter from
7 the posture of a natural scientist and came up with an hypothesis
8 which, one would suppose, would be of great interest to those
9 scientists whose subject matter is *Homo sapiens*, that strange
10 composite of body and mind. For Peirce's insight goes to the very
11 heart of those traits which seem to set man apart from other
12 species. In point of fact, the impact of Peirce on the modern
13 social and psychological sciences of man has been at or near zero.
14 That is to say, one will look in vain at standard works of
15 psychology, anthropology, linguistics, psycholinguistics,
16 sociology, to find so much as a mention of Peirce, let alone his
17 discovery.

18 And here is an even more melancholy fact. Peirce thought
19 that the old Cartesian mind-body split was all but done for in his
20 time and that he had polished off what remained of it with his
21 scientific realism. Alas, the present state of the sciences of
22 man can only be described as not only Cartesian by tacit agreement
23 —we don't even mention the word—but as having further
24 regressed to the ancient dualism of the earthly atoms of
25 Democritus and the heavenly ideas of Plato.
26 One need only look at a couple of familiar examples.

1 Take "psychology," Psych 101, the usual freshman course.
2 What is it about? It is about behavior and the nervous system

3   which controls it, neurones, axones, synapses, brain circuitry,
4   stimuli, responses, the operant conditioning of organisms.

5   But then you must also take the psychologies of modern
6   psychotherapies which everybody knows about, say Freudian or
7   Jungian psychology, which are the two most familiar of the hundred
8   or so schools of psychotherapy. Here, without batting an eye, we
9   find outselves [sic] talking about mental entities, the conscious, the
10 unconscious, ego, id, superego, archetypes. Isn't there a
11 discontinuity here? How did we get from one to the other? from
12 stimuli and synapses to dreams and archetypes? If one asks the
13 question, what one gets is the same frown and puzzlement the child
14 got who asked about the *naked* emperor.

15 We are back at the old Cartesian split with a vengeance,
16 worse than ever, straddling the split without admitting it.

17 The trouble then is not so much bad faith, say, the
18 superstitious arrogance of a Freud or a Darwin each of whom could
19 have explained each other, not so much that as it is the double
20 vision by which the rest of us see the world and ourselves as
21 incoherent. We are still haunted by the ghost of Descartes. The
22 case has been made, with some justification I think, that René
23 Descartes has had a more pernicious effect on the West than anyone
24 since Attila the Hun.

25 Then how did Peirce come at the Cartesian split which he
26 believed to be a wrongheaded view of reality which he saw as a

---

PAGE 24

1   continuum? It is important to understand that his approach is
2   neither religious or philosophical but that of natural science and
3   scientific logic, which is not surprising since he was a scientist
4   and a logician, the founder in fact of symbolic logic.

5   In a word, he said—and it is as easily demonstrated as
6   the molecular structure of water—that there are two kinds of

7   natural events in the world. One he called dyadic, the other
8   triadic.

9   Dyadic events are the familiar subject matter of the
10   physical and biological sciences: A interacting with B; A, B, C,
11   D interacting with each other. Peirce called it "a mutual action
12   between two things." It can apply to molecules interacting with
13   other molecules, a billiard ball hitting another billiard ball,
14   one galaxy colliding with another galaxy, an organism responding
15   to a stimulus. Even an event as complex as Pavlov's conditioned
16   dog salivating at the sound of a bell can be understood as a
17   complexus of dyads"—the sound waves from the bell, the
18   stimulation of the dog's auditory receptors, the electrical
19   impulses in the afferent nerves, the firing of the altered
20   synapses in the brain, the electrical impulses in the afferent
21   nerves to the salivary glands, and so on—the whole
22   understandable as a sequence of dyadic events. The entire event,
24   complex as it is, can be represented quite adequately by a simple
25   drawing which shows structures (dog, neurones, axones, glandular
26   cells) and arrows connecting them (energy exchanges, sound waves,
27   electrical impulses).

PAGE 25

1   Such events indeed are the familiar subject matter of the
2   natural sciences, from physics and chemistry to Psych 101.

3   But there is another kind of event, quite as "real," quite
4   as natural a phenomenon, quite as observable, which cannot be so
5   understood, that is, construed by the dyadic model. It is
6   language. The simplest example I can think of—and it is
7   anything but simple—is the child's early acquisition of
8   language, an eighteen-month-old suddenly learning that things have
9   names. What happens here is the same sort of thing that happens
10   when a lecturer utters a complex sentence about the poetics of T.
11   S. Eliot.

12 What happens when the child suddenly grasps that the
13 strange little sound *cat*, an explosion of air between tongue and
14 palate followed by a bleat of the larynx followed by a stop of
15 tongue against teeth, *means* this cat, not only this cat but all
16 cats? And means it in a very special way: does not mean: look
17 over there for cat, watch out for cat, want cat, go get cat—but
18 that *is* the cat. Naming is the new event. And of course soon
19 after this naming "sentence" appear other primitive sentences:
20 *there cat, cat all gone, where cat?*

21 As Peirce put it, this event cannot be explained by a
22 dyadic model, however complex. Words like *cat* he called symbols.
23 from the Greek *symballein*, to throw together, because the child
24 puts the two together, the word and the thing. A triadic model is
25 required. For even though many of the familiar dyadic events are
26 implicated, the heart of the matter is a throwing together, one

---

PAGE 26

1 entity throwing together two others, in this case *cat* the creature
2 and *cat* the sound.

3 This event is a piece of behavior, true enough, but any
4 behavioristic reading of it as a sequence of dyads will miss the
5 essence of it.

6 He, Peirce, was particularly interested in using the
7 dyadic-triadic distinction to understand communication by a
8 discipline which he called semiotic, the science of signs. He
9 distinguished between an index and a symbol. A low barometer is
10 for a human a sign, an index, of rain. The word *ball* is for my
11 dog an index to go fetch the ball. But if I say the word *ball* to
12 you, you will receive it as a symbol, look at me with puzzlement
13 and perhaps say, "Ball? What about it?" The difference between
14 the two, variously and confusedly called index and symbol, sign
15 and symbol, signal and sign, was perhaps most dramatically

16 illustrated by Helen Keller's famous account, her first
17 understanding of words spelled in her hand, like *cup, door, water,*
18 to mean go fetch cup, open door, I want water, and then the
19 memorable moment in the pump house when it dawned on her that
   the
20 word *water* spelled in one hand *meant* the water running over the
21 other. It was nothing less than the beginning of her life as a
22 person.

23 The triadic event, as Peirce would say, always involves
24 meaning, and meaning of a special sort. The copula "is," spoken
25 or implied, is nothing less than the tiny triadic lever that moves
26 the entire world into the reach of our peculiar species.

---

1 This strange capacity seems to be unique in *Homo sapiens*.
2 And even though, as psycholinguists have pointed out, there is
3 nothing unscientific about assigning a "species-specific" trait to
4 this or that species, if the evidence warrants many scientists
5 find this uniqueness offensive. We are all familiar with the
6 heroic attempts in recent years by psychologists and
7 primatologists to teach language to primates other than *Homo*
8 *sapiens*, particularly chimpanzees, using ASL, the sign language of
9 the deaf, the premise being that the vocal apparatus of the chimp
10 does not permit speech. The most famous chimp was Washoe whom
    the
11 Gardners claimed to have taught language, that is, the ability to
12 understand and "utter" not only "words," the common nouns of
13 language, but form these words into sentences. But we are also
14 familiar with the discrediting of these claims, mainly due to the
15 work of Herbert Terrace. Terrace adopted a chimp, which he named
16 Nim Chimsky, with every expectation of teaching Nim language as
17 one would a human infant. What he learned was that Nim, though
18 undoubtedly as smart as Washoe, was not really using language.

19 What he and Washoe were really doing was responding to small cues
20 by the trainer, probably unconsciously, to do this or that, the
21 appropriate behavior rewarded by a banana or whatever. What
22 Washoe and Nim Chimsky were exhibiting of course was not the
23 language behavior of the human two-year-old but the classical
24 reinforced response of the behaviorists. As Peirce would say,
25 both Washoe's and Nim's "language" can be understood as a
26 "complexus of dyads."

PAGE 2 8

1 One can draw a picture with things (matter) and arrows
2 (energy) connecting them setting forth the behavior both of the
3 chimp Washoe and the pre-language human infant with its responses
4 to sights and sounds, its crying for mama and milk.

5 But one cannot draw such a picture of an
6 eighteen-month-old human who looks at mama, points to cat and says
7 *da cat.* The new picture one draws has to have at least one
8 triangle, showing that something, some entity, has put together
9 *symballein*, cat and *cat.*

10 One would suppose that the appropriate scientist, the
11 developmental psychologist, the psycholinguist, whoever, would
12 zero in on this, the transformation of the responding organism
13 into the languaged human, undoubtedly the most extraordinary
14 natural phenomenon in all of biological behavior, if not in the
15 entire cosmos—and yet the most commonplace of events, one that
16 occurs everyday under our noses.

17 Unfortunately, such is not the case. What one finds in
18 the scientific literature is something like this: a huge amount
19 of information about the infant as organism, its needs and drives,
20 its behavior and physiology. But when it begins to speak, what?
21 What is thought to happen? What one finds are very careful
22 studies of the *structure* of the earliest utterances and their

23　development, the rules by which an eighteen-month-old will say
24　*that a my coat* but not *a that my coat. Rules, grammar, linguistic*
25　*structure*, the same formal approach which issues later in the
26　splendid disciplines of structural linguistics and even in

---

PAGE 29

1　"deconstruction."

2　The sciences of man, that is to say, do not find it odd to
3　jump from the natural science of biology to the formal science of
4　structures and rules. The scientist's behavior in any other human
5　would be called schizophrenic.

6　It is as if we lived in a California house atop the San
7　Andreas fault, a crack very deep but narrow, which has become as
8　familiar as an old shoe. We can hop back and forth, feed the
9　dyadic dog on one side, or sit on the other side and write a
10　triadic paper and never have a second thought about the
11　difference.

12　On one side are the dyadic sciences from atomic physics to
13　academic psychology with its behaviorism and its various
14　refinements and elaborations, operant conditioning, so-called
15　"cognitive" psychology, Gestalt psychology—and on the other,
16　"mental" psychologies with such entities as consciousness,
17　neuroses, dreams, ego, archetypes and suchlike. Then there's
18　sociology with things like culture, identity, role-taking.

19　Draw me a picture of role-taking. Who, what, takes the
20　role? The organism? How does an organism "take a role"?

21　Strangely enough, or perhaps not so strangely, a "mental"
22　discipline like Freudian psychology lends itself very well to the
23　Peircean dyadic model once one accepts the immateriality of the
24　entities. One can very easily make a diagram showing things like
25　ego, super-ego, the unconscious, and using arrows to represent
26　drives, repression, sublimation and such—even though one

1 recognizes that the whole drama takes place on the far side of the
2 chasm from such "real" things as organisms, neurones, stimuli,
3 responses.

4 Valuable though Freudian psychology might be, it must
5 nevertheless be understood as a transposition of dyadic theory to
6 the realm of mental entities with no account of how it got there.
7 But if scientists, both "physical" scientists and "mental"
8 scientists, can operate comfortably on both sides of the Cartesian
9 split, what happens when the serious scientist is obliged to look
10 straight down at the dysjunction? That is to say, what is one to
11 make of language, that apparently unique property of man,
12 considered not as a formal structure but as a natural phenomenon?
13 Where did it come from? What to make of it in anatomical,
14 physiological and evolutionary terms? The chasm must make one
15 dizzy. Not many psychologists or neuro-anatomists want to look
16 down. Norman Geschwind is one who has. He points out that there
17 are recently evolved structures in the human brain which have to
18 do with speech and understanding speech, such as the inferior
19 parietal lobule which receives information from the "primary
20 sensory projection system," that is, the cerebral cortex which
21 registers seeing and feeling water and hearing the word *water*.
22 But these are described as "association areas"—but Charles
23 Peirce would call "associations" dyadic events—and "information
24 processing systems," like a computer. But a computer is the
25 perfect dyadic machine.

26 What do biologists and anthropologists make of the

1 emergence of language in the evolutionary scheme? The advantages
2 of language in the process of natural selection are obvious.
3 Julian Jaynes would go further and say that "the language of men

4   was involved with only one hemisphere in order to leave the other
5   free for the language of gods." May be, but setting aside for the
6   moment "the language of gods," what goes on with the language of
7   men? Jaynes doesn't say.

8   This is what Richard Leakey, the anthropologist, says,
9   describing what happens in a human (not a chimp) when a human uses
10   a word as a symbol, in naming or in a sentence: "Speech is
11   controlled by a certain structure of the brain, located in the
12   outer cerebral cortex. Wernicke's area of the brain pulls out
13   appropriate words from the brain's filing system. The angular
14   gyrus . . . selects the appropriate word."

15   Pulls out? Selects? These are transitive verbs with
16   subjects and objects. The words are the objects. What is the
17   subject? Draw me a picture of Wernicke's area pulling out a word
18   or the angular gyrus selecting a word. Is there any way to
19   understand this other than supposing a little person, a
20   homunculus, in each place doing the pulling and selecting?

21   Then there is what is called speech-act theory of Austin,
22   Searle and others, promising because it is the actual utterance of
23   sentences which are studies [sic]. Thus Austin distinguishes between
24   sentences which say something and sentences which do something.
25   The sentence "I married her" is one kind of speech act, an
26   assertion about an event. "I do" uttered during the marriage is

---

PAGE 32

1   another kind, part of the performance of the ceremony itself. The
2   classes of speech-act behavior have multiplied amid ongoing
3   debate. But once again the naked emperor's little boy becomes
4   curious. "Speech acts?" he asks. "What do you mean by acts?
5   You never use the word acts in describing the behavior of other
6   creatures." An act entails an actor, an agent which initiates the

7   act. Draw me a picture of a speech act. Where, what, is the
8   actor?

9   Such are a few of the manifold discomforts of the natural
10   scientist who finds himself astride the Cartesian chasm, one foot
11   planted in dyadic territory, the other in triadic. What happens
12   is, he very quickly chooses one side or the other.

13   But how does Charles Sanders Peirce help us here? Are we
14   any better off with Peirce's Thirdness, his triadic theory, than
15   we were with Descartes' *res cogitans* and *res extensa*?

16   Let me first say that I do not have the competence to
17   speculate on the brain structures which may be implicated in
18   triadic behavior. Nor would I wish to if I had the competence.
19   Such a project is too uncomfortably close to Descartes' search for
20   the seat of the soul, which I believe he located in the pineal
21   gland.

22   No, what is important to note about the triadic event is
23   that it is there for all to see, that in fact it occurs hundreds
24   of times daily—whenever we talk or listen to somebody talking
25   —that its elements are open to inspection to everyone, including
26   natural scientists, and that it can not be reduced to a complexus

---

PAGE 33

1   of dyadic events. The chattering of an entire population of
2   rhesus monkeys is so reducible. But the single utterance of an
3   eighteen-month-old child who points and says *that a flower* cannot
4   be so understood—even though millions of dyadic events also
5   occur, light waves, excitation of nerve endings, electrical
6   impulses in neurones, muscle contractions and so on.

7   So what? one well might ask. Which is to say: admitting
8   that there is such a thing as an irreducible triadic event in
9   language behavior, are there any considerable consequences for our

10   anthropology in the strict sense of the word, the view of man
11   which comes as second nature to the educated denizen of modern
12   society?

13   There are indeed and they, the consequences, are startling
14   indeed.

15   For once one concedes the reality of the triadic event,
16   one is brought face to face with the nature of its elements. A
17   child points to a flower and says *flower*. One element of the
18   event is the flower as perceived by sight and registered by the
19   brain: blue, five-petalled, of a certain shape; and the spoken
20   word *flower*, a gestalt of a peculiar little sequence of sounds of
21   larynx vibrations, escape of air between lips and teeth and so on.
22   But what is the entity at the apex of the triangle, that which
23   links the other two? Peirce called it by various names,
24   interpretant, interpreter, judger. I have used the term coupler
25   as a minimal designation of that which couples name and thing,
26   subject and predicate, links them by the relation which we mean by

---

PAGE 34

1   the peculiar little word "is." It, the linking entity, was also
2   called by Peirce mind and even soul.

3   Here is the embarrassment and it cannot be gotten round,
4   so it might as well be said right out: by whatever name one
5   chooses to call it—interpretant, interpreter, coupler, whatever
6   —it, the third element, *is not material*.

7   It is as real as a cabbage or a king or a neurone, but it
8   is not material. No material structure of neurones, however
9   complex, and however intimately it may be related to the triadic
10   event, may in fact be the very means, ground, matrix of the event,
11   can itself assert anything.

12   A material substance cannot name or assert a proposition.

13   The initiator of a speech act is an act-or or agent. The
14   agent is not material.

15 Peirce's insistence on both the reality and nonmateriality
16 of the third element—whatever one choose to call it,
17 interpretant, mind, coupler—is of critical importance to
18 natural science because its claim to reality is grounded not on
19 this or that theology or metaphysic but on empirical observation
20 and the necessities of scientific logic.

21 Compare the rigor and clarity of Peirce's semiotic
22 approach to the ancient mind/body problem to current conventional
23 thinking about such matters. Ask a neurologist or psychologist
24 what the mind is. Here are some answers.

25 Mind is a property of the organization of neurones, their
26 circuitry and the neuro transmitters between them.

---

1 Or: The relation of brain to mind is analogous to that of
2 computer to its software.

3 Or: The step by step examination of the brain's circuitry
4 will demonstrate that the processes of mind are a consequence of
5 brain activity.

6 Or: Both brain and computer are information processors.

7 But here is the best statement I've come across of the
8 conventional dyadic understanding of such things as mind and
9 consciousness. It is from a textbook, *Physiology of Behavior* by
10 Neil R. Carlson. "What can a physiological psychologist say about
11 human self-awareness? We know that it is altered by changes in
12 the structure or chemistry of the brain; therefore, we conclude
13 that consciousness is a physiological function, just like
14 behavior."

15 These are something less useful than truisms. To say that
16 mind is a property or function of the organization of the brain is

17　like saying that Picasso's *Guernica* is a property of paint and
18　color.

19　But in any case and as the case may be, what, one well
20　might ask, what has this business, Peirce semiotic and so
21　forth, to do with the original statements about science and
22　religion?

23　Indeed one well might ask. And there is, I think, an
24　answer which is both significant and tentative, not to say
25　unclear.

1　What can one say about this entity and event, the reality
2　of which Charles Peirce demonstrated a hundred years ago and which
3　we ourselves encounter hundreds of times every day? What to make
4　of it, that is to say, not as a deduction from a theological
5　premise, not as an item in a linguistic structure, but from the
6　stance of natural science, as something out there to be made sense
7　of as one makes sense of a sunset or a bird migration?

8　To begin with, what to call it, this entity? Any number
9　of words have been used: not only Peirce's "interpretant," but
10　ego, self, "I," even soul. They may or may not be technically
11　accurate but for the educated denizen each suffers its own
12　semantic impairment. "Interpretant" is too noncommittal. "Soul"
13　carries too much furniture from the religious attic. "Ego" has a
14　different malodor, smelling as it does of the old festered
15　Cartesian split.

16　Then don't name it, but talk about it, like Lowell Thomas
17　coming upon a strange creature in his travels, in this case a
18　sure-enough beast in the jungle.

19　There are certain minimal things one can say about it,
20　this coupler, this apex of Peirce's triad.

21 For one thing, it is *there*. It is located in time and
22 space, but not as an organism. It has a different set of
23 parameters and variables.

24 For another, it is peculiarly and intimately involved with
25 others of its kind so that, unlike the biological organism, it is

---

1 impossible to imagine it functioning without the other, another.
2 All organisms have instinctive responses. But Helen Keller had to
3 receive the symbol *water* from Miss Sullivan before she became
4 *aware* of the water. Peirce's triad is social by its very nature.
5 Language is nothing if not intersubjective.

6 Here's another. It, this strange new creature, not only
7 has an environment. It has a *world*. The world is the totality of
8 that which is named. The environment has gaps. There are no gaps
9 in a world. Nectar is part of the environment of a bee. Cabbages
10 and kings and Buicks are not. There are no gaps in the world of
11 this new creature, because the gaps are called that, *gaps* or *out*
12 there or *what that?* or *them* or *don't know.*

13 In order to confirm some of the peculiar properties of
14 this entity, one does well to turn to some of those modern
15 thinkers known variously as philosophers, phenomenologists,
16 existentialists. I wish to use one or two of them here and to
17 take a liberty in doing so. That is to say, I wish to cite them
18 as anthropologists in the broad sense of the word, that is, as
19 scientists of human nature in the sense that their insights are
20 confirmable or disconfirmable by ourselves. One can do this, I
21 think, without buying into their various theologies, atheism,
22 Kantian subjectivities.

23 Heidegger, for example, uses the German word *Dasein*, to
24 name our subject matter here, this very entity. It is doubly

25 felicitous for our purpose because it bears no semantic freight;
26 it simply signifies what it says; a being there, and better still,

---

1   as Heidegger explicates it, a being there in the world—and by
2   world he means *Welt*, all that is out there and that we name, and
3   not *Umwelt*, the environment.

4   Another unique feature of this strange human creature is
5   that in becoming human he enters the world of the normative. As
6   the existentialists put it, he can live "authentically" or
7   "unauthentically."

8   Marcel speaks of an I-Thou relation which all too easily
9   deteriorates into an I-It.

10 For Sartre, it is altogether I-It, the I, the *en soi*, as
11 forever locked away as the Cartesian *res cogitans*. The It? What
12 if the It is another person? Here is Sartre on the other, the
13 Thou: *L'enfer c'est autri*. Hell is other people, a statement
14 which is, after all, as normative as Marcel's I-Thou and
15 Heidegger's Being-with.

16 One of the basic modes of existence of the *Dasein*.
17 according to Heidegger, is its primordial relation to language,
18 particularly spoken language. *Rede*, the German word Heidegger
19 uses, degenerates into *Gerede*, talk, gossip. *Verstehen*,
20 understanding, is in danger of turning into *Neugier*, idle
21 curiosity.

22 It is characteristic of the existentialists that the "I,"
23 self *Dasein*, is seen as capable of existing "authentically" or
24 "unauthentically." The authentic *Dasein* of Heidegger, the
25 being-with of Marcel, easily deteriorates into the anonymous *man*,
26 one, what one does, they, what they say. We are anxious to do

1 what one does under the circumstances, what they do.

2 Thus, the *Dasein*, can undergo a *Verfallen*, or "fall," from
3 the "authentic" to the "unauthentic."

4 But how can the modern psychologist or anthropologist take
5 account of the normative, of such relationships and behavior as
6 the I-Thou, the I-It, of "Falling" into an "unauthentic"
7 existence? (I find myself putting these expressions in quotes, so
8 strangely do they fall upon the ear of the positive scientist.)
9 He has difficulty since he is limited, on the one hand, to dyadic
10 biology as an explanatory model, and on the other, to purely
11 relativistic cultural "norms" of descriptive ethnology.

12 I cite these two philosophers, Heidegger and Marcel, as
13 alternative approaches to an anthropology. It does seem necessary
14 to look around for alternatives since anthropology, the science of
15 man, seems in its current version as a natural science both
16 impoverished and incoherent. Man is understood either as a dyadic
17 organism, as complex as you please, with a brain circuitry far
18 more advanced than the smartest chimp—or—and here the gap is
19 jumped—or as an "encultured" creature complete with the entire
20 apparatus of triadic phenomena, not merely culture but "mind,"
21 language, consciousness, the unconscious, "structural linguistics"
22 and so on.

23 Is the gap between the two so narrow that one can hop back
24 and forth without missing a step—from Psychology 101 about man
25 as responding organism to Sociology 102 about society and man as
26 role-taker—but so deep that one does not dare look down?

1 But what if one does look down, as Peirce did, and sees
2 the dark dipole where the spark jumps—or rather, and here is

3   precisely the point of all: it is not that the spark jumps as
4   it jumps across a million synapses in the brain. *It is rather*
5   *that the spark is jumped.* There is a jumper. It takes not two
6   but three to dance this strange little tango.

7   But so what about it? What if there is such a relation
8   and such a thing—Peirce hardly knew what to call it—but a
9   thing both nonmaterial and real?

10   And if there is such a thing as Peirce's "interpretant" or
11   Heidegger's *Dasein*, a thing which is both real and nonmaterial,
12   what has this got to do with the two original statements of
13   science and religion?

14   Well, one consequence is fairly obvious. It is safe to
15   predict that anthropologists of the future, as well as behavioral
16   scientists, will have to take into account such peculiar new
17   parameters of human relationships and behavior as the I-Thou,
18   I-It, "falling into unauthenticity."

19   I prophesy moreover that the behavioral scientist of the
20   future will be obliged to make sense of statements like this:
21   "The being-in-the-world of the scientist is different from the
22   being-in-the-world of the layman." Even though he, the scientist,
23   cannot presently make sense of it because he does not presently
24   have an adequate model or theory, I predict that he will have.

25   But, and finally, what has this new anthropology to do with
26   the original two statements, the scientific and the religious,

PAGE 41

1   in all their disparateness?

2   For one thing, the scientific statement will have to be amended
3   to take into account the new creature which is more than organism,
4   more than encuktured creature, is in fact a peculiar hybrid of mater-
5   ial and nonmaterial elemments [sic].

6 This new creaure [sic], moreover, can understand the world and be
7 understood by his new science—unlike the old—to a degree.
8 But on [sic] the end he can only understand himself, not as a problem,
9 not as an organism with needs, a creature of culture—though
10 he is all of these—but as a person in a mystery, a predicament,
11 a person moreover who is open to news appropriate to his predica-
12 ment.

13 Predicament? Mystery? News?

14 I think that is enough to say for the present.

December 11, 1988

Dear Walker,

Your letter and manuscript of the Jefferson Lecture, which was sent on 8 December, arrived at my Texas Tech office on Friday, 9 December, and I have been going over it since. I should respond now before Finals week duties overwhelm me for the next few days.

I'm deeply honored that you sent that over to the badlands. You can rest easy that I won't violate the confidence you have granted me. And you were right: It clears up a couple of points I have been fretting over in view of Jean Sebeok's request of me. (She may not like my response—I'll let you know.) I'm even more convinced that folks who have commented on your essays (leaving Robert Coles aside) have missed you badly. Patricia Poteat comes to mind. I'm not taking into account the descriptions of your novels. How dreary—not your novels, but folks who make a living telling us what a novel means. I chuckle when they fret about how to place you within literature.

This is a Jim Dandy essay. It thrills me to read it. Let me explain one part of the thrill. Old CSP is one of the greatest men of all times, yet he has rotted in the backwaters of human consciousness. He has a great deal to offer us, but there are almost no takers, and those who take, usually distort (the semiotikers for the most part being an excellent example—they are worse than the way you quite accurately view Freud: The semiotikers take up a triadic science by means of dyadic theories; they mouth around about triads and triangles, but it's only an act). You have done a wonderful thing here for old CSP in that your discussion of his ideas may just be the straw that will break through the curtain of disinterest (mixed my metaphors and proverbs there, but you know what I mean).

Bless me, I don't know a thing about the Jefferson Lecture (who, what, when, where?). Can you give me a clue?

I've read this over several times, and I found a few typ-o's and grammar-o's. I offer those in a helpful spirit. I will also argue-fy a little just to give you what is intended as a practice range for your golf shots. I'll refer to page number and line number as x:y, where x is page and y is line counted from top down, and x:yb is count the line from bottom up:

2:14. Dressed to kill. Do you intend "dressed for the killing about to be done" or proverbially "dressed fit to be killed"? It reads to me now in the former sense, but I suspect you intended "very prettily dressed."

3:6b. Conscious raising, or consciousness raising?

5:7b. "Validable"? But this could be one of your tricks.

5:5b. Transpose "learned."

Also the sentence that begins at the same 5:5b seems to "fall off." It starts: man has learned about x,y, and z—but in elaborating z, the grammatical trail is lost.

6:15. That wasn't Wittgenstein's line, at least I don't recall him writing anything like that. He did have, at the end of the *Tractatus Logico-Philosophicus* (Proposition 7), this famous remark: *Wovon man nicht sprechen kann, darüber muss man schweigen.* Wittgenstein talks about what one can speak; you talk through an attribution to him of what one can know. It seems to me that a possible reading of Wittgenstein's Proposition 7 is if we can't speak about it scientifically, our only option is to be silent. However, Wittgenstein's Proposition 7 comes just after a series of mystical remarks, which almost all Wittgenstein scholars studiously ignore. Yaas, Wittgenstein was a mystic, virtually a Catholic mystic. Sooo, his silence option is *nicht das Nichts*, but quite an option like that of your buddy the monk Merton. But I bet that virtually everyone who hears you would not be aware of the special meaning Wittgenstein attached to silence. So, couldn't you say, "Whereof one cannot speak, that is scientifically and empirically, one must be silent?"

6: last line, on to top of p. 7. This sentence seems to shift gears half way through, start on one track and end on another. Is there a missing phrase?

7:6. Do you want to capitalize or lowercase "christian"?

9. Do you want "i.e" in text? I try to prune 'em.

10. Not a complaint or a suggestion, but a thought that occurs to me. I follow you in regard to "hearing" ("The Message in the Bottle," get the news, and such). I follow you almost to the last point in the is-lander-getting-the news sequence. The last point in the sequence is the God-man telling us news. At that point I ask: "This is important news, but what does it mean?" Second point, which makes it relevant to your p. 10: "If I have to ask what the news means, then perhaps I have not *heard* it." Or better, if I hear the news, then I won't get the message, but if listening takes place, then the news is received, absorbed, taken in. Note the mysticism entailed by *listening*, but not by *hearing*. In other words, Jimmy Swaggart heard the God-man's news, but monk Merton listened to that news. If one hears news, one *has* to ask "What does it mean?," but if one listens to news, the act of "listening" eliminates somehow the need to ask for the meaning—it's just there. The Taoist's revenge. The last line of p. 10 about textual relativists is right on target. You shore know how to put your shoulder to the wheel and push a phrase.

13:6b. Goooood.

13:2b. You have captured books within this sentence: I'm a card-carrying folklorist, but don't practice much anymore, because in the old days when I got started out at UCLA, I couldn't overcome the schizoid nature of folklorists who on the one hand say "Myths are untrue sto-ries" and out the other side of their mouth mutter "But they—the 'folk'—think they are true." Also, I could never figger out who the folk were: Like the Hittites, they are nowhere. I told a colleague a story once, an untrue one, but he believed it; then I told him it was untrue, which surprised him. I asked him if it was a myth then. He said "No" because I wasn't a folk. I gave up folklore study.

14:10. Amen *re* values.

14.19. Christian bookstore. I see what you are up to here, but for me it didn't come off. A bunch of Baptists in your audience might holler "Me, me!" Baptist bookstores and Good News bookstores are big business—almost as big as Cox Cable: can't hardly get into them on Saturday afternoon, what with all the Sunday School teachers buying their supplies. There are some where you can go to buy your crystal, your subliminal tape, your Shirley MacLaine book, your Indian medicine pouch made in Santa Fe by real Hopis. Very popular.

14:last sentence. Salut! I could never get the deal about absurdity, as if it were something to rejoice about: "Absurdity—Oh hot damn!" I could never see that. I'm glad a distinguished scholar of existentialism gets me off that hook. I think the absurdity move is a cop out, a loss of courage, a loss of scientific nerve on the existentialists' part.

15:11. Rat own!

15:9b. Kinda harsh on pre-Christian science in ancient Greece, Egypt, China? Greeks invented astronomy, math, biology (Aristotle for instance) and made some progress; Egypt invented medicine and made some progress; China invented gunpowder and some other stuff.

15:last two lines. Well said.

16:7. Beyond a decade or less, most scientists are ahistorical!

20:6. . . . .ignored by natural (?and social?) science . . .

21:4. . . . .he came up with. . . . ?he developed; ?he devised; ?he argued for . . . .?

21:11. The "one of which" reference seems to jangle a bit. ?Better: . . . the first of which. . . .and the other. . . .

23:9. outselves = ourselves.

24:1. Might be worthwhile to add that CSP was deeply religious. I'm convinced that throughout his life he sought God through science, the evidence for which is in my chapter (and allied readings) on CSP in the Stuhr anthology for *Classical American Philosophy*.

24:5. easily demonstrated. I'm curious which demonstration you have in mind here. You're correct, of course; but which one?

24:10b. . . . .dyads" . . . .Beginning of the quote-marked passage?

25:5. . . . .that is, (?as?) construed. . . .

26:8. ?Better: . . .semeiotic, the science of semeiosis or sign action.

27:4. ?Better: . . .evidence warrants; but many scientists. . . .

28:12. responsing or responding or WP is up to something.

29. I don't know where one would put this, or even *if* one would put this, but the question arises. The dyadikers, when the discussion reaches about this point, wax eschatological. They say, "Sure, we don't know all those details now, but we have faith that someday by following out deterministic and causal ideas and methods we will have it all." I like Manicas's example in response to that: A big piece of rock finally splits off the side of a cliff in the Rockies, and begins to fall downhill—predict how that big rock will break up and where each tiny piece will land. In other words, would it be of any use to whack the eschatological determinists somewhere in here?

29:5. I know what you mean about the schizo claim, but I don't see it built up quite enough here so an audience would get it. ?Flesh out a bit.

30:4. Freud remark. A fine insight.

30:20. Your chasm talk here reminds me of a CSP passage—take a look at *CP* 6.264–65 (and when CSP says idealism, don't think of Hegel et al., but grit your teeth and think of Thirds as you have been discussing them). I'm interested in your medical opinion on all that slime.

30:4b. ?Better:. . .Peirce would call (?such?) associations. . . . I mention this because "association" is used by CSP in a number of places in a way consistent with Thirdness. What you are here calling associations he would indeed respond to as you say.

31. homunculus . . . A triad in other words.

31:4b. ?studies, change to "studied."

32:bottom few lines. hundreds (of) times. . . .

open to inspection (by) everyone. . . .

. . .there for all to see. You can say that again. That it is not seen is a curious phenomenon in itself. What you call the dyadicists is about equal to what CSP called Nominalists. Why is it so damned hard to be seen theoretically? It is seen, acted upon, but when explained it comes out dyadic only. There is a philosophical puzzle. I have found most persons cannot accept triads as primitive or irreducible—they can only count to two in their philosophy. Why is that?

33:top. Eschatological determinism appearing here in those you criticize.

33:middle. Do you want two "indeeds"?

33:last line. Would it be worth saying here that "links" is not equal to " = "?

34. Not material (meaning?). Hooray. Boy does that ever pickle their sassafras. Whup it on em. If they give you some trouble, ask them if math is material, if it is nonscientific. If that don't work, shoot 'em in the ear.

34:7–11. I can't make it through the second sentence of this paragraph. The last phrase seems to dangle.

34:mid-page. . . . .act-or or agent. . . . Do you intend to have two "or" together like that? ?is an act-or an agent. . . .

The nonmateriality is a good popular translation of what CSP would call reality. Would it be worthwhile to cite his definition of reality as that which has the properties it has independently of what any one of us wish, desire, hope, or dream those properties to be? That is, I had a dream. What I dreamed is not real; that I dreamed so-and-so, however, is real. Your character Tom More is not real (says so on the first page of the book!), but that your character More invented the Lapsometer is real.

34:11b. choose, change to "chooses"??

35. You're too kind to Carlson. It's a raw *non sequitur*, with the same form as the following argument. Mao Tse-tung sneezed in 1952, therefore Ketner is handsome. Both sentences are true, but the logical form is lousy, hence invalid.

37:6. Why *new* creature? The creature, persons, have been with us. If one takes St. John's prologue seriously, in the beginning was the *logos* (intelligibility, Thirdness has no beginning or end, another strange property of worlds, as opposed to environments). Later few lines, another new creature.

38.8. I know absolutely nothing about Marcel, other than I need to read him some day. So if you say he has an I-Thou/I-It distinction, you're the expert. But I thought that was Buber's distinction. Did Marcel have it too?

38: last full sentence. I can't decipher this sentence, especially its last part.

39.8. "positive scientist" Does this mean the bad guys, the followers of scientism? To be a positive scientist is OK; to be a positivist (e.g., Comte) is bad. A positive scientist is just someone like you and me who wants to find the truth and state it.

40: top. As a radioman, Choctaw, and fan of Mary Shelley, I love this spark talk.

40:7. relation. Isn't this the name? One could call CSP a developer of that philosophy called Relationism.

41:3. New creature. The creature isn't new is it? Just newly recognized per-haps (or re-recognized).

41:4. encuktured, change to "encultured."

41:5. elemments, change to "elements."

41:6. creaure, change to "creature."

41:8. But (?in?) the end. . . .

41:10. . . . .but (?primarily?) as a person. . . .

last sentence. Us mystical Choctaw Cenopythagoreans admire how at the end you leave the reader in the present, which is the only way to go.

This is a fine piece Walker. Ole CSP would be tickled with you. Now if you will just tell me where and when this here lecture is scheduled, I'll try to come and ask some bubble-headed questions about mysticism.

Thanks again for the expression of trust, and I hope this is of some little help.

Ken [s]

Ketner [t]

❧ .

December 14, 1988

Dear Ken,

Just received your letter. Haven't had time to digest it but wanted to dash off a note of thanks.

In fact, many thanks and extreme gratitude.

I gave myself the excuse of burdening you with that lecture (fresh from typist and, as you saw, full of mistakes) the possibility that it might be useful to you in deciding whether you want to write about the scribblings of this here sloppy amateurish armchair semioticist and story-teller [. . .].

More later. Meanwhile, the Jefferson Lecture is an NEH deal in Washington—the only money prize the feds give to folks in the humanities. To folks like distinguished professors Robert Nisbet last year, Robert Penn Warren, Cleanth Brooks and, once to a novelist, Saul Bellow. So it makes me nervous trying to talk to God knows who and don't know whether this CSP stuff is too heavy for a general audience. What do you think? I could write a much lighter lecture about storytelling.

More later. Again deepest thanks.

WP [s]

p.s.: It's a public lecture.[31]

❧

December 27, 1988

Dear Ken,

Thanks so much again. You make me feel better about having got into this.

If you're serious about attending this mess, and I wouldn't recommend it unless you're in D.C. on real business, I'll put you on my guest list (plus Berti and Kenny and whoever you like). I need a small claque to whistle and clap like mad whenever I mention triadicity, which nobody else will dig. Let me know.

All God's blessing for '89 to you and yours.

Walker [s]

≥⚬

January 1, 1989

Dear Walker,

It would be an honor to be on your guest list for the lecture in D.C. I see it is to be May 3, a Wednesday. Spouse and 8-year-old son beg forgiveness, as they will be (a) at work, and (b) at school. It seems a cultural rule in this case that only professors get to go somewhere. Seriously, it would be important business for me to attend your lecture—good enough that the U will let me out of class a couple days. That's what a professor calls serious business indeed. I include a card with official address. Come hell or high water, I'll be there whether invited or not—I'll make camp on a steam grate if I have to. It'll take an act of nature to keep me away [. . .].

I volunteer to organize your claque. Actually I've been thinking of starting a service, so this would be good practice. Maybe you will give me an endorsement I could use in advertising so would do it free—I find my misspent youth qualifies me. I can, for instance, execute the following: (1) South Texas Red Neck happiness expulsion, let fly when about four beers down and finally dancing the cotton-eye with that red head he's been after all evening = aAIIoooooooo; just a little threatening along the line of "in control now," but rather positive due to execution in high register with medium volume, interpretant is "Hot damn, at last, so get out of my way." (2) West Texas Rodeo victory whistle, done when your teen-age daughter like an avenging Attila the Hun on top of a two-thousand pound mare has charged a defenseless baby goat and roped it in record time, goes wheeEETT, WheeEETTT, wheeeEEETTTT, rising in register (medium w, high T, quick repetitions), each whistle executed with two dextral fingers stuffed high into the dorsal donto-lingual locus, loud, tantalizingly raucous, mildly aggressive as in "She can do it to any of you that hears this unless you join me in my pride for her." (3) The Mighty HO, it's unspeakable and unwritable, you have to hear it to believe it, was invented by the Malay Taoist priest *Ue Wonntu* to blow away the mental cobwebs of a slack-brained disciple, very useful for starting 8 A.M. freshman logic classes, verbally it is the sound HO, but it penetrates to the heart and blows away all past bad karma for a few seconds so that a new thought can get in, presented with deafening volume with infinite diaphragmatic support (it's all in the delivery). (4) Cajun expletives: Willing, but training required. (5) Emergency option when things aren't going too well: Moon a designated nay-saying person, always a laugh getter, a little hellacious, but acceptable even in conservative circles because it's approved by Johnny Carson.

Select your options, more than one allowed, state the sequence, and designate the cue(s) and/or target individual(s).

No, kidding aside, no need to be nervous or apprehensive. You deserve this honor. And, what is more important, you have something of the highest importance to say now. Part of its importance (a sign of our nominalistic times, the intellectual excuse-giving of the dying age) is that it may be hard for some to hear, really to listen to it. But such is the freedom of listeners, they can disinterpret. Some no doubt will use the very thing you are calling to attention to maintain their nominalism. A strange deal, eschatological dyadicism. Actually, I am growing in optimism that the world is about ready to receive the Cenopythagorean lesson. I see many little signs and portents. One is: "They picked Walker for this lecture, didn't they!" So, Al-ta-ha a-bi-ya, which is Choctaw (I think) for "Always able!"

I yearn to sit down sometime and talk Peirce, etc., with you. I'm hoping you'll tip me someday when the coast is clear.

Loyally,

Ken [s]

Ketner [t]

☙

January 17, 1989

Dear Ken,

Am just now reading a book you gave me last June, *Semiotic and Significs*, the correspondence of CSP and Lady Welby. It is extremely touching and enlightening. I've conceived the notion of some day making a pilgrimage to Milford, Pennsylvania, to see if I can locate CSP's house, which must have been way the hell and far from anything. I wonder if it's still there.

Again, thanks for this.

Best,

Walker [s]

☙

January 20, 1989

Dear Walker,

Yours about *Semiotic and Significs* received with much pleasure. You can't imagine how tickled I am that such a one as you read that. A deep and profound sense of tickled. Instigated my tickle. I think it is the best brief introduction to P's philosophy and *life* (I mean Life; that is, LIFE). I'm serious—one could write one hell of a novel about CSP's life—like Irving Stone's treatment of Freud, and such. Why dontcha come over to Lubbock and we'll barricade ourselves in the Institute rooms in the Library here and talk Peirce. Or, if you will say the word, I could come over to Covington by cheap air, stay in Motel 6, talk with you at your leisure about "stuff." With my schedule this semester, I could be in New Orleans Thursday by dark and leave as late as noon Monday. Or how about St. Paul's College in Covington (I got you mapped when I went down to our map collection to get US Geo Survey for Milford) might need a guest lecturer on Peirce (say on P and religion, or whatever might be desired) who would lecture for nothing, just for the excuse to get over to Covington because there is someone there the lecturer yearns to discuss Peirce with? You talk a lot about the Helen Keller Phenomenon. I've stumbled onto another phenomenon, and I'm trying to figure it out. I call it the St. Aelred Phenomenon, after the fact that he seems to have discovered it, or at least brought it to the consciousness of Western Man, and he seems to have exemplified it in a condensed way, as Helen did with her phenomenon. Ordinarily I'm the world's shyest skinny guy, but hell Walker, life is short. Forgive me for being so damned forward.

Your pilgrimage to CSP's house, Arisbe, should be easy.[32] I have driven over from New York City a couple of times. Its about a two-hour drive. Peirce would take the stage from the front of his house over to Port Jervis, New York, a few miles away, where he would get a train to New York or Baltimore or Boston. Since the advent of the Auto Age, it is no longer so easy! I inclose some poop that would help you. You might also want to read Fisch's essay on Arisbe in *Peirce, Semeiotic, and Pragmaticism* that I sent you. If the stuff I inclose suggests some other thing you would like to have, just ask. Mi stuffa su stuffa. Chances are I probably got it in the collection. I have two drawers of stuff on Arisbe, acquired from Dr. Preston Tuttle of Princeton, who was working on trying to make Arisbe a museum for the public. I tried to help him as much as possible from Texas. We didn't quite succeed, but we did get the house stabilized physically; it is on the National Register, and the Park Service owns it and has offices in it, treats it with respect, etc. Maybe someday the museum idea can develop. But anyway, in the Tuttle collection, I got photos, plans, tax records, video interviews with living CSP neighbors (kids in his day, now deceased), etc., etc. Anyway, by corresponding with the superintendent of Delaware Water Gap, one can arrange to go in the house. If you go, walk the old stagecoach road from the house toward Milford. At places as you step along, you will sense CSP's time, and feel the location in which he reported (on such a walk) he conducted musement (recall his paper "Neglected Argument for the Reality of God") on the starry heavens, where the neglected argument came to him.

Ken [s]

Ketner [t]

❧

January 29, 1989

Dear Ken,

What a lot of good stuff on Arisbe! I couldn't imagine it was still standing since CSP said it needed lots of work in his day. Too bad, or is it NRA didn't pay him $60,000 for it? Would he have been long gone to Italy as he said, to France, with Juliette? Somehow can't see him in Italy. I bet he'd have fixed up Arisbe.

Tomorrow I go into hospital for periodic dilatation of esophagus, which has a miserable stricture. Probably too much Early Times in U.N.C. Ain't fit to see anybody right now. Will be in touch. What a gorgeous map of Covington!

Best,

Walker [s]

p.s.: Ken, have just now spotted this too late. It is my daughter Ann's drawing of how the new bridge over the Bogue Falaya is going to mess up her book store, The Kumquat.[33] Sorry. WP p.p.s.: Why was Juliette "mystery woman"?

❧

February 13, 1989

Dear Ken,

Would be honored indeed to have you dedicate CSP's "Detached Ideas on Vitally Important Topics."

I'm somewhat poorly but wanted to tell you this.

Walker [s]

February 21, 1989

Dear Walker,

Your card reached me a couple of days ago. I am seriously pained to hear you are "somewhat poorly." Please get better quickly. I struggle for words. Let me put it this way: If you relax for a moment, you can surely feel my intense concern and devoted wishes for your welfare.

You may not be in a mood to correspond. But your expression of pleasure in my dedication to you of my edition of CSP's Cambridge Conference Lectures (Vitally Important Topics, etc.) has prompted my unconscious to speak to me. I woke up yesterday with this thought on my mind: Send the edition to Farrar, Straus & Giroux to see if they would be interested in publishing it. I had been talking to Harvard University Press, but that has been inconclusive (although not yet a definite "Yes" or "No"), and it is technically not in submission with anyone now. I've been trying to think what to do. I listen to my subconscious (remember Socrates' "spirit" that whispered in his ear). I know you publish with F, S & G. Perhaps you might be willing to guide me somewhat concerning whether it is the sort of thing in which they have any interest. Any "where and how to publish it" advice in general would also be welcome. I want it to be read by the general educated public. I think it is a wonderful introduction in CSP's own words to his late philosophy, knowledge of which is sorely lacking in said public. I feel like CSP's mouthpiece. On the other hand, if you are under the weather, just forget that I mentioned it.

I am exceedingly tickled—I mean ex-ceedingly—that you are happy about my little dedicatory tribute. It will be published somewhere good, someday. Then I will get to send you another book.

I got my steam grate reserved in D.C., and, God willing, the claque will be in place on 3 May 89.

Yours (truly),

Ken [s]

February 27, 1989

Dear Ken,

As CSP would say: It's a sweet thing, my dear Ken, for you to want to dedicate your book to me. But it may be misleading to dedicate to me CSP's *Reasoning and the Logic of Things*, your edition of the Cambridge Conferences Lectures. I'm not sure CSP would approve. Let me explain.

As you well know, I am not a student of Peirce. I am a thief of Peirce. I take from him what I want and let the rest go, most of it. I am only interested in CSP insofar as I understand his attack on nominalism and his rehabilitation of Scholastic realism. I am only interested in his "logic" insofar as it can be read as an ontology, or, as CSP said, insofar as he "takes the Kantian step of transferring the conceptions of logic to metaphysics."

Which is to say, I have not the slightest interest in his formal logic, existential graphs and such like. I use his "logic of relatives" for my own purposes, that is, as a foundation for my own categories. That means that I expropriate his two categories, Secondness and Thirdness, as the ground of an ontology, setting aside "Firstness" since it, Firstness, is an idealized notion and is not to be found exemplified in "reality." As CSP put it, "it is the mode in which anything would exist for itself, irrespective of anything else. . . ." But, of course, nothing exists like that but only in relation to something else.

Accordingly, if CSP defines himself as a logician, as he does in these Cambridge lectures, I am rather massively uninterested, same only when he strays from formal logic and allows his "logic" to stray into ontology.

But this is not the worst if it. What would set CSP spinning in his grave is the use I intend to put him to. As you probably already know, and if you don't, let us keep the secret between us, I intend to use CSP as one of the pillars of a Christian apologetic. CSP, of course, made himself clear about religion in general, "a barbaric superstition"—and Christianity in particular—especially "the miracle mongers of the synoptic gospels." To be specific, I think that CSP's notion that Christianity was a development out of earlier Asian traditions, especially Buddhism (to quote you), is the silliest kind of nonsense. I have seen it, ever since reading Kierkegaard, as quite the contrary. Kierkegaard (and I) would see Buddhism, and most of the great contemplative religions as "scientific" in a broad sense, that is, as professing general truths which can be arrived at by anyone, anywhere and at any time. Christianity (and Judaism) would fall into what Kierkegaard (and I) would call the "religious" stage, that is, the being open to "news," of the singular (scandalous) event, the Jewish covenant, the Christian incarnation and news of same.

As you may know, I have been at some pains to sketch out an "anthropology," a theory of man by virtue of which he is understood to be by his very nature open to the kerygma and "news." You can see why I not only diverge radically from CSP here, but find him in the enemy camp when he says things like: "The clergymen who do any good don't pay much attention to religion. They teach people the conduct of life, and on the whole in a high and noble way." So did "Booda," Socrates, Gandhi, and yes, Jesus. But Jesus taught something else far more subversive.

So if you want to dedicate this book to me, please do so with the understanding that I admire at the most one percent of it (two pages) and with the understanding to that it would spin CSP in his grave. Naturally I love the idea—using CSP as the foundation of a Catholic apologetic, which I have tentatively entitled (after Aquinas) *Contra Gentiles*.

As I was saying, what I hope to do is to use CSP's "ontology" of Secondness and Thirdness (not Firstness) as the ground for a more or less scientific introduction to a philosophical anthropology. Such an ontology, I think, would debouche directly into the phenomenology of the "existentialists," like Marcel, Heidegger, Buber, *et al.*

Anyhow I'm afraid you can't enlist me in your attempt to publish CSP's book and I think you see why. But good luck.

This is a pleasant way to spend a Sunday afternoon, sounding off at you.

Best,

Walker [s]

[On the flap of the envelope.] I think you already know the contents of the inclosed, but it is fun to make them explicit. w p

March 5, 1989

Dear Walker,

The six pages you penned last Sunday reached me a couple days later, and I have been pondering them until now. I knew (know):

(a) that your interest in logic is detectable only on a high-power Bausch and Lomb Lapsometer;
(b) that you have no use for Firstness:
(c) that you are hot after apologetics, using a little CSP in same;
(d) that you are unimpressed by Buddhism or Peirce's claims about same.

Something else I also came to know, not too long after I had the good fortune to be able to correspond with you, came in what I called my misunderstanding of you. Remember, hick that I am, I only came to read anything at all of yours about five years ago. Oh! Would that it had been in the late 1950's when I started. I would have been capable of understanding some at least of your ideas, for I was a philosophy major by 1960, after earlier thinking that I was destined by heaven to be a Double E. Twenty years without access to your work—what a schavoon I was (and perhaps am only slightly better now). My initial reading of your essays and novels (except for *Lost in the Cosmos* and *Lancelot*) made your ideas to be some of this and some of that, a kind of philosophical smorgasbord. Then I started reading all that I could find about you and trying to sort it onto my "classify Walker scheme." Then came some letter or other of yours and blew it all away, at which time I realized not what you are (a potentially misleading phrase, for you are a unique person, and besides, a very tricky one), but what hue your aura has (so to speak). I summarize that hue this way—Walker Percy is a Roman Catholic intellectual (or in place of the "I" word, plug in "novelist" or *littérateur* or whatever else big-sounding word of one's choice). You had disguised it in your works, you see—all this talk of a bad Catholic in novels, etc., etc. When I realized that, the scales fell from my eyes. I think I already told you before that I am a little slow, and easily gulled.

Now let me tell you a tidbit about myself which you will need in order that my words don't miss the target. I am not much of an appreciator of organized religion. I seem to get closer to God by myself or with just a few persons around. Remember "Where two or three are gathered in my name, there I will be also"? I sometimes suspect this means "*only* when two or three." But I accept that as a personal shortcoming and failing. Second thing, my closest friend and fraternity brother (I was a TKE, quite the opposite of DKE) in college at Oklahoma State University was a papist. I rented a room at Jim's house, took my meals with the family, who were quite devout, got to know the meaning of their religion as lived, not as from a book. These folks were like a second family. Mr. and Mrs. Barnes literally counseled me through a big part of college. I don't mean any of this in a condescending or patronizing way—quite the opposite. So when I came to my hypothesis that WP is a RC novelist, my affection and respect for WP was intensified, not decreased. (Now, don't start on me with that stuff about "Well now you've named me" as in "I feel better Doctor, now that I know what it is.") Although I was dipped in Rock Creek (just south of what is now the dam of the huge new Lake of the Arbuckles in the Chickasaw National Recreation Area near Sulphur, Oklahoma) when 12, by a Baptist revivalist, my religion has become "unorganized," although I make out religion to be tremendously important in this miserable age for reasons you know well.

Maybe all this will help you understand that I had a strong case of the "read Walker's books, then levitate above your old ways" syndrome, a phenomenon about which many have commented.

So when I finished this set of CSP lectures, I wanted to give you a tribute of some kind, to let you and the world know what I think of you. What I do, of course, is grub in manuscripts, and come up now and again to write mediocre essays. So I had the idea of trying to inscribe my efforts in the CSP edition to you. I didn't mean to imply by an inscription in this work that you are a Peircean. I just wanted to say that Ketner's part of this task should be understood by readers as a tribute to WP. I cooked up the Latin subphrase, *Doctor Humanitatis*, as a way of telling myself, if no one else, that the ancient Roman tradition is still active, still teaching humanity to humans. (After all, they are the folks who brought us the "Middle Ages," an appropriate mediation, wouldn't you think?) I had hoped to achieve a kind of double entendre by *Doctor Humanitatis* (with the help of a colleague from Classical Languages). I wanted to say "Humanity is who WP teaches (doctors), and what he teaches them is to be human."

What I didn't know, and concerning which your letter somewhat surprised me, was that you regard CSP as in the adversarial camp, or at least outside your pickets. I don't agree. If he is outside your picket line, then he is sleeping in tall grass on a moon-lit night about six inches away from the stump on which your sergeant of the guard is sitting, cooking gumbo, the same soldier who turns occasionally to spit tobacco juice over his shoulder into the tall grass (which is to say, close). Or put it this way, CSP was a medievalist and close student of the Scholastics when almost everyone near him thought that age a disaster and a desert. Still today, as one who takes Peirce seriously, I often get called names like "Scholastic," meaning you must be one if you mouth those weird doctrines of CSP's. Okay, maybe I am Scholastic. I'll admit to "monk-like" anyhow. Or put it yet another way: If CSP is in another camp, how come Father Vincent Potter, now the Provost of Fordham, is a top P scholar? The book by Donna Orange, *Peirce's Conception of God: A Developmental Study*, originated as a dissertation with Father Potter at Fordham.[34]

Some of the quotes from Peirce you mentioned are not anti-religious *per se* (as I interpret them) but anti-bad-things-people-do-sometimes-in-the-name-of-religion. He was an Episcopalian having earlier been a Cambridge Unitarian "under" his father. In 1891, in a very bad time in his life (he was sleeping on benches in Central Park in NYC, eating a cookie a day, struggling to earn some money on which to subsist), he made his way into the Church of St. Thomas in NYC ("Doubting Thomas' " church!) and the letter inclosed (from CSP to the minister of St. Thomas) tells what happened. There is a first bit of counter-evidence to your "enemy camp" hypothesis. There is a lot more where that came from.

The statistical odds are that when you were a student at College of Physicians and Surgeons in New York City you probably sat on some park bench on which CSP had slept!

I recently read big chunks of Merton's book on the Eucharist. Lordy, it's full of terminology that would make Peirce the arch-terminologist blush.

Rotten old heathen Taoist that I am, I found myself agreeing with Merton more than not.

You say you are a thief of Peirce's Scholastic realism. You can't be; he stole it from your gang! You reclaimed stolen property, remolded somewhat, but Thirdness is still distilled Scholastic realism—strong enough you can make an Old-Fashioned with it.

You say you only accept one percent of CSP. I think the percentage is higher. But who's to quibble. You picked the right one percent!!!—Thirdness, Secondness, and the thesis that former not reducible to latter. Or put it this way: If you had only written one piece and that "The Delta Factor," you would be deservedly famous, and what's more, honored by us Peirce fanatics.

You say you are concerned about CSP's postmortem circumrevolutions. I don't agree he would rotate. Might disagree with something or other you asserted, but what else is new?

You said you want to work up a Scientific Christian Apologetics, understanding science in a broad way. That is what P did in much of his own work. I'm convinced that a lot of his philosophy of science had religion as its ultimate destination (Orange argues that quite well in her book).

One big reason I would like to visit Covington is to see if I could add some CSP stuff to the list of things you could use in your project. Which is to say I applaud your project. Git tew it. Let me help you get access to the real Peirce, not the one of the CSP *Collected Papers*, which is so bad and incomplete that it is downright misleading and harmful.

If Walker Percy is going to do apologetics, then the future of apologetics is looking up considerably, and will amount to something the instant there is a book by WP in the field.

A while back I brought up the matter of the inscription of the CSP edition because I wanted to please you with it, and also to get permission. If it doesn't please you, I would remove it in an instant. Who knows, maybe no one will want to publish the project anyway. But I'm just getting started, and have only contacted two publishers. One said "No, not our thing"; the other, Harvard, said "Maybe," and "Let's talk some more," which is how it is now.

I have to add one more thing to this overly long mess. I want to try to describe not my ideas or thoughts but my feelings. I have an unshakable deep affection and devotion toward you. Don't ask me to explain it. I can't. I've tried. I'm not talking anything mushy or Freudian (I'll be 50 if I survive to the 24th of this month, and I know myself; I even like my own company). It's a strange phenomenon. The closest description of it I have been able to find is in the inclosed book, *De spiritali amicitia*, by Aelred of Rievaulx (sounds almost Cajun), a saint of your persuasion, I believe. I would change two jots and a title in Aelred's account, but it's close.

Greet them all,

Ken [s]

Ketner [t]

P.S.: Who is a Jew? The Israelites are even debating it now. Choosing presupposes identification. Would the child of a Hittite woman and a Jewish father be a Jew? Or, reverse the parentages? Boy or girl child, either parentage? Child of that child who married a Visigoth? Do I surmise correctly you are feeling better? Hope so.

[Editor's Note: The following letter (*MS* L483) was inclosed:

April 24, 1892

Dear and Reverend Sir:

I took the Holy Communion at St. Thomas's this morning—in fact just now, under peculiar circumstances, which it seems proper to report.

For many years I have not taken the Communion and have seldom entered a church, although I have always had a passionate love for the church and a complete faith that the essence of Christianity, whatever that might be, was Divine; but still I could not reconcile my notion of common sense and of evidence with the proposition of the creed, and I found going to church made me sophistical and gave me an impulse to play fast and loose with matters of intellectual integrity. Therefore, I gave it up; though it has been the cause of many a bitter reflection. Many times I have tried to cipher out some justification for my return to the communion of the church; but I could not. Especially, the last two nights I have lain awake thinking of the matter.

This morning after breakfast I felt I must go to church anyway. I wandered about, not knowing where to find a regular episcopal church, in which I was confirmed; but I finally came to St. Thomas. I had several times been in it on week days to look at the chancel. I therefore saw nothing new to me. But this time—I am not thinking of St. Thomas and his doubts, either—no sooner had I got into the church than I seemed to receive the direct permission of the Master to come. Still, I said to myself, I must not go to the communion without further reflection! I must go home and duly prepare myself before I venture. But when the instant came, I found myself carried up to the altar rail, almost without my own volition. I am perfectly sure that it was right. Anyway, I could not help it.

I may mention as a reason why I do not offer to put my gratitude for the bounty granted to me into some form of church work, that that which seemed to call me today seemed to promise that I should bear a cross like death for the Master's sake, and he would give me strength to bear it. I am sure that will happen. My part is to wait. I have never before been mystical; but now I am. After giving myself time to reflect upon this situation, I will call to see you. Yours very truly,

C. S. Peirce

It does not seem to me that it would be wise to make the circumstances known; but I conceive it my duty to report them to you. I am a man of 52, and married.]

March 8, 1989

Dear Ken,

You are very good to treat this papist so generously. I was writing in a state of shock fresh from reading CSP on religion, e.g.:

Religion *per se* seems to me a barbaric superstition. But when you come to Christianity, or as we ought to call it Buddhism, for surely the Indian Prince was an incomparably more perfect embodiment of it than the miracle mongers of the synoptic gospels, if that is to be called religion. . . .[35]

I was left stupefied. Buddhism as the forerunner to Christianity indeed. Us Jews and Christians have to smile. (I would say CSP was kidding, except that he didn't kid.)

Listen, if you folks get up to Washington, and I hope you do, please write this lady beforehand who will give you all the tickets you need. I've told her I got a claque of kinfolks and friends who might show up:

> Ms. Susan H. Metts
> Assistant Chairman for Administration
> National Endowment for the Humanities
> 1100 Pennsylvania Ave., N.W.
> Washington, D.C.

The lecture is May 3. We will be at the Henley Park Hotel May 1–4. Why don't you come by, give me a call and will have a drink or meal or something.

Best,

Walker [s]

☙

March 17, 1989

Dear Walker,

You eased my mind. I now understand your reaction and why you wrote a long letter expressing concern about CSP, Buddhism, etc. "Buddhism as a precursor of Christianity" was a historical hypothesis CSP entertained. It is no part of his thinking on Thirdness, or his neo-Scholasticism, which are parts of his philosophy. In other words, you ought not to be concerned, seems to me, that P entertained an unconventional historical thesis. Because that odd historical guess conflicts with the News, seems to me you could ignore it. On the other hand, P has a lot for your project in his philosophy, more than just the one percent you now like, if you can believe a sympathetic Choctaw.

As to the pronouncement on religion and ministers from the Cambridge Conferences Lectures (that long letter from P to William James), I read that as either (a) a disappointment with things done in the name of religion that are bad, that good religionists would also decry (e.g., Swaggart, Bakker, etc., etc., as examples of the bad religionists), or (b) CSP is in one of his moods or spells.[36] P had something like manic-depressive syndrome. Moreover, he would overwork, put in a week of allnighters, do that too many times, and enter into a kind of overall catatonia. Or he would be angelic at times, then suddenly bestial at others. His family was afflicted with this strange medical background, apparently. We Peirce fanatics (who know this side of him) don't talk about it much. That letter to James, by the way, was in effect a disguised plea for help. CSP was about to starve at that point, and his wife was deadly sick with what they thought was cancer. She was operated by Gill Wylie, a Johns Hopkins gynecologist, who removed a huge tumor (can't remember if it was 14 or 17 pounds) that was so intergrown with her organs that it was hard to tell where tumor started and intestine, etc., stopped. But Wylie got the right parts out in a marathon operation, and they turned out to be noncarcinomatical. So P was a bit out of his gourd from worry and malnutrition. It was so bad that he wrote to a friend that he would suicide if Juliette didn't make it. (Maybe there were also unknown heavy sodium domes under Arisbe.) Also, the remarks there about religion do not match most of the other (friendlier) remarks elsewhere on same topic.

Do you have Orange's book on CSP's religious thought? Can get you one at no cost to either of us.

Got my invite set with NEH, and I'll arrive in Washington Dulles at 4 P.M. on 2 May and leave at 4:50 P.M. on 4 May. It's very kind of you to ask me to drop by your hotel. I would hate to bounce in on you at an odd time. Hows about you let me buy you breakfast, lunch, or supper, or tea, or an Old-Fashioned at the time of your choosing? You say when, and I'll come to the place you appoint, and stay as long or as briefly as you desire. In D.C., I'll be just a lone Okie traveler, a spectator and opposition mooner, all easy and flexible—you, on the other hand, will have responsibilities and family with you, etc.

I inclose a warning about recent changes in D.C.[37] You might want to watch out.

Ken [s]

Ketner [t]

❧

March 22, 1989

Dear Ken,

I didn't know I was dealing with the head knocker in the CSP Society. Looks like you're doing a fine job honchoing that gang.

Please call me at Henley Park Hotel in D.C.

Best,

Walker [s]

❧

April 24, 1989

Dear Walker,

I'm finishing up an interesting year. Last semester I taught philosophy of religion, and now ending a semester with Asian philosophy. That on top of the class on Peirce-Percy gave my guts and chemicals a good stretching. Thanks to you, I find myself led by the pointing finger back to my old friends, the Catholic mystics (St. John of the Cross, St. Teresa, St. Augustine, Father Louis alias Thomas Merton, and such). I wanted to drop you this note and mention the thought recently discovered by me (not a new discovery, but new for me) that Wittgenstein has to be added to the list of Catholic mystics.

Wittgenstein was a mystic. This much I have known nominally. But lately I have been reading Tolstoy and an interesting book by Russell Nieli, *Wittgenstein: From Mysticism to Ordinary Language*, in which I find he was also a Catholic. Now I think I know the above un-nominally.

What this means is that Wittgenstein's interpreters and commentators have gotten him badly wrong. I had to survive a Ph.D. program in which some of his commentators dominated. I always suspected there was something bad wrong with Wittgenstein's approach to things, but now I see the principal fault is with those who have described him as a kind of revived Hume, or a slightly twerky Bertrand Russell. Wittgenstein's *Tractatus* also is a treatise on Signs! Of course, in Wittgenstein's revival as a mystic, there is still food for disagreement.

This is to say, here is another Catholic that is a mystic. Maybe they will take over the whole movement. I inclose some stuff on this I'm handing out in class, just in case you have any interest. I mark in red the mystical passages, including a few lines from Tolstoy's *My Confession; My Religion; The Gospel in Brief,* whose versions of the four Gospels influenced Wittgenstein quite a bit apparently.

Happy greetings to you on the eve of your voyage to the East.

Ken [s]

Ken Ketner [t]

❧

May 23, 1989

Dear Walker,

Since those outstanding few days I spent in D.C. with my old friend and fraternity brother Herb Huser and you, I have had to pay for my sins by going through ten pounds of stale mail in a five-pound sack, grading final exams for my courses, and getting caught up on the CSP International Congress work. Now I have a momentary breather, and my thoughts are a bit more collected, so I wanted to communicate a little with you. I been thinking you might be amused by a running account of my pilgrimage to hear the 18th Jefferson Lecture. You like *homines viatores*, and I was one.

First I had to scrounge like a sweaty supply sergeant to come up with some travel support. As it turned out, I cashed in a favor here at Tech, then ole Herb put me up at Chez Huser in Fairfax, Virginia. Now I owe *him* one. Got to the airport about 4:30 Tuesday and called you at hotel per directions. Heard your voice for the first time ever, and you sounded harried but cordial. You were covered up the next day, so you encouraged me to try to find you on Wednesday evening at the reception. Wednesday morning, Herb and I went to the lecture hall and scene of the reception across the street; we wanted to case both joints. They were setting up the hall, and we walked in like a couple of GSA accountants with clipboards, only in this case I had my little attaché, so the workers ignored us. Bluffing sometimes works. The hall looked good, but we couldn't figure out how the reception was going to be run.

I treated Herb to a neat supper at the Willard Hotel, about a block from the lecture hall, and then we mosyed (that is such a verbal as opposed to a written word, that I don't know how to spell it—mosy, mosey, mosie, mosee) over like we knew what we were doing, and got to the hall about 30 minutes in advance. It had already filled up somewhat, and the front few rows especially were already occupied. After we had sat down on the side of the hall that would have been to your far right, on the aisle, Judge Bork's beard came in and sat down behind us, the judge himself following ever so closely thereupon. Then the Secretary of Defense came in briskly and sat down just about 12 feet ahead of us on the front row. A TV camera guy came into our aisle and cranked up his rig about five feet away. Said CNN on it. Then came your family, which we couldn't see too well from where we were, and soon entered the Jefferson Lecturer himself and welcoming bigshots. Mrs. Cheney seemed to take charge right away, and the show was on the road. The guy from Princeton seemed all right, but I confess I didn't listen to him too well in anticipation of the main event. I had your first draft in my attaché under my legs, so as Mr. Princeton came to an end, I slithered it out to look at. I said to myself, "Walker is a tricky guy; I want to see how this draft survived." Immediately I knew you had made a revision, and I could track the pattern of it to some extent then, and later I tracked it even better. I think the revision was wise, for I doubt that the audience would have understood you. The first draft would have overloaded their interpretants. Or as we Okies say, "The way to cook a live frog is to. . . ."

The audience around us seemed to be composed of younger federals or D.C.-area academics. We made a fast estimate of the size of the audience, and computed a figure of 800.

Your voice came through very well. They had a PA system in the hall sufficient for a Rolling Stones Concert, and it was very clear. You have a good lecturing voice, but there were some ravening ferns on both sides of the lectern which I would have zapped if I had brought my laser beam. Those turkey ferns got in my way. And I could tell you were struggling with the lighting somehow. I had worried when all the TV lights came on at first—I thought "That's going to make him unhappy—all that light in his face." The audience was quite attentive and eagerly receptive. Your punch lines elicited some deeply wry chuckles, but no belly laughs.

It all ended with Mrs. Cheney inviting the audience to the reception, and her saying "I hope everyone will have a chance to meet our charming lecturer." Amen, but I poked Herb in the ribs, and he me, because we couldn't see how that was going to happen with 800 or so folks, give or take. As far as I could tell, the audience got up en masse and moved into the museum. So we moseyed in behind to see what would happen with the reception. It was disorganized, to say the least. I had thought there would be a receiving line. But it was a lot of pretty good food and a lot of people, clutching their copies of the Percy issue of *Humanities* with that autograph gleam in their eyes, stalking the prey, with no one in charge to direct traffic. We sorta strolled around, again trying to look like we knew what we were doing, looking for some sign. Then we split up, with an agreed rendezvous point. Soon here comes Herb saying, "Let's follow those popping flashbulbs." Herb's a born semiotician, who knows a good index when it appears. So sure enough there you were over by a Model T, heading toward the ice cream parlor section of the museum. There you sat down with some family members around, and a line of *Humanities* clutchers immediately appeared as if by magic. Herb (an old D.C. hand) whispered in my ear "Get in there, this is Washington, you have to be pushy." I said, "No way, José: I wouldn't interrupt on that gentleman for money." You see, I assumed that all this was somehow planned with your consent and cooperation, which you later dispelled, and which we quickly began to abduct was the case as the line grew and the flashbulbs became more insistent. So we stood about 10 feet directly in front of you, and watched you struggle with the line. Looked kinda like you were holding confessional, if you don't mind a friendly chuckle. We tried to look like your bodyguards, and even talked into our lapel buttons a couple of times to strengthen the impression. Must have worked, because we were left alone. If I had known then that you were under pressure, I would have charged in to rescue you. About the time our "abducting" told us that this ain't going the way it's supposed to go, your daughter came in and sprung you. We both were relieved as we followed, still talking into our lapels, watching you take shelter in a limo and then seeing it peel out. We were both happy that you were out of it, and back into the arms of your family. We took off for Chez Huser and a few winks.

From whence I called you the next morning about 9:30 to learn that our abductions were confirmed. You graciously invited us to see you Thursday afternoon at 2. So we lit out to see some antique stores (in your honor, since you seem to love antiques so well) outside Fairfax. Now don't get upset, but I collect old radios, and behold we found a great example of a 1925 two-tuber home-made set at a local junk shop—case was made from orange-crate material, the *omnia materia* for all the radios I built as a kid. I bought it and will restore it in my little shop at home.

We hit the Henley Park Hotel about 1 P.M., told one of the hotel lobby guys that we were going for lunch and pointed at the hotel restaurant, and would he please tell you in case you came early to the little room off the lobby where you told us to meet you. The hotel guy must have missed our gesture, hearing only "going to eat," and interpreting it as "eating out." Anyway, we were in the little room just before 2, and yakking away about this and that. Then about 10 after 2, looked up and there was the good doctor pacing the driveway outside. This time I jumped up and hollered at Herb, "There's Walker, let's go out and introduce ourselves."

And that is the story of how I got to spend an hour with Walker Percy on a bench in Gompers Park in D.C. on the fourth of May 1989. I see you also like to get out and case the area some, for you knew directly where a little bit of woods was located, even in the heart of decadent old D.C.

Turns out you was looking for me on Thursday about as much as I was hoping to contact you on the eve of the reception on Wednesday. I was looking for you and you were doing what you were supposed to do on Wednesday: Go to a reception. And turns out that I almost missed you on the afternoon of the following day when you were looking for me, and I was doing what I thought I was supposed to do: Wait in the little room. Ain't that a bit of life.

I was a bad conversation partner in Gompers Park. I was so pleased to be sitting on the same park bench with you and ole Herb that I must have been a little goofy. And I kept worrying that I was going to mess up something you had scheduled.

Anyway, it was a great trip, and a great lecture. Have you got any feedback or grousing from the social scientists? The nice write-up in *The Chronicle of Higher Education* (10 May issue—if you don't have a copy I can send you one) might bring some of them out of the woodwork.

You floored me by telling me on Gompers bench that I should write a life of CSP. You can't hit me with that and walk away. If you are serious (and I will take you extremely seriously if indeed you are), I need to talk with you some more on that and many things. I'm ready to zip over to Covington this summer if you will but say the word. I even have a frequent flyer credit now so I could get to New Orleans on Southwest Airlines, rent a car, and meet you at Wendy's in Covington or wherever (just mark it on the map).

I inclose some stuff on the CSP Congress next September. We are going to have a memorial meeting at 2 P.M. on Sunday the 10th of September, CSP's birthday, at Christ Church Cambridge, within a long stone's throw of the house where CSP was born 150 years ago (two or three blocks from Harvard Yard). Is there any way I could get you up to that Congress, either as someone just attending, or perhaps as a guy who would say a few words of memory about ole CSP in Christ Church? If everybody shows up, looks like we will have about 300 papers of one kind and another. A real Peirce orgy. Wish you could be there.

Ole Charley no doubt is happy in heaven or purgatory or wherever Episcopalians go because of the great honor you gave him. He yearned to hear "those wonderful words," perhaps because he didn't get enough love from his father: "Well done, thou good and faithful servant." The Jefferson Lecturer this year said them to him.

Faithfully,

Ken [s]

Ketner [t]

♨

May 29, 1989

Dear Ken,

Was very touched by the account of your peregrinations. I only blush to think of the disparity of the effort you took and the rather prosaic lecture.

But I appreciate it immensely (I don't stand around on street corners looking for many folks).

Yes, Gompers Park was just right. It was nice meeting in a tiny little park totally unknown to Washingtonians.

Re lecture: What do you think CSP would think of my idea that his Thirdness can be used as the foundation of a scientific anthropology?

Did you know that John Poinsot may have anticipated CSP by 200 years, with his ontology of relations, *relatio secundum esse* = dyads; *relatio secundum dici* = triads? The trouble is that the Scholastic language is all but impenetrable.

Am suffering from my yearly bout with diverticulitis, a real pain in the _____[sic].

Thanks again,

Walker [s]

P.S.: Congratulations on the NEH funding for the CSP Congress. By the way, why don't you apply for a grant to take some time off and write a biography of CSP? You can do it better than anyone else. I'd be glad to be the first to say so. W P

&

Lubbock, Texas 79464–5135

May 30, 1989

Dear Walker,

The age we occupy is well captured in the fact that all I need for an address are nine numbers above.

I've been tracking down ole Wittgenstein since I saw you. Alternatively I dig into his stuff, usually after I teach either religion or Asian (both recently done). I'm digging into his Christianity this time. It's clear that the late Tolstoy was a major influence on him. Wittgenstein carried Tolstoy's *The Four Gospels Harmonized and Translated* (see pp. 168–69) with him during his combat time in WWI. So, I try to get T's *Gospels*. No copy in Lubbock. I get interlibrary loan in gear, and in Texas there is a copy, at Sul Ross State University—Good old Sullie—patron of Texican culture, worshipped at Texas A & M to this day.

Now I'm sending you proof that Tolstoy knew your environment/ world distinction, and the notion of CSP that 3's are not equal to 2's. T claims that Jesus knew the distinction. I'm inclined to agree with T [. . .]. [The second page of Professor Ketner's letter is lost.]

꿈

June 12, 1989

Dear Walker,

Yes, I was truly honored that W. Percy, M.D., waited for me on a street corner. I guess that was actually, in a funny way, the highlight of the trip. I wasn't troubled by any of my adventures. It was a thrill to see you and hear your definitely antimediocre lecture. I also got you on video tape—a friend dubbed the lecture off C-SPAN on the cable.

You rattled my toes when you urged me on the park bench to take up CSP's biography. And since you repeated it in your last letter, I find that (having tried) I can't successfully ignore you. I'm also grateful and honored that you would be willing to critique such a project, and that you would support me in a request to NEH for a couple years off to gear it up.

However, the politics of the thing are not simple. I'm not talking Jim Wright versus Newt Gingrich politics, but the academic kind, which is . . . you know how. You're fortunate in having a nonacademic environment in which to produce.

Let me put it this way, your urging me to do this project means a great deal to me. No other person's urging could have the effect yours has had. So I will do it if I can find a way through the potholes in the road.

It would help me a lot if I could discuss these potholes with you, not that you can patch them (or maybe you can), but that you might have some ideas or advice. As you know, I could come over to Covington readily, easily, and inexpensively (I now have a free trip on a frequent flyer plan), at your convenience, for some conversation (not as a burden, but as a guy who stays in Motel 6 and happens to be in Wendy's when you eat lunch, and chats for a couple hours). I would love to do that, but would never barge in on you or interfere with your plans. OR, if you felt like it, you could call me some evening (or I you, as you wish) for a long telephone conversation on the potholes. I'm in most every evening (don't drink and carouse, but stay home with wife and kid, and when depressed, eat cholesterol-free cookies and watch "Matlock"). If any of this would put you out, then just don't do any of it.

In your last letter you raised the issue of whether Peirce had an anthropology. As you so eloquently stated in the lecture, our sciences of man today are reductionistic. What would a nonreductive science of man be like? I will tell you an intimate thought of mine. Such a science, in its fundamentals, would look a whole lot like the Gospel of Jesus. I think Peirce either knew this or contained it somewhere in his high unconsciousness. (Tolstoy, as I have recently found out, is another person who discovered this in his own way.) If true this would mean, wouldn't it, that the (correct and proper) science of man is the most fundamental of all sciences. (Why? because a scientist is a man, and to do science, one must be a man, which is not to say that one is simply a member of a biological species: Deng, the butcher, is a member of our species, but imagine him as a scientist!) I think P in effect claimed that when he argued that semeiotic logically precedes all the disciplines we now call sciences (which he called Special Sciences). There are a zillion insights within these (and other) great generalities which are worth pursuing. So my answer to your question is "Yes." Ayand futhamoah, this topic in its fundamental points is perhaps the main reason why hithertofore CSP has not been accepted or even considered by many folks today—or as you call them, denizens of this age. Scholars and scientists in particular take a look at CSP and say, "Dang, that's silly stuff," meaning that "here's a guy talking about something other than chemicals, or guts, or causes."

Walker's strategy: Get social science correct for good and sound nonreductive scientific reasons, and the Gospel of Jesus will be just around the next bush. *Nicht wahr?*

How can I be of further help to you?

Loyally,

Ken [s]

Ketner [t]

❧

June 15, 1989

Dear Ken,

Glad to hear you're considering a biography of CSP. I think you're
the man to do it. At least I don't know anybody else with the detailed
knowledge of his life and work, both.

I'd be glad to write you a letter of recommendation to NEH. But I
don't like nice long visits from anybody.

Best luck,

Walker [s]

❧

This is to commend to you the application for an National Endowment for the Humanities grant from Dr. Kenneth L. Ketner.[38]

I can recommend him very highly indeed.

Kenneth Ketner knows more about the great American philosopher,
Charles Sanders Peirce, both his life and his work, than anybody I know.

His accomplishment is to have contributed, perhaps more than any
other scholar, to the rehabilitation of this extraordinary scientist-philoso-
pher. Of particular value is his foundation of the Institute for Studies in
Pragmaticism at Texas Tech University, his collecting and editing of overlooked Peirce writings (e.g., Peirce's *The Nation* articles), his tireless efforts
at organizing seminars and congresses about Peirce all across the country,
his own writings about Peirce.

He is a modest and meticulous scholar. For example, I am acquainted
with several instances of his correcting other scholars' mistakes about
Peirce's life and work.

Of particular interest to me as a lay student of Peirce is Ketner's heuris-
tic approach in this project, of relating the facts of Peirce's life, which he
knows intimately, to the growth and changes in Peirce's thought.

In a word, Ketner's project is a much needed and certainly exciting venture. I don't know anyone else with the energy and intellectual competence to bring it off.

I recommend him without reservation.

᪾

June 29, 1989

Dear Dr. Ketner,

Inclosed are "preprints" of an article by novelist Walker Percy that will appear in the Summer 1989 issue of *The Wilson Quarterly*. Although our authors and editors conduct extensive research on featured topics, we know that we cannot cover all aspects of such a complex subject. We feel that we better serve our readers (some 90,000 academics, journalists, public officials, and professionals) by following up major articles with informed commentary, in the form of letters to the editor, from experts in the field.

We ask your assistance in providing additional perspectives on the subject. If you would be willing to help us out, we would appreciate your comments in the form of a brief (200- to 300-word letter) to the editor, and permission to publish the letter in the Autumn issue, space permitting, or a subsequent issue.

Unfortunately, we cannot offer any monetary reward, but we would be happy to send you a year's subscription to *The Wilson Quarterly* in exchange for your views.

In any case, we hope that you enjoy reading the articles. Thank you for your assistance.

Very truly yours,

Henry L. Mortimer, Jr. [s]

Henry L. Mortimer, Jr. [t]
Production Assistant
The Wilson Quarterly

370 L'Enfant Promenade, Suite 704
Washington, D.C.

P.S.: We would appreciate receiving your comments by Tuesday, August 1, 1989.

🙞

July 3, 1989

Dear Ken,

Thanks for the photos. They're lovely.

Peirce's yard looks like mine—a semiotic yard? [Peirce did not mow his yard.] It looks like it's up to you to solve the mystery of Juliette.

Best,

Walker [s]

🙞

July 19, 1989

Dear Mr. Mortimer,

I'm grateful for your invitation, and honored to comment on Walker Percy's Jefferson Lecture which will appear in *The Wilson Quarterly*. I had the memorable pleasure of hearing the lecture live at the Departmental Auditorium. The following material is yours to publish as you wish. I find it difficult to be profound in 200–300 words. At least it is from the heart.

"Walker Percy is a voice. That's good news and bad news. The good news is that the human spirit still speaks in such tones. The bad news is that our era may no longer have the capacity to listen well enough. Listeners are powerful beings, able to destroy communication in an ear's flick. Speaking to an incapable or unwilling listener is like trying to toss a cannonball into an egg cup. But Dr. Percy has his ways. He is a tricky man, widely loved for 'making up stories' full of good humor and beauty and transforming power, but which are ultimately designed to tempt listeners.

His Jefferson Lecture has no tricks, and the voice is pure and resonant. Will we then stop listening? It could happen. It could be said that Percy is not an expert social scientist, and since this is not a novel, he can be ignored as technically uninformed. In particular, it will be easy for some to reject out of hand (instead of fairly testing) the Peirce-Percy Conjecture, the hypothesis that no genuinely triadic relation can be reduced to collections composed exclusively of dyadic relations. This Conjecture has far-reaching consequences for social science. Peirce, one of the greatest logicians of all time, argued for its truth, successfully in my opinion. Several fine logicians today—for instance Hans Herzberger and Robert Burch—add strong support. Thus, my plea: This may be a fresh breeze; sniff it patiently. Don't automatically conclude it's rain, then run for Uncle Louie's worn-out old house where the San Andreas fault runs unnoticed through the kitchen."

Kenneth Laine Ketner [s]

Kenneth Laine Ketner [t]
Charles Sanders Peirce Professor of Philosophy
Texas Tech University
Lubbock, TX

❧

July 25, 1989

Dear Ken,

Thanks so much for your letter to *The Wilson Quarterly*. I don't know what they wanted or why, but it is gratifying—for a novelist, who is no social scientist, to level charges of dualism (latent) and mechanism (dyadic) models. My difficulty with social science is the latent dualism which is so powerful that they can't even take a triadic model seriously. My hope for you; that you may be the man who will come up with a new model or paradigm to allow scientists to take the human condition seriously.

Thanks again.

Cordially,

Walker Percy [s]

༄

August 1, 1989

Dear Professor Ketner,

This is to let you know that we received your commentary on the Walker Percy article, which appeared in the Summer issue of *The Wilson Quarterly*.

Many thanks for making the time for this exercise; we plan to run your letter in the upcoming Autumn issue, space permitting.

We hope you will enjoy future issues of the magazine—and, again, thank you very much for your contribution to *WQ*'s commentary section.

Very truly yours,

Henry L. Mortimer, Jr. [s]

Henry L. Mortimer, Jr. [t]

༄

August 5, 1989

Dear Mr. Mortimer,

Thanks for your unexpected call yesterday. I'll be glad to expand upon the social science consequences of what I call the Peirce-Percy Conjecture.

I think that my original piece had a certain unity about it for a short item. I hope my expansion would not mean that the other parts would be cut, for I labored long and hard to get mean and lean within your 300 word maximum. I was also warning about the possibility of a knee-jerk nonscientific reaction to Percy which it is important to keep in mind. In the expansion, I am continuing to write in the nonacademic style I was seeking in my first attempt. I didn't offer any references for my earlier name droppings, nor in this second try. However, if you want references, I can supply a bushel.

"Walker Percy is a voice. That's good news and bad news. The good news is that the human spirit still speaks in such tones. The bad news is that our era may no longer have the capacity to listen well enough. Listeners are powerful beings, able to destroy communication in an ear's flick. Speaking to an incapable or unwilling listener is like trying to toss a cannonball into an egg cup. But Dr. Percy has his ways. He is a tricky man, widely loved for 'making up stories' full of good humor and beauty and transforming power, but which are ultimately designed to tempt listeners.

His Jefferson Lecture has no tricks, and the voice is pure and resonant. Will we then stop listening? It could happen. It could be said that Percy is not an expert social scientist, and since this not a novel, he can be ignored as technically uninformed. In particular, it will be easy for some to reject out of hand (instead of fairly testing) the Peirce-Percy Conjecture, the hypothesis that no genuinely triadic relation can be reduced to collections composed exclusively of dyadic relations. This Conjecture has far-reaching consequences for social science. Peirce, one of the greatest logicians of all time, argued for its truth, successfully in my opinion. Several fine logicians today—for instance Hans Herzberger and Robert Burch—add strong support.

'And just what are those consequences?' says a poker-faced social scientist. One that is deeply important has to do with explanation. It would be quite easy to make a case that many social scientists do not regard any attempt at explanation to have been successful unless the explaining material is composed of dyadic relations. These are typically causal dyadic relations, often between quanta of matter. One could say that many social scientists today have an unconscious and rationally unfounded passion for explanations couched only in terms of dyadic relations. But, the central phenomena in social life are triadic relations: Percy has enumerated several. Therefore, if the Peirce-Percy Conjecture is correct, the most commonly preferred explanatory strategy in social science today is defunct, at least to the extent that explanations are actually sought for the central phenomena. Consider the situation carefully. It's worse than it appears; it isn't a matter of being patient until the right approach or the right experiment or the right device is found; no, we are looking in the wrong way, in the wrong places, with the wrong assumptions, the principal wrong assumption appearing in investigator's explanatory attempts to reduce crucial social phenomena—which are triadic relations—to collections of dyadic relations.

'I suppose you have something better?' says poker-face as a microbead of sweat appears over her left eyebrow. Maybe. The question might be whether the social scientific psyche is sufficiently strong to put such proposals to a fair test, or whether they will be rejected in an automatic manner. First, ask why the unconscious obsession with reduction to dyadic relations, typical causal patterns. Isn't it possible that it arises from a conviction that the aim of social science is control, of a rather mechanistic variety? But if the Conjecture is correct, understanding, not control, should be the aim of social science. And understanding a currently ill-grasped triadic phenomenon could be achieved through analogies with presently better-grasped triadic relations. This in a P-pod is Peirce's method of diagrammatic thought: Some relations are best understood by way of modelling them onto currently well-understood relations. This is not a matter that can be explicated during one short poker game; but it is one of the reasons that Percy is right in saying that 'most people have never heard of Peirce, but they will.'

Thus, my plea: This may be a fresh breeze; sniff it patiently. Don't automatically conclude it's a rain, then sprint for shelter in Uncle Louie's worn-out old house where the San Andreas fault runs unnoticed through the kitchen."

Kenneth Laine Ketner [s]

Kenneth Laine Ketner [t]

"Is Anyone Listening?"[39]

Walker Percy is a voice. That's good news and bad news. The good news is that the human spirit still speaks in such tones. The bad news is that our era may no longer have the capacity to listen. Speaking to an incapable or unwilling listener is like trying to toss a cannonball into an egg cup. But Percy has his ways. He's a tricky man, admired for "making up stories" that are full of good humor, beauty and transforming power, but ultimately designed to tempt listeners into thinking.

In "The Divided Creature," Percy has no tricks; his voice is pure and resonant. Will we then stop listening? Possibly. It could be said that Percy is not an expert social scientist, and since this is not a novel, he can be ignored as uninformed. It will be easy for some to reject out of hand (instead of fairly testing) the Peirce-Percy Conjecture, the hypothesis that no genuinely triadic relation can be reduced to collections composed exclusively of dyadic relations. This Conjecture has far-reaching consequences for social science.

"And just what are those consequences?" says a poker-faced social scientist. One that is deeply important has to do with explanation. It would be quite easy to make a case that many social scientists do not regard any attempt at explanation to have been successful unless the explaining material is composed of dyadic relations. These are typically causal dyadic relations, often between quanta of matter. But the central phenomena in social life are triadic relations: Percy has enumerated several. Therefore, if the Peirce-Percy Conjecture is correct, the most commonly preferred explanatory strategy in social science today is defunct, at least to the extent that explanations are actually sought for the central phenomena.

"So Percy has something better?" the social scientist asks. Maybe. The question is whether the social scientist is sufficiently courageous to put Percy's proposals to a fair test. If he isn't, we may question why he and so many other social scientists are obsessed with reducing phenomena to dyadic relations, typically causal patterns. Is it possible that such an obsession arises from a conviction that the aim of social science is control, of a rather

mechanistic variety? But if the Peirce-Percy Conjecture is correct, understanding, not control, would be the aim of social science—a development
that we would all applaud.

Kenneth Laine Ketner
Charles Sanders Peirce Professor of Philosophy
Texas Tech University

❧

August 19, 1989

Dear Ken,

Thanks for program for the Peirce International Congress. It is awe-
some, but my Lord, a whole week and 100 papers on CSP. By now it's over.
Hope it went well. (I didn't come across a projected paper by you. How
come? You know more about the guy than anybody I know.)

You won't mind my reaction to all that CSP. Actually I've had quite
enough from him, after swiping what I needed. My difficulty with CSP is
that he did not have an anthropology, which God knows he should have. I
am not talking about something vaguely Christian or Unitarian or Eastern
or what. I am talking about a scientific, i.e., rational, theory of man. He
has, God knows, a theory of everything else, from language to metaphysics,
but he is seriously disappointing here. If you can steer me something in the
collected work (I doubt you can, I've looked hard), I'd be grateful.

Yours as ever,

Walker [s]

September 11, 1989

Dear Ken,

Thanks. I'm sure the conference went fine, if you were running it. No excuse, though, for not having a paper by Ketner.

Re "philosophical anthropology"; an awkward term meaning no more than a scientific theory of man, without theological presuppositions.[40] In the same sense that we have a theory of organisms, a theory of evolution, a theory of molecular chemistry, a theory of the double star in Orion. I was hopeful that CSP, having it on triadicity as a beginning, would develop one. He didn't, aside from that vast goings-on about "interpretant," which in the end is so ambiguous as to be meaningless.

I'd be happy to be a NEH "referee," whatever that is. By the way, you'd better send me a résumé.

I understand that was not CSP's photo in *The Wilson Quarterly*. Nobody but KLK would have spotted it.

Best,

Walker [s]

September 21, 1989

Dear Ken,

Thanks so much for Milton Singer's *Man's Glassy Essence*. It is very valuable in its distinguishing between CSP's "semiotic" and Saussure's "semiology."

I have been pissed off for years by the hypocrisy of the Kultur boys, by the double whammy of: (1) all culture, including science is relative and so there is no "truth" to be arrived at, only cultural phenomenology, (2) I, the writer, am a scientist and am telling you the truth. If truth were "relative," why should I bother?

I had not seen clearly the importance of CSP's "ontology of objects," based on science and logic, which is based on "real objects of the external world."

So I'm back in the crusade and subscribe with pleasure to your credo: The only hope of overturning 300 years of dyadic crap—from Descartes to Freud—is the triadic revolution.

Hang in there. You're a good soldier. I'm off to Mayo clinic Monday for another treatment of my old prostate cancer, which is giving me trouble.

Best,

Walker [s]

P.S.: Only place Singer is wrong is listing Charles Morris as a proper heir of CSP. Morris is a dyadic subverter of CSP. W P

November 6, 1989

Dear Walker,

I think we got a movement starting up. Robert Burch, an industrial-strength logician from Texas A & M University, has just completed a book manuscript (which will be published here at Texas Tech University Press in the new series for which I will be the general editor: *Philosophical Inquiries*) that shows at the highest (or lowest, depending on one's biases) mathematical level that Peirce was right about the illogicality of reducing genuine triadic relations to bundles of only dyadic relations.[41] Math and logic has always been the den of the dyadicists, and ole Bob has bearded them there. He launches from Peirce's foundation, but in a semi-independent way that stands on its own merits. I sent it out to some strong logicians and mathematicians for reading and comes back a solid "He's right." Personally, I can read only the parts in English: When it goes to symbolese, I'm dead. Anyhow, I thought you would want to know, for it vindicates in a very strong way your half of the Peirce-Percy Conjecture, the Delta Factor. This will also be the end of the Saussurean-Morrisean dyadic hypothesis in semiotics. It is a straight disconfirmation of their hypothesis that dyads are fundamental in the theory of signs. We will now find out if dyadic semioticians are scientists or merely proponents of a worldview. If the former, they will say, "Oh goodie, a hypothesis disconfirmed; let's move on." If the latter, they will cry, "That's your view, but I still have mine; shall we be tolerant with each other or shall we fight?"

Have you had any reactions, up or down, to your *Wilson Quarterly* piece?

The *WQ* folks asked me to comment on it for their Letters to the Editor section. I also helped them with the erroneous photo caper. All that just appeared, and here's a copy for you. The peckerwoods edited my pithy proth in the last half of my little remarks; I guess Yankees can't stand bare-bark talk.

I've still got to write about you for Mrs. Sebeok's semiotic annual. I'm hoping to get that done over this Christmas holiday semester break.

You doing OK? Anything at all I can do for you or yours? All you need ever do is just ask.

Ken [s]

Ketner [t]

P.S.: No need to respond to this unless you're particularly inclined.

January 16, 1990

Dear Ken,

Many thanks for photo and your article.[42] You look much too young to be so smart!

If you don't mind a bit of advice on the article. While I am certainly flattered by your starting out with overly kind remarks about me, that is no way to write an expository article. Say what CSP meant plus KLK's comment, with maybe a footnote for WP and the like.

I'm not supposed to ask you, but any news about your gov't grant? I gave you a plug fit for an obituary.

Best,

Walker [s]

♣

January 17, 1990

Dear Walker,

I'm starting to get a rise from some logicians on my attempt to put Percy's antinomy on them. Maybe you will enjoy the inclosed (or maybe not).

Anyhow, warmest agape from me to dear old you.

Ken Ketner [s]

♣

May 17, 1990

Mrs. Walker Percy and Family
C/o The Kumquat
228 North Lee Lane
Covington, LA

Dear Mrs. Percy,

The loss of Dr. Percy came as a heavy blow to me. I hope you and your family will receive my deepest sympathy. I feel a profound sense of loss, and knowing your loss is much greater than mine, I yearn to do anything that could somehow contribute to your comfort.

Walker and I had corresponded for several years about our mutual interests in the work of Charles Peirce and topics in social science. It was a happy occasion for me to have been able to send Walker a few tidbits from Peirce that may have been useful to him as he prepared his Jefferson Lecture. It was a phenomenal experience for me to have attended that lecture in Washington, and on the following day to have been invited by Walker to chat with him for about an hour in Gompers Park.

I wish I could describe for you what Walker meant to me. Unfortunately my words are not adequate. Dr. Coles I'm sure knows the phenomenon, and maybe from the standpoint of his expertise could explain it or put the right name on it. I can only hint at it by saying that reading Walker's novels and nonfiction and essays was a transforming experience. The added privilege of having been in direct contact with him from time to time is something I will cherish always.

Walker's stature as a thinker and artist will only grow. He was one of the truly great men of our civilization, and the world is going to continue to grow in its realization of that fact. One of the amazements is that he himself was completely unaware of it.

As I used to say to Walker, I am a manuscript grubber, given that I work in the Peirce archive here. In looking back over Walker's letters in my correspondence file, I wonder if it would be of any value to you to have copies of what he wrote. Also, I hope you and your family and friends will eventually make plans to preserve Walker's library and his papers, because as recognition of Walker's accomplishments grows, those materials will be a treasure from which our children can gain an improved understanding of his unique contributions to humanity.

If there is anything I can do to assist you or your family, something that might remove even a milligram of a burden from you, or which might be helpful to you in some way, please call on me. Although I have not had the pleasure of meeting you, I hope you and your family will regard me as your loyal friend.

With warmest greetings,

Ken [s]

Kenneth Laine Ketner [t]

July 19, 1991

Mrs. Ann Percy Moores
C/o The Kumquat
228 Lee Lane
Covington, LA

Dear Mrs. Moores,

I appreciate very much receiving an invitation to the autograph party with Father Patrick Samway for his new book of essays by Walker. I am happy that I am on your mailing list. Unfortunately, I was unavoidably occupied, or I would have been sorely tempted to jump on Southwest Airlines and come on over to Covington for the first time ever. Please continue to keep me informed of activities of this kind. I am extremely interested in anything connected with Walker.

Could you let me know what kinds of things concerning the works of WP you have in the Kumquat? Could I leave my credit card number on file with you and order a book now and then? I need items occasionally and it would pleasure me to have you become my official bookstore, whatever that might be worth to you [. . .]. Let me begin by ordering a copy of *Signposts in a Strange Land*, preferably an autographed copy by Father Samway if you have one. (By the way, may I order books by telephone? If so, what is your number?)

By a strange coincidence, I had your notice, a letter from Roger Straus, and a letter from Father Samway all in the same mail. I include a copy of both of them for you.

I had the profound honor of corresponding with your father for about five years, off and on, principally about our mutual interest, Charles Peirce. Around the time of his Jefferson Lecture, Walker began urging me to write a life of Peirce, and to ask NEH for help. Initially I was extremely reluctant to take on the task, for I knew of several academic political mine fields I would have to cross. But he kept urging me. There is no one I respect more than WP, so I couldn't resist him. I applied to NEH in October 1989. In

June 1990, when the results were made known, I could be seen emerging from the smoke of several explosions. I could write a novel about what happened next, but suffice it to say, I eventually reapplied in October 1990 after several intelligence missions deep in enemy territory, and the upshot is that just a few weeks ago I was granted (from NEH) one year off (and possibly two if my university can raise some matching funds) to begin work in earnest on a life of Peirce, written for the average educated person, not for philosophical or mathematical specialists. I feel as if I had been directly commissioned by your father to do that job, so I am relieved that it is beginning at last. I know it may be fallacious and silly of me to speak as I did in that last sentence, but it was an attempt to express my feelings accurately.

I have carefully preserved the letters Walker sent me, and copies of much of what I sent him. Is there to be a repository somewhere of his correspondence? Someday, if it is ever possible, I would like to get copies of the letters I sent to him; that side of my file is weak. I inclose one copy of a letter to the Nobel Prize Committee from my file that is an attempt to express what Walker meant to me. Unfortunately, what I proposed in it didn't come to pass.

Please let me know if I can ever be of any service to you or Walker's family.

Cordially,

Ken [s]

Ken Ketner [t]

❧

October 29, 1991

Dear Mrs. Percy,

[. . .] Meeting for about an hour with Walker outside your hotel in Washington the day after the Jefferson Lecture was certainly a high point for me. It was there he urged this Peirce bio project upon me. I was unable to resist him. And thank goodness NEH finally supported it. The job seems to be unfolding reasonably well, but I suspect I now feel a little bit like Walker told me he felt when he was hatching a book.

I have a box full of correspondence with Walker. Usually I kept my side of the letters, but sometimes I didn't. So if it would not inconvenience you to send me a xerox copy of any of mine that you find, I would appreciate it. And I will keep the whole correspondence set intact here. If you will advise me, I hope some day to send a copy of the completed correspondence between us to the place you designate as a repository. Likewise, if there are any of Walker's letters I might have that you want to see, please let me know.

Fundamentally we corresponded about our mutual interest in Charles Peirce (and, of course, on my side, about my interest in WP). And, since Walker planned to feature Peirce in the Jefferson Lecture, I am proud that I could help him by sending over some references from our Peirce archive here.

I sent your daughter Ann at the Kumquat a copy of a letter I had sent to the Swedish Academy nominating Walker for a Nobel Prize. I never told him that I wrote such a letter. Did you see it?

Through a stroke of good luck, Father Samway is going to visit me in late November for a few days. We will go through the letters I have here and discuss Percy and Peirce. I rather suspect that the Percys and the Peirces have common distant ancestors back in England. I know that is the source for the Peirce clan. They spelled their family name in many ways: Pers, Pearce, Perse. Remembering Walker's essay, "Metaphor as Mistake," I can just hear someone making a two-syllable word out of one syllable by mispronouncing "Perse"—not as "Pers" but as "Per-see."

I am just now finishing proofreading a book on Peirce, entitled *Reasoning and the Logic of Things*, which will appear in 1992 with Harvard University Press. I had asked Walker's permission to dedicate it to him. He eventually agreed. I will look forward to presenting copies to your family members next year, with my utmost respect.

Loyally yours,

Ken [s]

Kenneth Laine Ketner [t]
Peirce Professor of Philosophy

p.s.: I'm sending Father Samway a copy of this—hope you don't mind.

✣

December 17, 1992

Dear Ken,

I remember seeing Walker greeting you in a little park across from the hotel in Washington and how pleased Walker was. He had on several occasions told me, "Bunt, this man knows what I'm getting at." I have found several of your letters to him and will be pleased to send them to you—I haven't done so already because I find them stuck in books so it may be an ongoing situation.

I was deeply touched that you would dedicate your *Reasoning and the Logic of Things: The Cambridge Conferences Lectures of 1898 by Charles Sanders Peirce* to Walker. I know that Walker's brothers and Bob Coles would like to have a copy [. . .]. Come to Covington if you ever get a chance.

Sincerely,

Bunt Percy [s]

Appendix I

August 17, 1982

Dear Walker,

I was delighted to hear from you, just as I got back from the Eastern Seaboard, and had a lot of fun with your book [Walker Percy had sent Thomas A. Sebeok a typescript copy of *Lost in the Cosmos*]. I hope you won't think this out of order, but I did call your manuscript to the attention of the Director of the Indiana University Press, Mr. John Gallman.

I am used to colleagues disagreeing with me about the prevalence of all sorts of signs throughout the animal kingdom, but none of them have convinced me that I am wrong (although particular examples could be). I guess I am just as much an epigone of Peirce as you may be one of Cassirer!

About the Cosmos: My personal views are, roughly, identical with those of John Archibald Wheeler, but these, too, hark back to Peirce: "The Universe as an argument is necessarily a great work of art, a great poem—for every fine argument is a poem and a symphony—just as every true poem is a sound argument. . . . That total effect is beyond our ken." See *CP* 5.119. And further: "Mind is First, Matter is Second, Evolution is Third" (*CP* 6.32). See also *CP* 8.317.

Jean and I also have fond memories of you in Toronto, and, while speaking of Toronto, I might mention that, next June, the Institute will be repeated here in Bloomington. Is there any chance of your paying us a visit?

Cordially,

Tom [s]

Thomas A. Sebeok [t]
Research Center for Language and Semiotic Studies
Indiana University
Bloomington, IN

✤

August 19, 1982,

Dear Tom [Sebeok],

Am most grateful for your letter and that *Lost in the Cosmos* might have given you some pleasure.

I'm glad you mentioned it to John Gallman, whom I've heard from. I told him if my publisher doesn't like it, he might well have a look at it.

Your summer Institute sounds great. I'd really enjoy being there. I might.

Tom, could you refer me to a statement in English of von Uexküll's notions about *Welt, Umwelt, Innenwelt, und so weiter*? He is positively unavailable hereabouts, even in German.

Sincerely,

Walker [s]

✤

August 28, 1982

Dear Walker,

I devoted Chapter Ten of my book, *The Sign & Its Masters* (Austin: University of Texas Press, 1979), wholly to Jakob von Uexküll.

An entire issue of *Semiotica* to appear during the latter part of 1982 will feature an English translation of his *Bedeutungslehre*, with extensive commentary by his eldest son, Thure von Uexküll, a prominent German physician.

Finally, Chapter Seven (pp. 233–75) of a recent (Berlin, 1981) book deals with Jakob von Uexküll, and includes a good working bibliography as well. The book is entitled *Die Welt als Zeichen*. It is being translated into English, but won't, I am afraid, appear until later next year, or early 1984.

Best,

Tom [s]

Thomas A. Sebeok [t]

ॐ

October 27, 1986

Professor John N. Deely
C/o University of California Press
Berkeley, CA

Dear Professor Deely,

This is, first, an expression of gratitude for what you have given us in your magnificent rendering of John Poinsot's *Tractatus de Signis*. Besides being a very handsome volume, it is of great value to anyone interested in semiotics, both in presenting the *Tractatus* complete in English for the first time (for me anyhow—I had earlier read the Simon's *Material Logic*, but couldn't make much of it) and for the clarifications of your "semiotic markers" and afterword.

But this is also a cry for help. I don't have to tell you about the double difficulty of reading a text which was somewhat muffled even in its own time and dressed up to look like the standard Scholasticism of the times, but also set across a gulf of three hundred years of Anglo-Saxon nominalism and Cartesian dualism.

But I will ask your help in only two brief passages, which are of particular interest to me.

(1) I am both fascinated and tantalized by what he says about the "relation of stipulated signs to the signified" (p. 141, ll. 11–27). This addresses the heart of my interest in semiotics. He says that "the relation in this case is mind-dependent, yet the sign does not consist only in the extrinsic denomination whereby it is rendered imposed or appointed for signifying by common usage, as some philosophers think. . . ." Okay, right. Now here comes the heart of the matter: Yes, a stipulated sign is imposed, but—"this imposition is indeed required as the fundament of the relation and rationale of the sign, because it is through this imposition that *something is habilitated and appointed to be a stipulated sign,* just as it is through some natural sign's being proportioned and connected with a given significate that there is founded a relation of the sign to that significate" (my emphasis).

Now this is fascinating, indeed seeming to foreshadow as it does some extremely recent developments in semiotic theory which suggest that the relation of conventional sign to signified is much more than the standard notion of word-as-tag-to-idea. The conventional sign is indeed utterly unlike the signified (as in *Cratylus,* Locke and all the rest), but there seems to occur in the acquisition and retention of language a sort of interpretation of "word" and "thing" toward the end of a transformation of a sort of the former—perhaps the latter too.

My question: What does John Poinsot mean by: *quia per illam habilitatur et destinatur aliquid?*

Habilitatur. A strange expression. Does he mean it in one root sense of habiliment? Clothe? Deck out? And something *aliquid.* What? What is habilitated? (I could have stood a little more of Aquinas's precision here.)

I would like to think, to use Peirce's example, that he means something like this: That when a child learns a word—father pointing to a balloon, saying word *balloon,* child looking at balloon, fitting one to the other so that in the end by a sort of false onomatopoeia, the word also becomes (*in alio esse*) something of a round, inflated object.

But I am not at all sure he means anything of the sort.

Could you help here?

(2) A similar question. In the extremely important Q.3, Part II, p. 254: Whether an Impressed Specification is a Formal Sign. This business of specifier of *species* is obviously central—you must think so since you give the

expression over two pages in your *index rerum*. But I am almost at a total loss to know what he means either by impressed specifier or expressed specifier. One can only guess. Sometimes these bloody schoolmen can make one think they deserved what they got what with their distaste for the concrete example.

Do you think it possible to translate these terms into something remotely Saussurean or Peircean or Cassireran?

Thus, given this statement (p. 183, ll. 37–40) ". . . a cognitive power is passive both in respect of the agent or thing impressing a specified form, and in respect to the form impressed." What is the "agent"? "Thing impressing"? "Specifying form"? "Form impressed"?

I am tempted to translate this into my own version of the Saussurean sign as *signifiant/signifié*. The sign *tree* being a union of the two, the signifier or "sound-image" tree and the "concept" (I'd call it "percept") tree.

To translate the Poinsot version into my own semiotic, I'd say something like this about the linguistic sign as observed in the acquisition of language in children: The *signifiant* or sound-image *tree* which the child hears is the impressed species being "impressed" by the percept tree which the child sees—itself a sort of general as Peirce would say, since the child can apply it to all trees—the agent or thing impressing being the percept-concept tree—for a cognitive power.

Now this does not suit me at all. I think of the process in more triadic or Peircean terms as the "agent" being itself the "cognitive power" or interpretant which "throws together" (e.g. *symballein*) the *signifier* and *signified*.

A fine mess, as you see. Perhaps you could say a magic word or two. Current semiotics is crazy enough without trying to connect up with John of St. Thomas. Yet I feel, reaching a hand across three hundred years, that he is onto something of the utmost value.

At any rate, my thanks again for this wonderful achievement. I have no doubt that a few years from now John will be recognized as one of the major founders, if not the founder, of modern semiotic, thanks in no small way to you.

Sincerely yours,

Walker Percy [s]

Walker Percy [t]

≈

October 29, 1986

Dear Tom [Sebeok],

Since you are one of the few semioticists I trust—this because your approach is biological; you start with organisms and what happens between them, inside them, unlike the ever increasing number of structuralists-textualists-post-structuralists who seem to start with the Platonic realm of the text or nontext; I think they're all English teachers at heart and I find myself as I read them wanting to ask dumb questions like: *Where* is the text?—As Hippocrates might say, draw me a picture.

Since, as I say, you (and perhaps Harley Shands and Hippocrates) are perhaps the last surviving sober semioticist, it is to you I apply for a bit of information.

I keep coming across the name of a guy variously spelled Sklovskij, Schlovsky—one of the Russian formalists. The point is I think he is onto something with his notion of the evolution and "devolution" of the esthetic symbol, and an esthetic device which he calls *priëm ostrannenja* which Eco translates as the "device of making strange," others as "fresh."

This interests me very much because, both as a novelist and an amateur semioticist, I am very much aware of the vicissitudes of the linguistic sign (sign in the Saussurean sense of word uniting *signifiant* and *signifié*) both in its devaluation by quotidian use (Marcel spoke of this process as simulacrum-making)—and the recovery and rebirth of the sign by poets, metaphor restoring freshness—and by ordeal (Prince Andrey recovering *clouds* as he lay dying at Borodino).

I am hoping that Sklovskij may have descried some order in this vague business. What I am asking you is how I can get hold of him in English. Perhaps you can direct me to an anthology of Russian formalists which has him.

I will also take this occasion to thank you (as I have already thanked John Deely) for reviving interest in John of St. Thomas—very well, John Poinsot. I've just finished a novel at which I've been hacking away for four years, and so have a bit of time before the proofs come in and have spent the last few days toiling away at Deely's gorgeous edition of *Tractatus de Signis*. It is the source of endless frustration, sweats, even rage—why couldn't these guys use more *examples* to illustrate such alluring yet mysterious entities as "impressed species"? At any rate I am persuaded that he is the seminal man indeed. For example, I am endlessly intrigued by his insistence that "even in the case of stipulated signs the rationale of the sign must be explained by a relation to the signified." Thus it won't do to explain "stipulated signs" either as tags for ideas or as stimuli which evoke responses. Locke and Skinner don't work. So how does a word mean what it does? "Because it is this imposition (of 'stipulated signs' or 'denomination') that something is habilitated and appointed to be a stipulated sign (*quia per illam habilitatur et destinatur aliquid*), just as it is through some natural sign's being proportioned and connected with a given significate—" e.g. smoke and fire.

How do you like that? I wish I had John Poinsot here right now to grab by the cassock and pester him until he told me what he meant—by *habilitatur*, by *aliquid*—something? What something?

At any rate I suspect that thanks to you and Deely, that Dominican will be hooked up with Peirce and de Saussure as a Founding Father, if not the Founding Father.

All I meant to do was to ask you for a reference to Sklovskij.

All best to you and Jean [Umiker-Sebeok],

Sincerely,

Walker [s]

꙳

November 4, 1986

Dear Walker,

There are diverse adits to the work of Viktor Shklovskij (as I prefer to transliterate from the Cyrillic—but this is of little consequence). Perhaps still the best is via a 1955 book (revised in 1965) by Victor Erlich: *Russian Formalism—History—Doctrine*, published by Mouton, in The Hague, and certainly still in print (although Mouton, renamed Mouton de Gruyter, now operates out of Berlin). There are numerous references there (on p. 274) to this great figure.

Perhaps of lesser interest to you, but still relevant, would be the book co-edited by Ladislav, Matejka and Krystyna Pomorska [i.e., Jakobson's "third" widow], *Readings in Russian Poetics: Formalist and Structuralist Views* (Cambridge: Massachusetts Institute of Technology Press, 1971), which includes Shklovskij's witty piece on the mystery novel (specifically, Dickens's *Little Dorrit*). See further his "Art as Technique," available in English in L.T. Lemon and M. J. Reis's *Russian Formalist Criticism: Four Essays* (Lincoln: University of Nebraska Press, 1965).

The poetic term *ostranenie* is variously renderable as "making strange" or "defamiliarizing," and is later related to the Brechtian concept of "alienation" (in Germany *Verfremdung*).

There is also a periodical published in England (No. 1, in 1975), bearing the over-all title *Russian Poetics in Translation*, which exhibits the influence of Shklovskij throughout.

Finally, you might want to glance at Chapter 25, "Semiotics in the U.S.S.R.," in a recent (1986) book I co-edited with Jean, *The Semiotic Sphere* (Plenum). This is one of the best chapters in this book of ours, and may be considered definitive (anyhow, for time being); it is long, occupying (oversized) pp. 555–582. The author of this piece is Stephan Rudy, one of Jakobson's last and better students.

I am grateful for your trust in me, and hope it isn't misplaced. My approach *is*—and continues to be—anchored in the life sciences (see also my new book, *I Think I Am a Verb*, likewise published by Plenum this

Fall), although there are some exciting developments at the borderline of physics and semiotics as well.

It is also good to learn of your interest in Poinsot (I suppose you have read my review of the book in the past Easter Sunday issue of *The New York Times Book Review*). However, there is more to all this: namely, that there are other more-or-less contemporary figures, equally or even more obscure, who wrote some fascinating things about meaning and signification, and whose ideas need urgent editing, with as much care lavished upon them as Deely did on his really-not-all-that-unique hero. But who can spare ten or fifteen years of our lives to undertake such an archeological chore? If it hadn't been for Maritain's dedication, Poinsot might never have been "revived" in the manner as he now has been!

Well, I hope this will get you started on Shklovskij. Let me know if you want more.

Do you ever leave Covington? We would love to see you again, to talk with you of many things. And, of course, we look forward to reading your new novel.

Best,

Tom [s]

Thomas A. Sebeok [t]

❧

November 12, 1986

Dear Tom [Sebeok],

I am deeply grateful for your trouble in supplying me with references to the work of Viktor Shklovskij. I knew you would know.

The work I most want to get hold of is "Semiotics in the U.S.S.R." in *The Semiotic Sphere*.

Cordially,

Walker [s]

ა⁊

March 27, 1987

Dear Walker,

Thank you for your letter of October 27 of last year, which was forwarded to me, embarrassingly many weeks ago, by the University of California Press.

I can't tell you how pleased I am that my own message in a bottle has washed up on your shores. The President of our College here, Pasquale DiPasquale, never fails to ask me if I have "answered Walker Percy's questions yet."

At least now I will be able to say that I have answered, if not his questions, at least his letter.

Shortly I will be sending you a long manuscript in reply to an extremely vicious review which has a section specifically addressing, and with you in mind, the problem of the "species."

For the moment, please be assured that your letter has been received, your questions pondered, and your interest appreciated; and assured further that I will be writing you anon.

Warmly,

John [s]

John Deely [t]
195 West 17th Street
Dubuque, IA

June 8, 1987

Dear John Deely,

First, let me say that I was both awed by this sumptuous book, your translation of Poinsot, *Tractatus de Signis*, which I have been reading at— and then floored by yours and Dean MacCannell's invitation to review it for *The American Journal of Semiotics*.

I fear I must then say next that there is no way I would feel up to doing a review of it. The simple truth is I don't have the competence. If I did it, I would have to take off six months, pour over Poinsot—about whom I have the unerring feeling that he is onto something extremely important—so important that he might even heal the ancient Cartesian split and the current semiotic split between the neurone scientists and the literary structuralist-post-structuralists—all this along with the huge difficulty of access to Poinsot's language and ways of thinking. Which is to say, I can read Deely on Poinsot but Poinsot with difficulty and sweats. And I don't have the time.

This is an extremely valuable contribution you've made (since I'd known Poinsot only through Maritain and that book *The Material Logic of John of St. Thomas*—no matter what Earline J. Ashworth says). A gorgeous book and a gorgeous piece of scholarship.

Of course I am reading it with the view toward reconciling it with Peirce's triadic theory—and furthering triadic theory because Peirce, as seminal as he was, left us in something of a muddle. Thus, Peirce's "interpretant" is a very unsatisfactory notion which he never explains to my satisfaction. Is the "interpretant" a passive sort of business "caused" by the action of the sign on the receiving organism? Or is it the active agent which unites sign and signified—e.g., when Helen put together *water* (sign) and water (stuff)?

So I'm thinking Poinsot is going to tell me and I am reading with considerable excitement, say, the article of "What are the Divisions of Categorial Relations and What Are Its Essential Types?" especially when he comes to "relations of the second type" (p. 110). It is quite exciting when he talks about these sign relations as *secundum esse*. And when he talks about these relations being founded upon action and reception, he's really got my attention. And also (p. 110, ll. 43–45): "And we do not doubt that some relations are founded immediately upon an active power itself. . . ." The trouble is he does not specify what is the "actor." If there is an act, there must be an actor. Is it, as he suggests somewhere, the *intellectus*? What part? The soul? And his repeated use of power, *potentia*, is as ambiguous as Peirce's interpretant, sometimes "active" but mostly it seems passive.

Also exciting to me: His notion of "habilitation of a sign to its significate" as a mind-independent relation, is most suggestive to me in the way I am thinking of my own reading of triadic theory.

More later. This is just to say thanks for a great book.

Walker [s]

⁂

October 13, 1987

Dear Tom [Sebeok],

Thanks for the info on *The Encyclopedic Dictionary of Semiotics*. I just ordered it.

Since you are always for us the court of last resort, maybe you can help me. There's a Russian formalist who was onto something. Last name spelled variously Schklovshij, Sklovskij, Schkloviskij—first name: Viktor I think. I can only find indirect references, but what he's onto is variously called the "devolution" of the sign and its opposite: "defamiliarization."

Trouble is, I can't locate anything by him, translation or even a good commentary.

Any help would be much appreciated.

Am working on something about "Thirdness"—beginning not with Peirce but Poinsot, whom I think you also put me onto.

My best,

Walker [s]

ﭏ

October 20, 1987

Dear Walker,

The problem with Viktor Shklovskij (1893–1984—as I prefer to transcribe his name) is not that references are scarce, but precisely the opposite—that there is an *embarras de richesses*. I would certainly urge you to begin with Victor Erlich's *Russian Formalism* (The Hague: Mouton, 1955), on p. 274 of which you will find no less than 13 lines of his index devoted to this distinguished figure. You can then work forwards from there, up to the *The Encyclopedic Dictionary of Semiotics* (of which, by now, you presumably own a copy), where Aage Hansen-Love has a fair-sized lemma on "Russian Formalism."

In this country, and, in the West generally, knowledge of the movement known as *Opojaz* was propagated chiefly by my old teacher, Roman Jakobson, who makes frequent references to his friend, Viktor Shklovskij, especially in Volume 5 [1979] of his (i.e., R.J.'s) *Selected Writings*.

The opposed concepts of *obnazhenie* and *ostranenie* are discussed in the aforementioned works and elsewhere.

For a popularization of all this, let me refer you to Terence Hawkes's little book, *Structuralism and Semiotics* (Berkeley: University of California Press, 1977), where there is a lot about Viktor Shklovskij and the concepts you are interested in.

Let me see please, your piece about "Thirdness"!

Hoping that the above will be helpful (but if not enough, I'll try harder), and with all good wishes.

Cordially,

Tom [s]

Thomas A. Sebeok [t]

September 28, 1988

Dear Walker,

We have contracted with Mouton de Gruyter Publishers to produce a yearbook of semiotics, entitled *The Semiotic Web*. *Web* volumes feature state-of-the-art accounts of selected sub-disciplines, such as "Semiotics and Cognitive Science," and countries, such as "Semiotics and Japan." They also include reports of meetings, institutes, associations, research projects, and teaching programs.

The books are typeset here at the Research Center for Language and Semiotic Studies in order to produce the volumes as quickly as possible, thus assuring that the information in them will be current at publication. The 1986 volume was published in November 1987, and the 1987 volume will appear this month. The contents of the 1988 volume have been set and that book will be published in July 1989.

Tom and I would like to have an article on your work for the 1989 volume, and I am writing to ask you for help in selecting the best person to write about "your semiotics." Tom had thought of William H. Poteat, but is not certain that would be the best choice. Could you suggest one or two people who might be able to undertake such an assignment?

We have not seen you in quite a while! I trust that you and Mrs. Percy are well and happy. Our two daughters are now 9 and 12, and growing fast. Why not pop in at one or more of the events described in the enclosed announcements?

With all good wishes, and looking forward to hearing from you.

Sincerely,

Jean [s]

Jean Umiker-Sebeok [t]
Research Center for Language and Semiotic Studies
Indiana University
Bloomington, IN

❧

October 6, 1988

Dear Jean [Umiker-Sebeok],

Many thanks for your letter. I'm honored you'd want a piece on my semiotics.

I'm not sure about Poteat. I'd prefer Ken Ketner (Prof. Kenneth Ketner, Institute for Studies in Pragmaticism, Texas Tech University, Lubbock, TX)—him or you or Tom. Ketner is a true Peircean and understands my and C.S.P.'s "triadicity."

Best to Tom.

Cordially,

Walker [s]

❧

November 1, 1988

Dear Walker,

Thank you for your letter of October 6th, received in my absence. It was nice to hear from you. I am writing to Ken Ketner today, in the hope that he will contribute an article for the *Web*.

Tom and I wish that you would resume your visits with the Semiotic Society of America and I.S.I.S.S.S. meetings, so that we could see you again. Any chance of that?

With warm personal regards, also from Tom.

Sincerely,

Jean [s]

Jean Umiker-Sebeok [t]

＊

November 1, 1988

Dear Ken,

. . . I am writing you to invite you to write a report on the semiotics of Walker Percy, for the 1989 volume of *Web*. Your report would be due December 1, 1989. There is no page limitation for *Web* entries. . . .

Sincerely,

Jean [s]

Jean Umiker-Sebeok [t]

＊

December 5, 1988

Dr. Jean Umiker-Sebeok

Dear Jean,

Your letter inviting me to write about Walker for *The Semiotic Web* came as quite a surprise. Percy is a profound fellow as well as a great artist. That is a real combination. I am very honored that you consider me equal to the task.

As you might guess, I'm busy with the preparations for the Peirce congress next September at Harvard. However, for some time I have wanted to write something about Percy on the very topic you mentioned. My problem is that I can't sincerely promise to have it by next December. I strive to be on time for my academic obligations, but I can see that my present responsibilities might get in the way. On the other hand, I can pledge my devotion to the undertaking, so if I am slowed, it will not be because of my inclinations. (That is to say, I *think* I can make your deadline, but I can't *promise* it.) I hasten to add that the Scholastic nit-picking here is arising from my respect for Walker, than which I have none greater.

If you can live with the contingency that I may not be on time, then I will accept the assignment. If you can't work within that context, I completely understand your wish to seek another writer for the topic. Let me know your thoughts about my somewhat hedged response. If you say "Yes," then I'll get to the matter using the time available.

After my first plunge into Percy's works, I emerged confident I had understood him. Subsequent events proved otherwise. So I plunged in again. I have recently re-emerged, thinking that my earlier ideas were much too narrow and technical. He may even give me another baptism—he's a tricky guy.

What I would like to write would involve Percy's novels as well as his essays. I put equal weight upon each category. It is my thesis that persons who have written on what "Percy is about" have missed the mark. My claim is that both his essays and novels are fundamentally about how to live. That sounds rather trite. But if Percy is correct, there are good reasons why that sounds trite in our age. Percy first tried to address this question in the context of our age through essays, but then I suspect made the tremendous discovery that novels could be used to address the same point with better *general* results. If my interpretation is correct, then Walker's basic essay is "Loss of the Creature": "The Delta Factor" (also the place where Peirce-like notions arise) would be the spectacular follow-on account of why the creature is lost. The novels enter the scene as an almost scientific use of brilliant literary skills in giving teachings about the same topic. This is the art of medicine (which is after all ultimately the ancient art of teaching persons how to live), in a highly developed and generalized form. That explains why Walker so soundly deserves the title of Doctor of Medicine.

Peirce's semeiotic is strongly implicated in much of this, although until recently, implicitly so.

Cordial greetings,

Ken [s]

Kenneth Laine Ketner [t]

January 14, 1990

Dear Ken,

Thanks for the Tursman paper. I see it is too technical to read in a hurry, so I'll have to take my time with it.

I've been thinking a couple of days about your analysis of ordered pairs and your interchanges with Hilary Putnam; and, though the issues are, it seems to me, *extremely* complicated, I do have a few intuitions about what is going on. It seems to me that there are two different levels of analysis involved: that Putnam is working at the level of "purely logico-mathematical analysis," while you are working at the level of analysis that might be called the "philosophy of logic and mathematics." In other words, you are a meta-level removed from Putnam.

His point, taken at the level he intends, seems to me to be correct. That is, suppose we start by removing from our discussions of mathematical objects all reference to the logician-mathematician who invents, frames, discovers, etc., these objects. Let us discuss mathematical objects just as the mathematician does, without reference to any meta-questions. Then, as Kazimierz Kuratowski, Norbert Wiener, and others have shown, the ordered pair as so defined is sufficient to do full mathematical duty, for the only property requisite for doing this mathematical duty is the property that if $(a,b) = (c,d)$ then $a = c$ and $b = d$.

But, at this point, you retort in two ways: (1) the ordered pair as so defined is not *really* an ordered pair; it has at most the property that is a necessary condition of an ordered pair. But possession of this property is not sufficient for making something into a real *ordered* pair; for that, something additional is needed. (2) What *is* needed in order that something be a *real* ordered pair is for it to contain two elements that are *ordered* as first and second in it; now for anything actually to contain two elements that are ordered in this way, there must be some consciousness (that of the logician-mathematician) that does the *ordering*. Hence, the formation of an ordered pair, a *real* ordered pair, involves essentially *three* "things," two elements *and* an ordering consciousness.

Now, it is easy to see why Putnam and virtually all mathematicians are going to object to your analysis: They think that you are intending to offer the *same* sort of analysis *they* typically offer; and it, therefore, seems to them that you are importing some sort of weird, unintelligible reference to the mathematician into the discussion of mathematical objects. They consider such importations to be illegitimate.

But you are, I think, not even remotely attempting to offer the same sort of analysis, at the same level, as the mathematicians. You are rather offering a piece of philosophical analysis of the formation of mathematical concepts. In effect you are saying that a *full* analysis of what is going on when mathematical concepts are formed *must* import reference to the concept-forming consciousness; and that a full analysis necessarily involves triadic relations (specifically, those in which the mathematician is one of the *relata*). For this reason, even though Willard Van Orman Quine has "reduced" at the purely logical/mathematical level mathematical triads to dyads, a full philosophical account of the matter would show that a triadic relation (one involving Quine himself) is involved. It would, therefore, be wrong to cite Quine's reduction as showing that Peirce's ideas are mistaken (since Peirce's ideas do take the mathematician into consideration).

What, I suspect, makes it difficult for logicians and mathematicians to appreciate your argument is that they do not see that you have shifted from the level of analysis with which they are concerned to a different level: that of the philosophical analysis of concept formation and use. They think that you are merely offering up, at the very same level they work on, a confused claim that triadic relations are still involved.

Partly, if you don't mind my saying so, this seems to be your own fault, for much of your language in "Novel Science" suggests that you think that the triadic relations you appeal to are nothing but the ordered triples that the mathematicians are concerned about. You don't take, I think, sufficient pains to distinguish your project from the ordinary non-philosophically analytical project of the mathematical logician. You need, I think, clearly to identify the philosophically analytical level of your argument, and to say that the triadic relations you are talking about are not the merely ordered triples that were already on the scene. You need to make clear that you have shifted by a meta-level.

Also, I think when you do shift levels in the manner that you are doing (if I am right), then not only does the formation of the concept of ordered pair involve reference to the mathematician, but also the formation of the concept of the *unordered* pair does so, as indeed the formation of the concept of a singleton and the concept of set in general. The suggestions in your paper "Novel Science" that the unordered pair is merely dyadic, I believe, must be cut out. For consider a closely analogous line of argument: How did these two elements *get placed together in a single identity*? Etc., etc. In other words, your argument extends to unordered pairs as well as ordered pairs.

In other words, what you do with the idea of ordering can also be done with the idea of *assembling together, independent of order, into a unit.* You might ask, what is it that makes the pair into a unit that contains two elements. *Real* sets, as opposed to items that merely have one or two crucially necessary structural properties of sets, necessarily involve a consciousness which holds two elements together and considers them (as so held together) as a unit.

The issue as to what is a *real* ordered pair, as opposed to what merely has a structural feature of an ordered pair, is a piece of a broader issue in the philosophy of mathematics: It is related to the famous issue of what the numbers *really* are. (This whole topic is deeply complicated, and it is notorious for dividing Platonists from Kantians, Pragmatists, and others.) You are essentially taking, here, a somewhat Platonistic position: That is, you consider that there is something like what is a *real* ordered pair; and that a particular mathematical formulation may get the real notion either right or wrong. Accordingly, in your reformulation of your argument, I think you will need to be self-conscious about the Platonistic elements in your view, and you will need to be prepared to deal with constructionists/intuitionists of all varieties, who will rabidly attack you.

I think that *The Journal of Symbolic Logic* would be a waste of time for a joint article on this subject. More likely would be *The Journal for Philosophical Logic.* (However, it seems that Rich Thomason is now running this journal, and his approach would not very likely be sympathetic.) Give me some more time to think this whole business out. It goes down to the roots of the philosophy of mathematics and logic. And it is very difficult.

But I think that the different levels on which you and Putnam are considering the problem are causing some of the sense (that I assume both of you probably have) that you are not quite addressing each other.

More later, when I learn something about Peirce. (I wish I had time to study him.)

Bob [s]

[Robert Burch]
Professor of Philosophy
Texas A & M University
College Station, TX

ॐ৬

January 18, 1990

[To Robert Burch]

Dear Bob,

Yours of 14 January probably crossed in the mail with my latest (had a copy of my letter to Hilary Putnam in it). We've got to get together on Bitnet. It's free and instant—computer to computer over the phone.

Your comments about HP and me are very helpful.

I have nailed the unordered pair in my chapter in Hartshorne's book. Should I bring that into my essay on "Novel Science," which is already too big?

I thought HP and I might be talking about different things. You and I may be too. You say in your letter "[HP's] point . . . is . . . suppose we start by removing from our discussion of math objects all reference to the person who invents, frames, discovers, etc., these objects." There could be no better statement of the syndrome Percy is criticizing in his "antinomy" essay in *The Message in the Bottle*, and which he also refers to as the transcending or orbiting (completely detached from *life*, in other words) scientist. Ketner's way of saying it: OK, fine, show me someone who can actually *do* that, i.e., discuss math objects without referring to persons who invent, frame, discover. Any *act* of discussing is an implicit reference to some other mind, whether yours or my (future) mind. This is Peirce's primitive element in Existential Graphs, and Percy's primitive in his semiotic. This is the mathematician's antinomy. They want to become ghosts hovering disembodied over their symbols. Others say: "Let _____ be considered as _____." Or "Take _____ as the object language and _____ as the metalanguage." On and on the examples can be multiplied. These are all acts of people that are being addressed. In other words, the "level" you attribute to HP *doesn't exist*. (Better—it isn't real.) This is parallel to John Searle's smash of strong Artificial Intelligence. Searle shows that syntax, pure disembodied Hilbertian symbols, cannot create meaning, just Percy's antinomy in other language.

Ken [s]

꙰

January 21, 1990

Dear Ken,

I've been thinking the last couple of days about you and Putnam and pairs; and it seems to me that the real heart of what you are arguing goes much deeper than any point about logic (considered in the typical way as abstracted from the thinking of the logician). You are really, I think, trying to make a point about the philosophy of mathematics, about the nature of mathematical signs.

That is to say, I think the real essence of your point is that it is a mistake to think (as mathematicians/logicians typically do) that mathematical signs, concepts, etc., can be divorced from the use of those signs, the conceiving acts, the semeiosis, of the thinker who transacts them. In other words, your point is really a point about semeiotic in general. You are attacking the whole formalist tendency in mathematics and logic, with its assumption that mathematical/logical signs have a life of their own, independently of employers of them. In effect, you are really, I think, arguing that there is something totally illegitimate about the level of abstraction at which Quine and Putnam are working. You are saying, "OK, leave the third element of a triadic relation out of the picture, and of course (à la Quine) only two elements are left."

In other words, your point is really a semeiotic point.

Does this make sense? Or am I barking up the wrong tree here? If it strikes you as harmonious with what you are saying, I think you have the embryo of a major work in the philosophy of mathematics contained in your "Novel Science."

Bob [s]

[Robert Burch]

❧

February 18, 1990

Dear Mr. Percy,

I have just read your piece on "The Divided Creature." While I'm in deep sympathy concerning what I take to be the main thrust of this essay, I wonder if the source of the incoherence of our worldview lies even more deeply within science than you suggest here or, for that matter, elsewhere. The problem might surface most evidently in reference to the so-called human sciences, but the roots of the problem are to be traced to the implicit metaphysics of the natural sciences themselves, a reductionist metaphysics in which purely dyadic reactions are presumed to exist *in re* rather than only in our highly abstract perspective (i.e., the highly abstract perspective of natural science). Should we not be careful to replace the dualisms of modern thought (e.g., the Cartesian dualism of mind as unextended thing and matter as extended thing, the Humean dualisms of reason and custom and of reason and passion, the Kantian dualism of phenomena and nou-mena) with the dualism of purely dyadic reactions and genuinely triadic ones? Perhaps there are only triadic reactions, though with regard to some of these (the ones Charles Sanders Peirce called "degenerate") it may be profitable, within certain contexts and for certain purposes, to treat them as though they were essentially dyadic.

As Peirce himself suggests or, at least, implies, we have to become as little children again (*CP* 1.349). This means, in part, recognizing—*re*-cognizing the cosmos as a perfusion of signs (*CP* 5.448, note 1). This is the guess of a *physicist* at the riddle of the universe (*CP* 1.7).

My purpose in writing is not to elicit a response from you, but to pose a question that might be of some interest and perhaps even importance to you as an intellectual wayfarer.

Best wishes,

Vincent Colapietro [s]

Vincent Colapietro [t]
192 Midland Avenue
Tuckahoe, N.Y.

❧

February 23, 1990

Dear Mr. Colapietro,

You are quite right, of course. The temptation is to find inadequacies in the "dyadic" theory of natural phenomenon, suggesting a "triadic" theory in its place. But, of course, the difficulty is the mind-set of the entire Western world, beginning with Descartes, which is supposed to be based on the scientific revolution but is not. Descartes is the villain in my book.

A curious fact: You can point out to scientists and to modern philosophers the contradictions and errors in Cartesian dualism. They will nod, shrug, agree—and continue in their *scientism*.

The mind-set of a era is all-powerful and all-construing.

Thanks,

Walker Percy [s]

❧

March 10, 1990

Associate Dean Thomas A. Langford
The Graduate School
Texas Tech University
Lubbock, TX

Dear Dean Langford,

I am very grateful to you for your article.[43] It gives me some hope.

Who knows? Someday serious scientists may become excited by discovering the incoherence of their "dyadic" science and actually explore—
scientifically—the alternatives.

Again, my thanks. It is heartening.

Cordially,

Walker Percy [s]

❧

[n.d.]

To: Ken Ketner
From: Thomas A. Langford
The Graduate School
Texas Tech University
Lubbock, TX

I thought you might be interested in the note I received last week from
Percy.

Thanks for suggesting that I send him the paper. I would not have
thought of it otherwise.

Tom [s]

Appendix II

Peirce's "Most Lucid and Interesting Paper": An Introduction to Cenopythagoreanism

Kenneth Laine Ketner

"Mathematicians have always been the very best reasoners in the world; while metaphysicians have always been the very worst. Therein is reason enough why students of philosophy should not neglect mathematics." (*MS* 316)

Approximately six months before his death on April 14, 1914, in a long letter to his friend, Frederick Adams Woods, Charles Sanders Peirce reflected upon some of his previous work:

> It was 17 years ago, lacking between 2 and 3 calendar months, that it first forcibly struck me . . . that my paper of Jan. 1897 ["The Logic of Relatives"] . . . required considerable modification. Not that I had said anything *false* but that I had failed to state the matter in the simplest and best form. Thereupon, I wrote the most lucid and interesting paper I have ever written; but I had no way of publishing it. The editor to whom I sent it refused it on the ground that he was afraid I should soon make some further discovery; so he preferred the old mumpsimus to my sumpsimus.
>
> Nine years later, [I] found that system of expressing assertions that I had given in my rejected article to have been a perfect Calumet mine in my own work [the letter was interrupted here, but continued on November 7] I under-took to write such an account of that system as no *stultus stultorum* could

refuse to print; and as a natural consequence, it was far the worst I ever perpetrated [probably a reference to "Prolegomena to an Apology for Pragmaticism"]. (*MS* L477.30–32)

Peirce is widely respected as America's most original and versatile intellect. It seems obvious that the best essay of a great scholar might be quite important for increasing our understanding of the true nature of that thinker's overall efforts. So when I first read this passage, it immediately raised the prospect of locating a piece of writing that Peirce regarded very highly. Hoping for these results, I began searching for clues that might lead to identifying this work among the extant manuscripts. Because there are a number of places (in addition to the above letter) where Peirce mentioned and described that "rejected article," we know several of its properties. On the basis of an analysis of the contents of the surviving *MS* 482, "On Logical Graphs," I have argued that it fits Peirce's descriptions well, and that it is a nearly complete version of the essay Peirce regarded so highly.

It is clear from the beginning of *MS* 482 that topology is its context. Explanation of that background, and of a number of other important and relevant themes, must be reserved for later projects; the purpose of this one was first to undertake the collateral efforts of identifying the important manuscript and analyzing it. Then as a way of showing that it is indeed important for gaining a better understanding of Peirce, I have prepared an account of an important formal system implicit in it. On this basis we can vindicate Peirce's claim that the contents (this formal system, for one example) of his "most lucid and interesting paper," did indeed become a central part of the "perfect Calumet mine in [his own later] work."

The system presented here—which I name "valency analysis"—has been prepared by me using clues from *MS* 482. I have attempted to be consistent with what I take Peirce's insights to have been. He gave the system no special name. What I present is in the spirit of fleshing out and organizing (didactically) what he outlined.

One of the effects of this study of *MS* 482 will be an addition to our knowledge of the basis of Peirce's categoriology. Students of that topic have often lamented that there seems to be no place in the extant papers where he wrote out the proof he claimed to have that tetrads or higher order relations could be reduced to combinations of triads. Many persons have without success searched his writings for an account of this "reduction proof," presumably seeking something that is like a contemporary mathematical or logical proof, expressed algebraically. But perhaps they have been looking for the wrong thing. After having been one of the pioneer developers of logical algebras, Peirce came to favor a topological and diagrammatic approach in logic and logical analysis. Hence it would be quite natural for him to have expressed the reduction proof in some (nonalgebraic) diagrammatic form. If so, then students of the reduction proof ought to be familiar with Peirce's topological interests and with "existential graphs," his system of logical diagrams. Indeed, if we were to use the contemporary name of the mathematical field that seems to lie under the reduction proof, it would be "graph theory," an offshoot of topology. Peirce's awareness of, and participation in, the early development of graph theory is a story yet to be told.

I believe that *MS* 482 represents at least one place where Peirce came very close to stating explicitly the reduction proof in terms of valency analysis. So what I present here (based on *MS* 482 and allied items) will include a reconstruction of what that proof might have been if it had been fully displayed.

Why did Peirce not present valency analysis or this proof in an explicit manner? The best speculation I can produce so far is that it was simple, as he often stated (for example, *MS* 292.80). Peirce was an accomplished mathematician, and it might have been a potential source of embarrassment to him to have written out such a "simple" presentation—he may have thought other mathematicians might regard it, and him, as trivial. And perhaps it is in the context of research-level mathematics, but the application of it in the theory of categories, and elsewhere in Peirce's system of science, is far from trivial. I should add that I have presented only one aspect of *MS* 482, and when the whole piece has been fully studied it may involve items that even a research mathematician would regard as important.

Part One: Valency Analysis

Let

FIGURE I

represent an entity with one "loose end," and let it be named "monad." Let an entity with two loose ends

FIGURE 2

be named "dyad." Let

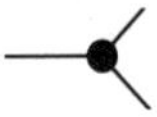

FIGURE 3

an entity with three loose ends, be named "triad." Let an entity with N loose ends be named a "spot." (Monads, dyads, and triads are also spots.) What I am here describing as an "entity" is some as yet unanalyzed relation name. For example, consider a triad: the entity could be specified as

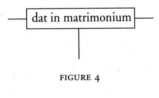

FIGURE 4

or as

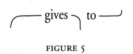

FIGURE 5

The point of concentrating upon valency, and leaving the "content" of the relation unspecified is precisely to achieve results that will apply to any triad, no matter what its content (or to any spot of valency N no matter what its content).

Loose ends may connect with other loose ends to form a "bond" or bonds. Each bond always requires two and only two loose ends. Any series of spots with or without bonds is a "valental graph" (VG). "Valency" (V) refers to the total number of loose ends in a valental graph. The valency of a monad is one, of a dyad two, of a triad three, of a spot with N loose ends is N. (My terminology is sometimes not quite that used by Peirce, but I think the overall effect is the same.)

An "unbonded," or equivalently, a "simple" valental graph, is one that contains no bonds. This allows the statement of a rule.

alpha: *V* simple *VG* = Sum *V* spots

That is, the valency of a valental graph composed only of unbonded spots is equal to the sum of the valencies of all the spots in the graph. Here are three examples of simple valental graphs, I, II, III, together with their valencies:

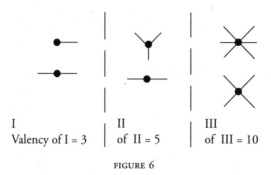

FIGURE 6

A valental graph that contains at least one bond we shall name a "complex valental graph." Here are eight examples of complex valental graphs:

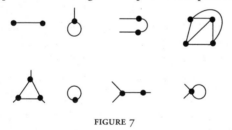

FIGURE 7

The valency of a complex graph is:

beta: *V* complex *VG* = sum *V* spots minus 2x sum bonds

That is, the valency of a complex valental graph equals the sum of valency spots (imagined as if they were simple and unbonded) minus 2x the sum of bonds. In *MS* 482, Peirce established this rule on the basis of general topological considerations. However, we can see that one subtracts 2x sum bonds because each bond is seen as the result of joining two loose ends, starting from an appropriate simple valental graph. That is, a complex valental graph can be understood as having been created from an appropriate collection of nonbonded spots plus the act of bonding (called "composition") two or more loose ends at a time. Because each bond consumes exactly two loose ends, each bonding act decreases overall valency (of the imagined simple spots) by two. Here are some (eight) examples (letting " + " = compose):

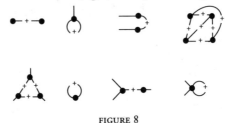

FIGURE 8

A corollary of *beta* is:

> *gamma*: It is not the case that any "perissid" (odd valency) spot can be composed exclusively from "artiads" (even valency) spots.

Gamma may be established from *beta* by means of a *reductio ad absurdum*:

Assume as an hypothesis the contradiction of *gamma*, which would be: Some perissid of valency $2N + 1 =$ sum V spots minus 2x sum bonds, and that "sum V spots" includes only artiads. That is, by hypothesis there is at least one perissid that can be composed exclusively of artiads. We can see that "sum V spots" is even by hypothesis, and "2x sum bonds" is necessarily even in any case. An even number subtracted from an even number always gives an even number. Therefore, the right side of the hypothesis equation would always be even. That creates a contradiction in the hypothesis, since by assumption, the left side is odd. This means the hypothesis is not the case. This completes a proof that establishes the truth of Rule *gamma*.

Two valental graphs are "valency equivalent" if the two graphs have the same valency, no matter what other properties they might have. Thus, these four graphs are valency equivalent (the valency of each is four):

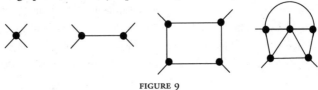

FIGURE 9

While valental graph composition is accomplished by bonding loose ends, exactly two at a time, "decomposition" may be accomplished by breaking bonds, one bond at a time, each broken bond always creating exactly two loose ends.

The result of composing any collection of two or more monads, whether simple or complex, is that only "medads" (graphs of valency zero) are created. Simple monads cannot be decomposed, for there are no bonds to be broken. But complex monads may be decomposed. For example (letting " → com" = "may be composed into," and " → decom" = "may be decomposed into"):

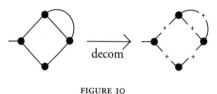

FIGURE 10

If any simple or complex monad and any simple or complex dyad are composed, a monad results, thus:

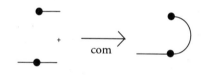

FIGURE 11

Any simple dyad, like a simple monad, cannot be decomposed, because there are no bonds to break. But any complex dyad may be decomposed.

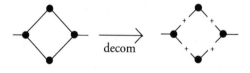

FIGURE 12

If any dyad and any other dyad (either dyad being simple or complex) are composed, a dyad results, thus:

201 *Appendix II*

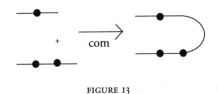

FIGURE 13

From the definition of bonding by two loose ends at a time, it follows that no set of monads only can compose a triad (either simple or complex), and no set of dyads and monads can compose a triad (either simple or complex). By Rule *gamma*, no set of dyads alone can compose a triad (either simple or complex). Hence it follows that:

delta: A triad (either simple or complex) cannot be composed of dyads exclusively, nor of dyads and monads exclusively, nor of just monads.

However,

epsilon: For any spot S which has a valency of four or more, a graph which will be the valency equivalent of S may be composed from triads exclusively.

Here are some examples (the sign " $= V =$ " means "is valency equivalent to"):

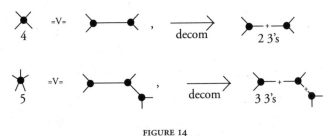

FIGURE 14

We can see that Rule *epsilon* is established by the "Fermatian Inference" (mathematical induction). From *epsilon* will follow:

zeta: Any spot of valency four or higher is decomposable into (may be seen as the valency equivalent composition from) N minus two triads, or: spot V (greater than or equal to four) $= V =$ comp (V minus two) triads.

That is, any spot of valency N, where N is greater than or equal to four, is valency equivalent to the composition of some N minus two triads.

To summarize, within this system of valency analysis:

(1) triads may not be composed exclusively from only monads, or only monads and dyads, or only dyads;
(2) but any tetrad or higher valency spot (of valency N) is valency equivalent to the composition of some series of N minus two triads;
(3) thus tetrads and above are not indecomposable, but can be expressed as the valency equivalent composition of triads;
(4) simple monads, dyads, and triads are, however, indecomposable.

Peirce's principal focus in *MS* 482 and elsewhere was on keeping track of bonding, or "putting things together." He was not especially interested in "medads," graphs with zero valency, except perhaps in how they came to be zero (how they came to be bonded as they are). This is the attitude of a chemist who sees a finished reaction (comparable to a medad) as the result of the activity of combining some more elemental compounds that have free ions (comparable to loose ends). We might object to this decision to bond two at a time. We might want to say, "let there be bondings greater than two," bonding five at a time, for example:

FIGURE 15

But Peirce could respond: "I can analyze that with my two at a time bonding and with my unique and elemental 1's, 2's, and 3's, especially my lovely 3's. Perhaps your bond $2N + 1$ at a time method will work, but my bond two at a time method works also, and mine is simpler."

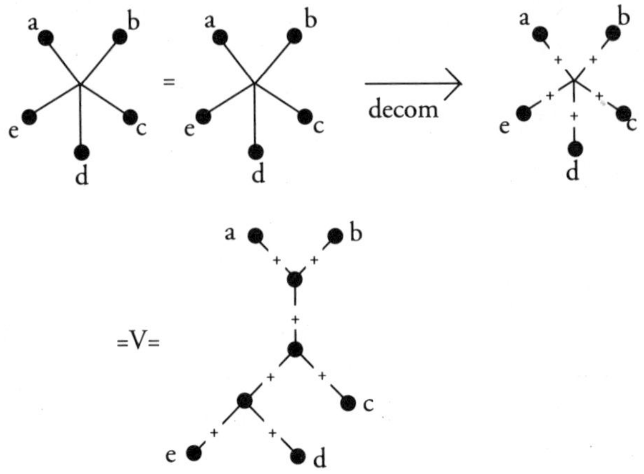

FIGURE 16

I worked out the above before I first noticed Peirce's nearly identical solution.

The Significance of Valency Analysis

One who has followed the discussion thus far might be inclined at this point to ask if valency analysis is of any importance, either in understanding Peirce's system of science, or perhaps in a broader context. The germ of an answer to that very appropriate question lies within Peirce's 1913 letter to Woods, in his remark that "nine years later" (which would be 1897, plus nine, or about 1906) he found the results of *MS* 482 to have been "a perfect Calumet mine in my own work." This suggests that the answer to part of this question might perhaps be found in works from 1906 or a few years earlier. A study of the whole period 1897–1906 is needed, especially the last two years. I have space only for briefly considering one of the more relevant groupings of essays. The principal published works of 1906 are: "Recent Developments of Existential Graphs and their Consequences for Logic," read before the Washington meeting of the National Academy of Sciences in April (*MS* 490 is probably a set of notes for this presentation); "Prolegomena to an Apology for Pragmaticism" (*MS* 292 and 295 are earlier drafts of that article), and "Phaneroscopy, or Natural History of Signs, Relations,

Categories, etc.: A Method of Investigating this Subject Expounded and Illustrated," a paper read before the Boston meeting of the National Academy of Sciences in November (*MS* 299 is probably a draft of this lecture). I think that we should take particularly careful notice of the title of this last mentioned presentation, and of the fact that in his description of it in *The New York Sun* for November 8, 1906; Peirce revealed that it emphasized valency analysis and diagrammatic thought.

In *MS* 292.33ff., while applying valency analysis to a graphical analysis of logic, Peirce stated:

> Every graph has a definite valency. . . . A number of dyads can only make a chain, and the compound will still be a dyad . . . unless the two ends are joined making it a medad. . . . But a number of triads can be joined so as to make a compound of any valency not exceeding the number of triads by more than two, and any odd number giving any odd valency under the same restriction. This shows that there are five natural classes of forms of graphs; namely, medads, monads, dyads, triads and higher perissids [odd valents], tetrads and higher artiads [even valents]. . . .

It is noteworthy that here, nine years later, the discussion given by Peirce in outline form in part of *MS* 482 (which I have fleshed out in the first part of this essay) reappears virtually intact, and even with the same terminology. A new finding is added to valency analysis, namely that there are but five natural classes of forms of valental graphs.

Valency analysis, according to Peirce, has an important application (continuing *MS* 292.34ff.):

> In classification generally, it may fairly be said to be established, if it ever was doubted [remember that Peirce was an expert in scientific classification], that Form, in the sense of structure is of far higher significance than Material. Valency is the basis of all external structure; and where indecomposibility precludes internal structure—as in the classification of elementary concepts—valency ought to be made the first consideration. I term [this] the doctrine of Cenopythagoreanism [compare *MS* 292.98].

That term was an appropriate choice, given Peirce's wish to honor his scientific ancestors, and given his own conclusion that mathematics is the most fundamental science, the ultimate basis for all intellectual activity. I don't recall seeing any essay in the literature on Peirce in which this doctrine of classification according to form, which he called Cenopythagoreanism, has been noticed accurately. Usually it is simply taken as an odd name for the categories. But it is clearly something much broader than that, for we find Peirce classifying according to external form in many areas of his thinking. In a number of places in his later work, Peirce gave a careful analysis of form in terms of icons, diagrammatic thought, and mathematics. A late name for some of his more familiar pragmatic thought is indeed Cenopythagorean pragmaticism.

Now we are beginning to discover the significance of Peirce's "most lucid and interesting paper." For a further brief exploration of the classificatory doctrine of Cenopythagoreanism and how it can be further applied in cenoscopic philosophy, let us examine a parallel passage in *MS* 292: "The chief purpose which governed the construction of [Peirce's logical] algebras and still more exclusively that of existential graphs has been the facilitation of logical analysis, and the resolution of problems in logic. . . . For example, one of the puzzling questions of logic is how concepts can be combined." Peirce classified sciences of research according to the following hierarchy:

Mathematics
Philosophy
    Phenomenology, or Ideoscopy (also Phaneroscopy)
    Normative Science
        Esthetics
        Ethics
        Logic (or Semeiotic)
            Speculative Grammar
            Critic
            Methodeutic
    Metaphysics
Idioscopy (Special Sciences, physics, psychics, etc.)

He also stated in 1904, "In order to understand [my] doctrine, which has little in common with those of modern schools, it is necessary to know, first of all, how [I classify] the sciences." If we add to this Peirce's well-known identification of logic (the third of the normative sciences) with semeiotic, we can see that valency analysis, which originated in mathematics, has found its way down the scale of sciences, now appearing as the fuller doctrine of Cenopythagoreanism, which is being used to analyze and explicate a puzzling problem in semeiotic/logic. The proposed solution of the problem of concept combination, found at *MS* 292.62–67, is too lengthy to consider now, but we note that valency analysis is a part of it. Indeed, the graphical representation of concept combination is "bonding of loose ends." The way this lies at the basis of existential graphs will be displayed shortly. This same manuscript sequence, by the way, contains evidence that the classification of signs is done according to the doctrine of Cenopythagoreanism.

Valency Analysis in the Existential Graphs

The purpose now is to show how valency analysis and bonding is fundamental in Peirce's existential graphs. In order to gain that understanding, we must quickly review the *alpha* part, roughly truth-functional logic. It contains no valency analysis elements, but is essential for progress later. One should supplement this very condensed outline by studying some of the more complete accounts of existential graphs.

A single capital letter represents a simple proposition, and writing that letter on an appropriately designated surface called "the sheet of assertion" asserts the proposition. Writing two such letters side by side on the sheet of assertion conjoins them. Thus juxtaposition is the sign of conjunction. If a circle or other lightly drawn self-closing figure, called a "cut," is drawn around a capital letter, then the proposition represented by the letter is understood to have been denied. With these two conventions, all the truth-functional connectives, and hence any truth-functional proposition, can be generated. Here are a few examples (where "&" is "and," and "-" is "deny," "im" is material implication, and "eq" is material equivalence):

Algebra	Language	EG
A	atomic sentence	A
−A	deny sentence A	(A)
−−A	not not A	((A))
A & B	A and B	AB
A &−B	A and deny B	A (B)
−(A &−B)	A materially implies B	(A (B))
A or B	A or (inclusive) B	((A) (B))
A eq B	A equivalent to B	(A (B))(B (A))

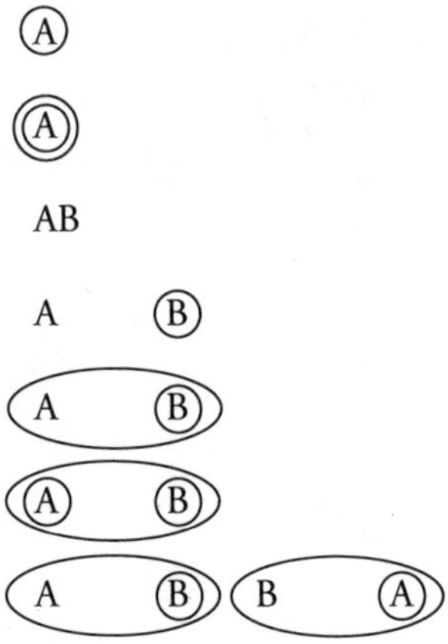

FIGURE 17

If one insists upon reading each existential graph by first translating back into the equivalent not-and algebraic form, the power of existential graphs will be unnecessarily lost. To realize its considerable facility, one should learn to see the connectives directly as cut patterns. Here are several important ones (where $ and @ represent any truth functional sentence of any complexity).

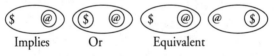

Implies   Or   Equivalent

FIGURE 18

Thus, one quickly learns to think of each "implication" connective as generating a kind of one-eyed binocular cut pattern, while an "or" connective generates a binocular pattern, and so on. To create the graph of a complex proposition, simply begin with the proper cut pattern of the principal connector in the proposition, then progress toward the least connectors, adding the appropriate graphs on top of cuts already drawn. Once one grasps this simple technique, the full computational power of the graphs is released.

Peirce developed five easily remembered and powerful transformation rules, but a discussion of them is not possible here.

If we add a bit more, properties may be represented in the system. A required new symbol is a heavy line drawn from the left of a capital letter. The heavy line, called the line of identity, means "something exists." Moreover, we think of the line as composed of dots that touch. And we also understand it as asserting the identity of all dots within it. So, a simple unattached line states that something exists and that the dots on its extremities are identical to each other and to every other dot in the line. A capital letter having such a line attached to its left side represents a property. In valency analysis terms, this is a monad. By employing the "matrix" of truth-functional logic, we can generate the following parallels (where "SS" is the existential quantifier and "II" is the universal quantifier).

Algebra	Language	EG
SSxAx	Something is A	 —A
IIx−Ax	There is no A	 (—A)
SSx−Ax	Something is not A	 —(A)
IIxAx	Everything is A	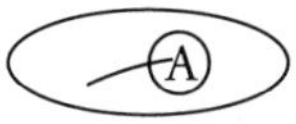 (—(A))

FIGURE 19

If we introduce two monads involving two different properties, by using an act of assertion/bonding, we can produce the kind of medads traditionally known as the Aristotelian categorical propositions. Notice that the assertory act of bonding amounts to taking up two loose ends and asserting that the dots at their unattached extremities are identical, so that what before were two separate lines (two individuals), now through a new act of assertion (bonding) become one individual. In the examples to follow I will use " + " to show where bonding occurred. Try to imagine before and after bonding conditions by means of these + signs. Ordinarily one omits + in writing existential graphs.

Algebra	Language	EG
SSx(Ax&Bx)	Some A is B	cA⟋ + ——B
IIx(Axim−Bx)	No A is B	(cA⟋ + ——B)
SSx(Ax&−Bx)	Some A is not B	cA⟋ + ——Ⓑ
IIx(AximBx)	All A is B	(cA⟋ + ——Ⓑ)

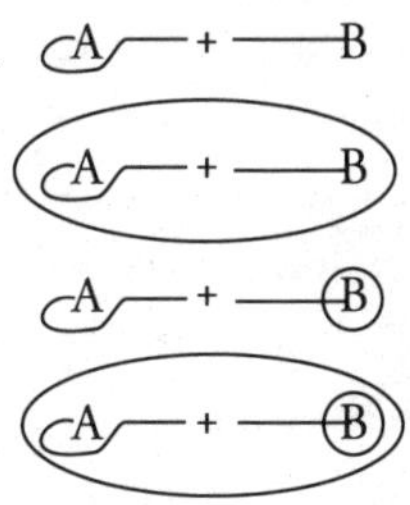

FIGURE 20

Notice that these are Boolean contradictories. A full Aristotelian square of opposition is obtained if one adds 𝒜 as an extra premise to both the universal propositions. This, of course, is an advantage for a system designed to analyze as deeply as possible.

Dyadic relations may be introduced into existential graphs in the following manner (where R is a dyadic relation):

Algebra	Language	EG
SSxyRxy	Some x is R to some y	$\overset{x}{\text{——}}\text{-R-}\overset{y}{\text{——}}$
IIxy−Rxy	No x is R to no y	(⊂——R——⊃)
SSxy−Rxy	Some x is not R to some y	——Ⓡ——
IIxyRxy	All x is R to all y	(⊂——Ⓡ——⊃)

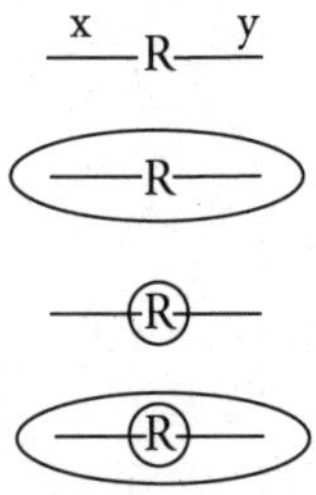

FIGURE 21

Notice that our convention will be that the left line of the R represents the x placeholder, and the right line represents that for y. Generally, in existential graphs, in a given graph there are as many individuals as there are separate lines of identity. Mixed quantification can be represented in ways illustrated by these examples:

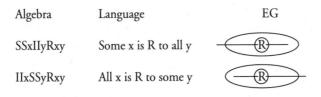

Algebra	Language	EG
SSxIIyRxy	Some x is R to all y	
IIxSSyRxy	All x is R to some y	

FIGURE 22

It works out that a line of identity, the least enclosed part of which is on an even area, expresses existential quantification, while one, the least enclosed part of which is odd, expresses universal quantification. Odd and even enclosures can readily be ascertained by regarding the paper or other surface on which graphs are written as even. Then the area within one cut is odd, within two cuts is even, and so on.

The six examples just given are unbonded dyads. We may represent the bonding of dyads and monads in these ways (where a lower case letter with a line of identity at its left represents a definite individual):

Algebra	Language	EG
Rab	Alice is R to Bob	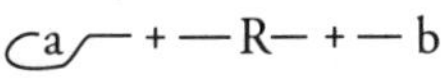 ca⌒ + —R— + — b
SSy(Yy&−Rby)	Bob is not R to a Yankee	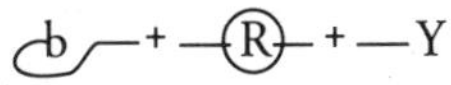 cb⌒ + —(R)— + —Y

FIGURE 23

Two monads representing definite individuals may be bonded to represent their numerical identity. Nonidentity may be expressed by having a line of identity pass through a cut:

Algebra	Language	EG
t = c	Twain is Clemens	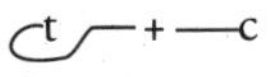 ct⌒ + —c
−(t = j)	Twain is not Jones	 ct⌒ + —◯— + —j

FIGURE 24

211 *Appendix II*

Triadic relations may be represented in the following way, where, to provide a useful example, S will mean the sign relation "_____ stands for _____ to _____."

Algebra	Language	EG
SSxyzSxyz	Some x stands for some y to some z	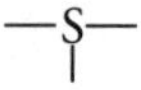
IIxyz−Sxyz	No x stands for no y to no z	
SSxyz−Sxyz	Some x does not stand for some y to some z	
IIxyzSxyz	All x stands for all y to all z	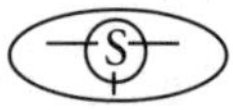

FIGURE 25

We could bond three monads to the above to get a full sign relation (where *r* is a specific representamen, *o* is the object, and *i* the interpretant):

Algebra	Language	EG
Sroi	r stands for o to i	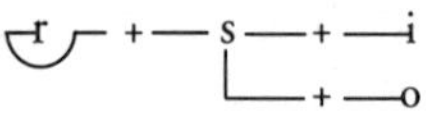

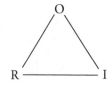

FIGURE 26

Of course, given the results of valency analysis, one does not need to introduce symbols for tetrads or relations of higher valency because according to valency analysis they are in principle reducible to patterns of triads.

In terms of valency analysis and existential graphs, something in the spirit of the above is how one would represent sign relations. I can recall no place where Peirce represented a sign relation as a triangle such as this:

O

R ——————— I

FIGURE 27

This is often attributed to him, but falsely so, for this portrays a triadic relation as composed exclusively of dyads, something that was disproved in valency analysis at Rule *gamma*.

We can now use these ideas to experiment briefly with adapting the techniques of valency analysis and existential graphs to an important principle of Peirce's semeiotic, that "Every $sign_1$ is interpretable in another $sign_2$." Consider the following graph (where S_1 is the first temporally occurring sign relation and S_2 is a later occurring sign relation):

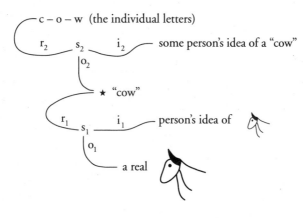

FIGURE 28

At ★, two elements that are the same entity in both of the two triadic relations are bonded, allowing lines to be joined. This would enable us to read Peirce's principle in the following way: "$sign_1$ means r_1 in the diagram, and "interpretable" means "in a second triadic relation like S_2" and "another $sign_2$" means the r_2 of the S_2 mentioned in the interpretable clause. There are a number of other permutations that one might try. Also, because each of the extremities is a sign, that means that there is potentially some additional triad bonded to each such sign, and triads on the signs of those extremities, and so on *ad infinitum*. So we see that we have made but a limited and tiny snapshot of the vast network of semiosis which is the intelligible world.

I hope this outline will make plausible the claim that valency analysis underlies existential graphs, and that both are important tools which Peirce used in applying diagrammatic thought to study semeiotic scientifically (using hypothesis, experiment, and observation). These considerations seem to vindicate remarks like those at *CP* 2.227.

Valency Analysis and Phaneroscopy

If we return to *MS* 292, we can find Peirce using valency analysis and Cenopythagoreanism to resolve one more issue within another of the sciences in his classification scheme: I mean the science of phaneroscopy:

> I invite you, Reader, to turn your attention to a subject which, at first sight, seems to have as little to do with signs as anything could. It is what I call the *Phaneron*, meaning the totality of all that is before or in your mind, or mine, or any man's in any sense in which that expression is ever used. There can be no psychological difficulty in determining whether anything belongs to the Phaneron, or not; for whatever seems to be before the mind *ipso facto* is so, in my sense of the phrase. I invite you to consider, not everything in the Phaneron, but only its indecomposable elements, that is, those that are logically indecomposable, or indecomposable to direct inspection. I wish to make out a classification, or division, of these indecomposable elements; that is, I want to sort them into their different kinds according to their real characters. I have some acquaintance with two different such classifications, both quite true; and there may be others. Of these I know of, one is a division according to the Form of Structure of the elements, the other according to their Matter. The two most passionately laborious years of my life were exclusively devoted to trying to ascertain something for certain about the latter; but I abandoned the attempt as beyond my powers, or, at any rate, unsuited to my genius. I had not neglected to examine what others had done but could not persuade myself that they had been more successful than I. Fortunately, however, all taxonomists of every department have found classifications according to structure to be most important.
>
> A reader may very intelligently ask, "How is it possible for an indecomposable element to have any differences of structure?" Of internal logical structure it would be clearly impossible. But of external structure, that is to say, structure of its possible compounds [bondings!], limited differences of

structure are possible; witness the chemical elements, of which the "groups," or vertical columns of Mendeleef's table, are universally and justly recognized as ever so much more important than the "series," or horizontal ranks in the same table. Those columns are characterized by their several valencies, thus . . . [here Peirce gave long lists of chemical elements that are medads, monads, dyads, triads, tetrads, pentads, hexads, heptads, and octads].

So, then, since elements may have structure through valency, I invite the reader to join me in a direct inspection of the valency of elements in the Phaneron. (*MS* 292.71–75)

* * *

If, then, there be any formal division of elements of the Phaneron, there must be a division according to valency; and we may expect medads, monads, dyads, triads, tetrads, etc. Some of these, however, can be antecedently excluded, as impossible. . . . In the present application, a medad must mean an indecomposable idea, altogether severed logically from every other; a monad will mean an element which, except that it is thought as applying to some subject, has no other characters than these which are complete in it without any reference to anything else; a dyad will be an elementary idea of something that would possess such characters it does possess relatively to something else but regardless of any third object of any category, a triad would be an elementary idea of something which should be such as it were relatively to two others in different ways, but regardless of any fourth, and so on. Some of these, I repeat, are plainly impossible. A medad would be a flash of mental "heat-lightning" absolutely instantaneous, thunderless, unremembered, and altogether without effect. It can further be said in advance, not, indeed, purely *a priori* but with the degree of apriority that is proper to logic, namely as a necessary deduction from the fact that there are signs, that there must be an elementary triad. For were every element of the Phaneron a monad or a dyad, without the relative of teridentity [which is, of course, a triad] it is evident that no triad could ever be built up. [That conclusion is a direct application of valency analysis]. Now the relation of every sign to its Object and Interpretant is plainly a triad. A triad might be built up of pentads or of any higher perissid elements in many ways. But it can be proved—and with extreme simplicity . . . that no element can have a higher valency than three [the reduction theorem from valency analysis]. (*MS* 292.78)

Experienced students of Peirce will readily recognize that this long passage terminates in a short presentation of his famous categories, First-ness, Secondness, and Thirdness. It is quite enlightening to notice that he referred to them as his Cenopythagorean categories. Perhaps more importantly, what the foregoing shows can be summarized in the following way. It is well known that Peirce argued that mathematics was the most fundamental science, even more basic than philosophy. In *MS 482*, he developed in outline the mathematical system of valency analysis. In conjunction with his classification of the sciences, and with his own training as a scientist lurking in the background, he applied these fundamentals of valency analysis to sciences below mathematics, the first being philosophy. In other words, he interpreted this abstract mathematical system onto the structures of other subject matters, fundamentally a movement of diagrammatic reasoning (mathematical reasoning), but one that any expert mathematical physicist such as Peirce would regard as a mere routine, almost unconscious, aspect of scientific work.

Conclusion

It is important to re-emphasize clearly that the doctrine of Cenopythagoreanism is not to be equated with Peirce's doctrine of the categories, as some scholars have done. It is a doctrine of classification based upon valency analysis of external form, developed within the science of mathematics, and deployed into the sciences that come later in Peirce's system of science. Its appearance with the categories within phaneroscopy is but the first of many applications of it in a number of different sciences.

Indeed, application of the technique of classifying and analyzing in terms of the results of valency analysis, named the doctrine of Cenopythagoreanism, created a number of other results within Peirce's whole system, for example: the existential graph method of logical diagrammatization, the doctrine of the categories which is a central part of phaneroscopy; and the classification of signs. It has been possible to consider only some of these topics here briefly.

Given all these extensions and ramifications, it is clear that the doctrine of Cenopythagoreanism (classify in terms of external form by means of valency analysis) occupied a central and fundamental position in Peirce's later works. That is a result which appears to vindicate our initial hypothesis that identifying and understanding the "most lucid and interesting article" would produce a more accurate understanding of Peirce.

My only goal has been to develop a truthful account of Peirce's thinking, or at least a part of it. I have not raised the other question, namely, "Are his hypotheses correct?" He thought they were on the basis of evidence that he sifted. Perhaps it seems odd to ask, within philosophy, "Is this hypothesis correct?" But Peirce argued that philosophy was a science; hence we should not simply say, about his hypotheses, that they are his views. They are that, of course, but if they are also correct, then they should become the view of every scientific intelligence.

And indeed, if Peirce's hypothesis in the present matter is correct, it would have far-reaching consequences. Among these would be that mathematics, the science of diagrammatic thought, provides a way to "see into" (comprehend) mind, which is a semeiosis, a bundle of relations. As a telescope is used in astronomy, so mathematics is the "scope" of phaneroscopy, and the means whereby mind can be scientifically observed and studied. That was clearly expressed by Peirce more than once, the earliest I have found being from a review of Frank Abbot's *Scientific Theism* in *The Nation* from 1886:

> The knowledge of relations [according to Abbot] depends upon a special "perceptive use of the understanding." This view, although it is not adequately set forth, is the centre of all that is original in the book, and it is sure to excite a fruitful discussion of the question of the mode of discernment of relations. Of all the sciences—at least of those whose reality no one disputes—mathematics is the one which deals with relations in the abstractest form; and it never deals with them except as embodied in a diagram or construction, geometrical or algebraical. The mathematical study of a construction consists in experimenting with it: after a number of such experiments, their separate results suddenly become united in one rule, and our immediate consciousness of this rule is our discernment of the relation. It is a strong secondary sensation, like the sense of beauty. To call it a perception may perhaps be understood as implying that to understand each special relation requires a special faculty, or determi-

nation of our nature. But it should not be overlooked that we come to it by a process analogous to induction.

Moreover, this tool (diagrammatic thought, or general mathematical method) for objectively observing the highest kind of reality is the technique for making scientific progress in semeiotic, as Peirce clearly stated (for instance, at *CP* 2.227). This means that diagrammatic thought with its valency analysis background (especially as ultimately embodied in existential graphs) is a vital tool for Peirce's conduct of scientific inquiry in semeiotic.

On a more general level, Peirce's conception of general mathematical method may be a means for our very survival as a civilization. Briefly, by this cryptic remark, I mean that because much of what now constitutes our civilization are systems of relations (food distribution systems, power grids, computer networks, and so on), and because we may be rapidly reaching the point where we may lose control of those systems (remember the shorter response times in missile defense computers, as one prominent example, not to mention other systems involving our environment), we may thus be blindly going about creating the kinds of systems which, if they fail or get out of control in a certain kind of way, may bring our species to extinction. Indeed, we may be the first species on earth to have created a kind of artificial environmental niche (our various systems) which has the potential to make extinct our whole species, either through being out of control or through collapsing. Systems of relations, so it is plausible to think, are more than the things and motions of things one associates with them—thus a functioning computer is more than a collection of parts, even electrified parts. Perhaps this "something more" could properly be called relations. It is clear that we know how to observe *things* and their motions. Peirce's Cenopythagoreanism and associated topics offer us, however, a way in which we might begin to develop a theory of how better to be able to observe and experiment upon relations. That, in turn, might yield a better understanding of the relational part of systems, a result which, if attained, might possibly allow us to control them, as opposed to the other unhappy possibility which now seems to be steadily drawing closer.

The foregoing point has been eloquently expressed by Walker Percy in "The Delta Factor," an independent discoverer of Cenopythagoreanism about one hundred years after Peirce found it; I refer Percy's essay to those who would like to continue this line of thought, and who, like me at this juncture, may be saying to themselves, "I think I may be a Cenopythagorean."

Charles Sanders Peirce: An Introduction

Kenneth Laine Ketner

". . . if I were asked to nominate the two native Americans of greatest intellectual genius, I think they would both be 19th-century figures—Willard Gibbs and . . . C. S. Peirce."—(C.P. Snow, *Saturday Review*, Dec. 13, 1975)

Although now considered by many to be the founder of serious philosophic study in the United States, late in his career, which was a study in extremes of triumph and misery, Peirce sometimes complained, usually without bitterness, that most of his contemporaries did not fully understand or appreciate his work. He was aware that he had something valuable to give mankind, and often felt frustrated that circumstances were preventing him from making that contribution. Today that complaint is still valid, although the flow of scholarship is now in the direction of responding to it. The response will be possible because almost all the books and essays that Peirce wrote, even without support from publishers or universities, have survived and are beginning to appear in convenient editions. In effect, Peirce overcame his lack of resources by writing out his contributions any way he could, sometimes with home-made ink and scrap paper, so that there would be at least one copy of his thoughts which would survive him. In this prologue for a set of materials designed to introduce readers to the work of the man widely considered to be the most original and profound American intellect, let us pursue the question of his complaint, both from within the context of his era and of ours. As a necessary preparation for that task, we should first quickly review the status of Peirce's writings, both published and unpublished.

He published a great deal during his lifetime, more than received opinion has registered. Perhaps the reason for this misregistration was that many of his publications were unsigned, or appeared in government scientific reports not widely distributed to the public, or in reference works (for example, he contributed to *The Century Dictionary*). Recent bibliographic research has identified almost all such items. That he was a severe recluse has also been a favored allegation among some students of his life and work. A look at the evidence shows this to be false, for as late as 1906 he wrote published reports as an eyewitness of meetings of the National Academy of Sciences which he attended as a member and where he also gave papers. He often expressed pride in the fact that he was elected to the National Academy on the basis of his work in logic, which he understood broadly as the science of scientific method. Another nonreclusive theme one can detect in the same way is the amount of influence Peirce exercised upon others during his lifetime, and the amount of influence others exercised upon him. It is also fashionable to proclaim that Peirce's intellectual ability or output suffered because he lacked a permanent academic chair. Such a position, it is further said, would have provided him with appropriate critical feedback from students and colleagues, which he is supposed to have needed to forestall certain difficulties considered to exist in his works. Yet, by looking over his complete published output one can see that he was constantly, almost until the day he died, responding to and arguing with friends and detractors. Whether there are difficulties in his works is a matter for argumentation, not speculation.

For the most part, Peirce's manuscripts (like his publications, also voluminous) have survived and are widely available for study. Some scholars have described these as fragmentary. It is true that one can find some that fit this category, but one can also find several virtually complete and unified book manuscripts or complete series of lecture notebooks. Furthermore, his system—whether expressed in a series of fragments or in complete essays—is present for examination. At the moment, in addition to Harvard, there are four other centers at which scholars are welcomed to pursue studies of these and related materials: Institute for Studies in Pragmaticism at Texas

Tech University, the Peirce Edition Project at University of Indiana, l'Institut de Recherche en Sciences de la Communication et de l'Education Universitaire de Perpignan, and the Philosophisches Seminar Universität Hamburg. The effort to make Peirce's writings more widely available in conveniently accessible formats began in 1923 and continues today.

From Peirce's literary production, which has been estimated to be enough to fill more than one hundred volumes, it is difficult to present a representative selection of Peirce's writings within a narrow scope. That difficulty is increased by the fact that he was a systematic thinker, whose work is poorly appreciated if broken up and perused in isolated chunks. However, clues from a study of Peirce's life career suggest a way to organize a set of introductory texts, and these same considerations will begin to suggest an answer to the complaint initially mentioned. In this way we can start to understand why his contemporaries misunderstood him, something that will help us to overcome this barrier insofar as it still affects us.

Biographical Summary

The first and most important thing one notices by looking carefully at his total life, especially if one avoids preconceived conclusions about it, is that he was not a philosopher, but was a scientist and mathematician. You, dear reader, at this point might have experienced a voice from your inner dialogue, which said "That can't possibly be true." If I may join your dialogue, it is clear that the key word of that statement, "philosophy," must be explicated. If we today look back upon a figure from the past, surely we bring our own vocabulary (at least initially) to that task. So the issue amounts to a question about the meaning of the word "philosophy" in our time. It is clear that philosophy today is usually and upon first presumption considered to be a discipline within the humanities, as opposed to being a part of the sciences. It isn't pertinent whether that widespread public and academic notion is correct. It is relevant that this is the perspective from which most persons would judge the matter now; thus that is the sense in which the above claim states that Peirce is not a philosopher, as considered by those in the humanities. One of the lessons to be gained from reading Peirce's intellectual autobiography is that Peirce had concluded that philosophy is (or could easily become) a science, which is embedded within a context of other sciences or presuppositions of science; it isn't even the most basic science, a position he reserved for mathematics. This simple fact has been systematically overlooked and ignored by almost all commentators on Peirce, who usually approach his works from the humanistic standpoint of philosophy. To proceed in that manner is an invitation to serious misunderstanding of what he believed he had accomplished. Indeed, this simple fact is a convenient touchstone for judging the accuracy of any account of Peirce's works one might encounter. Another barrier has to do with his laboratory cast of mind; a reader who lacks experience with the inner life of a laboratory has a distinct disadvantage to overcome in understanding him.

Perhaps we could identify Peirce's sense as philosophy in a more technical, scientific sense. This means that he should be compared to scientific philosophers such as Aristotle, Bacon, Leibniz, H. L. F. von Helmholtz, Ernst Mach, or Einstein, and contrasted with philosophers (again, as used in the humanities) such as Plato, Ockham, Hegel, William James, or Wittgenstein. His boldly announced allegiance to Aristotle as scientist and distaste of the Hellenic tendency to mingle philosophy and practice are (as used in the humanities) very unphilosophic.

It is not surprising that he would have that outlook, for he was born on September 10, 1839, into the family and extended circle of friends of Benjamin Peirce, professor of mathematics and astronomy at Harvard, an acknowledged leader among American scientists. His father, realizing the son's intellectual gifts, took charge of his early education, submitting him to strict intellectual exercises which especially emphasized rigor, detail, and long perseverance. Charles also made a study of chemistry at a tender age. His graduate degree was in chemistry, and throughout his life he often referred to himself simply as a chemist, who had in effect been born in a scientific laboratory, for such was the atmosphere of his father's house and social orbit.

When about 12 years old, in his brother's room he came across a copy of Whatley's *Logic*, read it, and began his lifelong fascination with that subject, understood as the scientific study of scientific method. After his first degree from Harvard in 1859, wanting direct experience with the methods of science, he entered the employ of the United States Coast Survey, then the premier government scientific agency. He spent the Civil War years on field surveys in Louisiana, or working in Cambridge with his father, the Survey's consulting geometer. In 1865, he made his academic debut with a series of lectures at Harvard entitled "On the Logic of Science." During 1867, he commenced astronomical work at the Harvard Observatory which eventually culminated in *Photometric Researches*, a pioneering attempt at mapping our galaxy, the Milky Way. During the early 1870's, he was one of the participants in the well-known Metaphysical Club, an informal but serious Cambridge discussion group consisting of Peirce, James, Oliver Wendell Holmes, J. B. Warner, and sometimes Frank Abbot and John Fiske. In November 1872, his father, now superintendent of the Survey, commissioned him to take charge of its pendulum experiments, by which means one could determine the relative force of gravity at various locations on the globe. With sufficient information of that kind one could more accurately determine the shape of the earth, thus permitting one to make more accurate maps, not to mention increasing knowledge of the value of the force of gravity, which is among the most important physical constants. During the 1870's and early 1880's, he travelled widely in the United States and in Europe, conducting gravity surveys. In the course of his research, he discovered a serious error in what was then regarded as the best pendulum work in Europe. He defended and sustained his critique at a meeting of the International Geodetic Association in Geneva in 1877. Based on this and related work, he designed the Peirce pendulum, which became the standard apparatus for this kind of research. As a result of these efforts, he became world famous as a mathematical physicist in geodesy.

As a consequence of his need in pendulum work for very accurate measurements, in 1879 he was directed by the Survey to study the possibility of using a wavelength of light as a standard for the length of the meter. This he succeeded in doing in a "Report on the Spectrum Meter," tendered to the Survey. Peirce's findings on that topic later contributed to the work of Michelson and Rowland. During 1879 to 1884, while retaining his full-time position with the Survey, Peirce accepted a part-time position as lecturer in logic at the Johns Hopkins University. There he was closely associated with members of the mathematics department under James J. Sylvester. He was abruptly dismissed from his position in Baltimore, probably because some members of the governing board of Hopkins were told he had taken up residence with Juliette Froissy (who later became his second wife) before concluding his divorce from Melusina Fay (who had deserted him, according to their divorce decree). He returned full time to Survey work, but a number of changes had begun to take place in its policies, perhaps the most important being that its new leaders no longer insisted upon the kind of high standards Peirce brought to his physical and geodetic research. For this and other reasons, Peirce resigned from the Coast Survey in 1891, after first submitting an exhaustive summary report upon his long gravity researches. Perhaps this all too brief account of his scientific accomplishments helps one to understand why in 1895 Peirce remarked that "My philosophy may be described as the attempt of a physicist to make such conjecture as to the constitution of the universe as the methods of science may permit, with the aid of all that has been done by previous philosophers."

While undertaking his astronomical, geodetic, and metrological researches Peirce was also busily involved in helping to create modern symbolic logic. His very important role there has been ill treated, misdescribed, or ignored, as Hilary Putnam has recently explained in "Peirce the Logician" in *Historia Mathematica* (1982). Peirce's research in formal logic (roughly that part of semeiotic or general logic which he labeled as "critic") were important contributions toward a number of contemporary developments, the most notable among which is computer science. In fact, Peirce's legacy to computing may include more than having provided some of its software—it is also likely he contributed somewhat to hardware and to a kind of limitative thesis similar to that advanced by Alan Turing.

The end of his government employment meant a serious loss of income for Peirce, and he spent the 1890's attempting to secure an adequate means of support for himself and his chronically ill second wife. He participated in a number of money-making schemes, including projects such as the commercialization of acetylene gas or the development of hydro-electrical power. More than once some well-known businessmen cheated him of his share in such projects. His luck, which had favored him in earlier days, had inexorably and irreversibly turned. On March 13, 1897, he wrote the following to his old friend, William James:

I have learned a great deal about philosophy in the last few years, because they have been very miserable and unsuccessful years—terrible beyond anything the man of ordinary experience can possibly understand or conceive. Thus, I have had a great deal of idleness & time that could not be employed in the duties of ordinary life, deprived of books, of laboratory, everything: and so there was nothing to prevent my elaborating my thoughts, and I have done a great deal of work which has cleared up and arranged my thoughts. Besides this, a new world of which I knew nothing, and of which I cannot find that anybody who has written has really known much, has been disclosed to me, the world of misery. It is absurd to say that Hugo, who has written the least foolishly about it, really knew anything of it. I would like to write a physiology of it. How many days did Hugo ever go at a time without a morsel of food or any idea where food was coming from, my case at this moment for very near three days, and yet that is the most insignificant of the experiences which go to make up misery? Much have I learned of life and of the world, throwing strong lights upon philosophy in these years. Undoubtedly its tendency is to make one value the spiritual more, but not an abstract spirituality. . . . On the other hand, it increases the sense of awe with which one regards Gautama Booda.

This letter led eventually (with background assistance from James) to Peirce being invited to give a series of eight lectures about one year later at the Cambridge Conferences, a kind of auxiliary education activity conducted just off Harvard Yard. It is in those 1898 lectures that Peirce first began to set down his mature thought. Surviving correspondence also shows that the Harvard philosophy department was solidly impressed with them, especially Josiah Royce and James. Subsequent essays by both men confirm that this and other works had a lasting and profound influence upon their own thought, although the Peirce-James debate is one that still continues today. Yet still no steady employment or other source of adequate income came Peirce's way; eventually he came to spend most of his time on his homestead "Arisbe," near Milford, Pike County, Pennsylvania. He was able to continue publishing articles and book reviews, and occasionally to give lectures—notably his 1903 Lowell lectures, which followed other lectures before the Lowell Institute in 1866 and 1892. But more important, he continued to write essays, and even complete whole books, for which he could find no publisher, yet which have survived and will appear in due time.

After the loss in 1910 of his friend and supporter James (in whose honor he informally adopted the additional name "Santiago"—Saint James), full-time misery once again sought him out. He contracted cancer, possibly as a result of being exposed to radiation at the National Academy of Sciences' meeting for April 1904, where "Professor Barker . . . showed one specimen of a salt of uranium . . . [that] shone so brightly as to be visible all over the darkened . . . hall." As the disease reached its terminus, he often asked for pen and paper, writing eventually having become the only way available to him for relieving his pain. At about 10 A.M. on the morning of April 19, 1914, he died in the arms of a concerned young neighbor lad who had come to offer assistance.

A System of Science

Peirce's system is not a system of philosophy, but is a system of science, the organizing principle of which is method as revealed in *The New Elements of Mathematics*: "I have now sketched my doctrine of Logical Critic, skipping a good deal. I recognize two other parts of Logic. One which may be called *Analytic* examines the nature of thought, not psychologically, but simply to define what it is to doubt, to believe, to learn, etc., and then to base critic on these methods is my real method, though in this letter I have taken the third branch of logic *Methodeutic*, which shows how to conduct an inquiry. This is what the greater part of my life has been devoted to, though I base it upon Critic" (Vol. 3, p. 207). Peirce's intellectual career is in effect a lifelong search for a correct account of the nature and function of methods that permit the discovery of truth by those that have the will and capacity to learn from experience, a personality type he designated as "scientific intelligence." Moreover, the method whereby Peirce conducted this lifelong search was itself science, aided by a powerful historical consciousness by means of which he sought in the history of science lessons for his own life search. He concluded that scientific intelligences do not begin their activities in an intellectual vacuum—there are presuppositions of science and scientific method. Basically these fall into two large classes: religion and common sense. Peirce distinguished sharply between religion and theory of religion (or theology). Roughly the difference is parallel to that between someone like Gautama and someone who equates religion to following a creed or living according to a mechanical recipe (the kind of orthodoxy that the early pragmatist Jesus spent his career disclaiming). One might say that Gautama or Jesus acted, without thinking or theory or premeditated recipe, in good ways because their instincts were good. What disturbed Peirce about theology was that it proposed to give mankind a stone when bread was needed—the stone of theory, which is not right instinct (which would be the bread of religion within his system). Within metaphysics he admitted theorizing about religion, but always insisted that such metaphysics could influence true religion only by a slow, almost evolutionary, process of percolation. Scientific activity is based upon religion, no matter if the particular scientific intelligence is aware of it or not, because the ideals of that method presuppose a search for the truth about a reality not yet known. The influence of George Boole is strong here, in a way not yet fully studied.

Common sense is that set of instinctive beliefs which all normal human beings do not doubt. Peirce considered that these were the result of evolutionary change over millennia. Again, like religion, such "original beliefs" are not theory, and like religion, there is a place in his system for theorizing about them ("critic," under critical common-sensism), but again one should not take the theory in place of the fact of the presence and current nature of such beliefs in all humans. These themes bear a strong resemblance to those pursued by Wittgenstein in *On Certainty*.

The system proper begins with mathematics. This is the fundament of his entire intellectual effort. A good way of accurately describing Peirce's career would be to say that he was a student of the method of mathematics in all its ramifications. He regarded mathematics as diagrammatic thinking. His treatment of diagrams in this sense arose from his study of figures like Helmholtz and Johann Benedict Listing. Again and again, the general notion of diagram appeared throughout his system, and it, along with his concept of mathematics, is a central unifying theme. His treatment of method in mathematics makes induction, observation, and experiment basic there, a stance in sharp contrast to the deductivism of today.

His science of philosophy, which in the system of science is called cenoscopy, is thoroughly based upon his studies of mathematics. A mythical conception of Peirce can be developed if this important fact is discounted. The first and perhaps most important application of mathematics to philosophy comes in phaneroscopy (or categoriology). There Peirce applied the results of his studies of the graph theory of Leonhard Euler, Alfred Bray Kempe, William Kingdom Clifford, and Listing. These results led him to the doctrine of Cenopythagoreanism—that classification of basic concepts should be according to their external valency. That notion, taken directly from graph theory within 19th-century topology, became the basis for phaneroscopy and the existential graph approach to logic.

Now functioning under the control of the Cenopythagorean categories, Peirce continued to work out the additional branches of his system. He argued that logic was the third of the normative sciences, preceded there by esthetics and ethics. Again by operating under the inspiration of mathematics, he explicated the several branches of logic (or semeiotic). There is a contemporary study, called semiotics, that traces its history to Peirce, but his semeiotic (logic) is radically different from this current phenomenon. Within semeiotic, Peirce included branches for basic definitions (called "stechiotic"), formal logic (roughly designated as "critic"), and methodology. Perhaps critic is the most difficult to anthologize, for it is principally technical formal logic, the aim of which is to analyze reasoning instead of creating a calculus for reasoning. Methodology, of course, was his ultimate destination, and all that preceded it within the system contributed toward its final explication. Peirce's most well-known doctrine, pragmaticism, is a theorem of methodeutic—he often remarked that pragmaticism amounted to little more than a description of a typical (generalized) laboratory experimenter's procedure. After thus securing a methodological base, and only then, did Peirce consider it possible scientifically to undertake philosophy in the central sense, the problems of metaphysics in other words. Thus, Peirce's Copernican revolution is to make metaphysical philosophy depend upon science, which he understood as reliable methods for seeking truth in all areas of study, in opposition to the usual inverse image in which metaphysical philosophy is prior to science.

One Hundred Fifty Years Later

Five years after George Orwell's apocalypse, the 150th anniversary of Peirce's birth was celebrated. Given that occasion, it is appropriate to ask whether and in what ways Peirce's contributions to mankind have been helpful, or will continue to be helpful, as he thought they would be. This is a large subject, and like other subjects taken up in this introduction, it can only be considered briefly.

The contribution that John J. Stuhr's anthology urges upon us is the fact that Peirce's work has deeply influenced every other thinker represented here, some of whom were his pupils in one form or another. And because he and the other five thinkers exemplify the best in America, at least in that period, Peirce has either directly or through these others had a far-reaching impact upon intellectual life in the United States. Opinions of James and Royce about Peirce's importance are well known—let us add a sample remark from one more: John Dewey: "The readers who are acquainted with the logical writings of Peirce will note my great indebtedness to him in the general position taken. As far as I am aware, he was the first writer on logic to make inquiry and its methods the primary and ultimate source of logical subject-matter" (John Dewey, *Logic, The Theory of Inquiry*, Note 9). But today Peirce's influence is international, not limited by a national boundary. Neither is it limited to mathematics, natural sciences, or philosophy; for instance, Walker Percy in "Toward a Triadic Theory of Meaning" in *The Message in the Bottle* stated, "I . . . suspect that the state of the behavioral sciences vis-à-vis language is currently in such low spirits, not to say default, that Peirce's time may have come" (p. 159). Perhaps a similar remark is in order for literary criticism and art.

Perhaps one reason for this is the fact that Peirce's works address problems with which we still wrestle. Of course, the writings of all thinkers of quality possess this property to some extent, but Peirce's output has it more strongly. Perhaps this is because he was ahead of his time, this being yet another of the barriers to accessing his works, one which is slowly falling away. There is space to exemplify but one such problem to which his findings may indicate a solution, once his genuine conclusions are better known.

At the International Congress of Mathematicians in 1900, David Hilbert presented a challenging series of questions, the 23rd of which asked if there was a mechanical way (a precise, finite, determinate algorithm) that would decisively establish the truth or falsity of any statement within the predicate calculus—a calculus, by the way, that Peirce had helped to develop. In 1936, Alan Turing showed that if a mechanical algorithm was assumed, then on the most reasonable definition of "mechanical," the answer to Hilbert's question was "No." Turing's method was classically Peircean. First, he asked for the meaning of "mechanical," which he produced using the technique Peirce called pragmaticism and had introduced as the pragmatic maxim in the Metaphysical Club in the early 1870's in Cambridge, the very technique that had inspired James, Royce, Dewey, and a host of others. The result of Turing's application of pragmaticism (he did not call it that, and may never have known of Peirce) was later called a Turing Machine. Basically a Turing Machine is not a real machine at all (yet its principles can be instantiated in actual machines), but instead is a way of constructing a kind of diagram in which later states of modification of the diagram are completely determined or caused by previous states. Thus, it is a machine in the requisite sense: namely, that its rules must function to cause it to change its states (change the marks in its diagram) deterministically as opposed to nondeterministically. That is to say, there is no provision in the "machine" for creating, experimenting, or serendipity.

Turing was able to show that if "mechanical algorithm" is what one means by the method of mathematics, then that pragmatically implies that there are things such a method cannot produce. Yet these are things (theorems, computations) that human mathematicians can produce through an exercise of their nondeterministic ingenuity, creativity, experimentation, and observation—what Peirce called abduction, induction, and deduction (his general semeiotic or logic of science, in other words). Thus, it seems to me, that Turing's results are very similar to Peirce's results, except expressed in an alternative but equivalent language, or notation (if you will). Peirce took the positive mode and said that mathematics is an experimental, observational, hypothesis-seeking, and confirming science, just as all other sciences are, the only difference being that mathematics proceeds with operations upon written or mental diagrams, where "diagram" includes figures as well as algebras. Turing, who took the negative mode, coming from an opposite direction, began by assuming that the mathematical method was mechanical, and by using pragmaticism and experiments with diagrams, showed that such an assumption was absurd, thus establishing that the mathematical method could not be strictly mechanical. I think the results achieved by both Peirce and Turing amount to approximately the same thing, and that it would profit us immensely now to return to Peirce's more elaborate and interconnected system of science to pursue further details and ramifications of this matter. There are several other major contemporary issues, ranging from the arts to physics, to which the same assertion could be accurately applied.

Who Was Charles Sanders Peirce? And Does He Deserve Our Homage?

Kenneth Laine Ketner

There might be persons who would think that the first question in the title of this essay is frivolous, for, they might say, by now everyone knows who Charles Peirce was—the great American philosopher, etc., and so forth; and of course, it would be right to give homage to such a great philosopher, etc., and so forth. If there existed in the cosmos such strawpersons who would obligingly charge me with this frivolity, I would want to disagree with them, and to address them along these general lines: The man you are most likely conceiving did not exist; such a man is principally a myth that came into being, piece by piece, through the offices of some inaccurate biographical sketches (for example, the one in *The Dictionary of American Biography*), and by a change in scholarly habits among some academics who have tended to disavow historical antecedents, and who have created or tolerated a false gulf between philosophy and science that has grown up (or at least widened) since the real Peirce died in 1914. Without going into further detail, I hope you may grant me that there could be some little grain of truth in what I have in mind, and that you will therefore permit me to begin again from scratch with the two questions in my title, as if we had never heard anything about Peirce. I shall try to answer those questions in outline, a contingency imposed by the present format.

The place to begin, naturally, is not with the first question, but with some things one might presuppose in asking it. Chief among such presuppositions might be, "How shall we find out who Peirce was?" In fact, this issue has been begged by some scholars who have sought to deal with the matter. Many have merely assumed their procedures without argument or comment. In general, often the procedures used lack some of the following, which seem to be among the essential principles for this task: (1) read carefully what Peirce says about himself and his work, and accept it until evidence forces one away from it; (2) learn what the intellectual atmosphere of his time was and use that information to better understand his expressions and goals; (3) try to understand the longer range historical antecedents of Peirce's activities; (4) look at all that Peirce wrote, not just at what he wrote that is conveniently accessible; (5) avoid preconceptions by remembering that interpretational hypotheses are not facts.

"Very well and good," say the strawpersons, "but get on with it." And so I will. Because this is a *little* essay, to begin to answer "Who was Peirce?" I will use a *little* description, almost surely written by Peirce himself: namely, his entry in *American Men of Science*, edited by Peirce's friend at Columbia University, J. McKeen Cattell. But before citing this paragraph, consider a few preliminaries. The directory includes a bit more than four thousand entries. Of these, about one thousand have an asterisk by the name of the person's principal field of scientific research. Asterisk-holders were considered by their peers, according to Cattell's introduction, to be the top men of science in the United States. Peirce has an asterisk, and his principal field of science is logic, which in *MS* 364 Peirce described (circa 1872) as "the doctrine of truth, its nature, and the manner in which it is to be discovered." Here, then, is the paragraph, which has been virtually ignored in the Peirce literature:

Peirce, C(harles) S(antiago Sanders), "Arisbe," Milford, Pa. *Logic*. Cambridge, Mass. Sept. 10, 39. A.B. Harvard, 59, A.M. 62, B.S. 63. Asst. U.S. Coast and

Geod. Surv, 73–93. Lecturer, Harvard, 64–65, 69–71, 03; Hopkins, 80–82; Lowell Inst, 66, 95, 03. Delegate for U.S. Int. Gradmessung Conf, Stuttgart. Nat. Acad; fel. Am. Acad. Logic, especially logic of relations, probabilities, theory of inductive and retroductive validity and of definition, epistemology; metrology; history of science; multiple algebra; doctrine of the nature and constitution of numbers; gravity; wave-lengths; phonetics of Elizabethan English; great men; ethics; phaneroscopy; speculative cosmology; experimental psychology; physical geometry.—Foundations of mathematics; classification of science; code of terminology; topical geometry.

In a long and important autobiographical letter written to J. H. Kehler, dated June 22, 1911 (*MS* L231), Peirce explained that there are three parts or aspects of logic: "I have now sketched my doctrine of Logical Critic, skipping a good deal. I recognize two other parts of Logic. One which may be called *Analytic* examines the nature of thought, not psychologically but simply to define what it is to doubt, to believe, to learn, etc., and then to base critic on these definitions is my real method, though in this letter I have taken the third branch of logic *Methodeutic*, which shows how to conduct an inquiry. This is what the greater part of my life has been devoted to, though I base it upon Critic. Of course, in order to study methodeutic it is necessary to make researches in as great a variety of sciences as possible—*real* researches, not the two penny half penny 'research work' that students of colleges do" (p. 207). From this data we can syllogize that Peirce devoted his life to a study of methodeutic. His standards were high, for contrary to the mythical Peirce's lack of persistence or of purpose, the real Peirce mastered several natural and exact sciences to the extent that he made original and important research contributions in them.

Why should Peirce go to science to find a basis for methodeutic? Because, as he said, "Men, the principal occupation of whose lives is finding out the truth, are called *scientific men*; and their occupation is called Science. . . ." Thus we see that science is the activity (method) that in general finds truth, so in order to accurately describe such methods (the activities of scientific men, or of scientific intelligences), such a description being the object of methodeutic, the real Peirce became a scientific intelligence of the first rank in his own day, and was so recognized by his contemporaries. The mythical Peirce was a philosopher, so it is said, and when it is said, what is usually meant by the word "philosophy" in such cases is "a student of systematic knowledge," a person who subscribes to the truth of a system or a party, not the truth that is "as yet unknown." The real Peirce declared this kind of activity to be philodoxy, and repudiated it (see *P* 779), but added that if by "philosophy" and by "science" were meant an older sense of each—the objective pursuit of truth—then he was certainly both a philosopher and a scientist, for the two words then described the same activity.

This then explains the rather large number of scientific endeavors in Peirce's entry in the Cattell volume, and his accomplishments in them constitute a da Vinci-like mastery of universal science. This can be further appreciated by considering a little bit of detail from sample sciences. In metrology, he served the United States government through the Office of Weights and Measures, of which he was the head for a while. In such capacity, he undertook wavelength studies and developed pioneer techniques for using light as an exact standard for length measurement. He was the first experimental psychologist in the United States, producing, among other things, a classic experiment in psychophysics. His study of gravity and the values he developed for its strength were the best in the 19th century and compare favorably with present values. Peirce was apparently the first astronomer to prepare a reasonably accurate map of our galaxy, the Milky Way. He was most likely the first historian of science in the United States. He was also a great scholar of medieval science, and this in a time when that era was widely supposed to be mostly a barren darkness. He theoretically studied the medieval logicians, treating their terminology and principles with respect. The real Peirce, by the way, did not simply study history as a pastime, as the mythical Peirce did, but for a very sound and serious reason. He thought that "each chief step in science has been a lesson in logic." As far as I can see, this means that a vital part of the way to study methods for finding truth (logic) is to study their careers in time, including their successes and failures. No wonder then, that the real Peirce declared that "the history of the human intellect has been one of my chief interests, especially in reference to the physical and philosophical sciences." Peirce's knowledge of the history of science was vast. A part of that expertise was his understanding of the crucial role that an effective terminology has in science. Thus, he made a careful study of that matter to which he made some original contributions.

The mythical Peirce is supposed to be dark and difficult to read. This charge exasperated the real Peirce, the careful student of scientific terminology who was struggling to reform philosophy, in part by trying to give it a terminology on principles similar to those that gave natural science its successful terminology. Thus, in a letter the real Peirce replied to William James, who had accused him of dark expression, by saying:

> Now I will speak first of my meaning of which you "don't understand a word" and then of what you say. It is very vexatious to be told at every turn that I am utterly incomprehensible, notwithstanding my careful study of language. [Toward the end of this letter, Peirce chided James for violating the Ethics of Terminology, a part of what Peirce called the Ethics of Science.] It is downright bad morals so to misuse words, for it prevents philosophy from becoming a science. One of the things I urge in my forthcoming *Monist* paper [*P* 1078] is that it is an indispensable requisite of science that it should have a recognized technical vocabulary composed of words so unattractive that loose thinkers are not tempted to use them, and a recognized and legitimated way of making up new words freely when a new conception is introduced, and that it is vital for science that he who introduces a new conception should be held to have a *duty* imposed upon him to invent a sufficiently disagreeable series of words to express it. I wish you would reflect seriously upon the moral aspect of terminology.

A person who complains about the mythical Peirce's obscurity of expression will profit in many ways from this advice from the real Peirce.

One other aspect of Peirce's entry in Cattell stands forth—his obvious interest in and pursuit of mathematics. This pursuit is something the mythical Peirce undertook independently of his work in philosophy. But, said the real Peirce (in a letter to his friend Judge Francis C. Russell of Chicago): "My special business is to bring mathematical exactitude—I mean *modern* mathematical exactitude into philosophy—and to apply the ideas of mathematics in philosophy. . . ." Peirce's doctrine of exact philosophy, he explained, "is that all danger of error in philosophy will be reduced to a minimum by treating the problem as mathematically as possible, that is, by constructing some sort of diagram representing that which is supposed to be open to the observation of every scientific intelligence, and thereupon mathematically—that is, intuitionally—deducing the consequences of that hypothesis." In other places we find that mathematical thought equals diagrammatic thought, and as a method, it precedes those normally associated with philosophy, at least in the classification of the sciences the real Peirce made. Hence, Peirce, the profound student of methodeutic, is telling us that in order to practice what would be genuine philosophy, we need to practice a general kind of mathematical method in which experiments and observations are performed upon actual or imaginary diagrams.

Peirce's name is associated today with something called semiotics, but again, this is the mythical Peirce. The real guy, consistent with the doctrine of the ethics of terminology, called his work semeiotic (pronounced seem-eye-OH-tick, which means it is pronounced in English much like it is pronounced in German [*Semiotik*] and French [*sémiotique*]). In the mythical world, some persons seem to regard this aspect of Peirce as a handy little chunk that can be chopped away, ground up, and sprinkled about to provide a distinctive flavor. In reality, if semeiotic is broken away from the methodeutic trunk, it becomes some kind of contemporary semiotics, and something different. In *MS* 798 (circa 1897), Peirce tells us that semeiotic is "the quasi-necessary, or formal, doctrine of signs. By describing the doctrine as 'quasi-necessary,' or formal, I mean that we observe the characters of such signs as we know, and from such an observation, by a process which I will not object to naming Abstraction, we are led to statements, eminently fallible, and therefore in one sense by no means necessary, as to what *must be* the characters of all signs used by a 'scientific' intelligence, that is to say, by an intelligence capable of learning by experience. As to that process of abstraction, it is itself a sort of observation."

This often-quoted passage takes on a new light if one examines it in terms of our discussion thus far. First, consider that the entire description of semeiotic is based on the notion of a "scientific intelligence," which, briefly put, is an intelligence functioning according to the ethics and standards and general principles of science, which items are the object of study in methodeutic. Thus, the "must be" of this passage is an ethical one, not one from formalistic logic, or from metaphysics. As one or more scientific intelligences begin to *observe* signs in action in scientific intelligence, by means of mathematical (diagrammatic) methods, an account, eminently fallible, hence eminently testable, of the real nature of signs, is developed. Notice how the whole thing arises out of methodeutic and mathematics, not out of philosophy in the contemporary sense of the word. That is to say, some scholars have interpreted this passage to mean that Peirce's "must be" is a philosopher's way of telling us what logically has to be the case in "sign-use by a scientific intelligence." But such an interpretation is exactly backwards. Peirce is telling us here that we observe sign-use in scientific intelligences, looking for the general principles of what scientifically has to be the case in such sign-usage. And mathematics will be crucial and basic in that undertaking. Peirce has elsewhere told us exactly that his "study of the formal laws of signs [is] a study guided by mathematics and by the familiar facts of everyday experience and by no other science whatever."

Moreover, notice that only scientific intelligences can be semioticians. Thus, if you ever were to meet a semiotician so-called who would be unable to make a mind change, you would know that this is not a genuine semiotician, at least in the sense of the word meant by the genuine Peirce. This is to say that semioticians (students of semeiosis) are scientific intelligences (users of scientific methodeutic) who are studying semeiosis(sign)-use-by-scientific-intelligence in order to develop and confirm hypotheses about whatever formal (quasi-necessary) laws might be detectable in such semeiosis(sign)-use, just as a chemist (a user of scientific methodeutic) might seek to develop and confirm hypotheses about the laws of chemical combination. To complete the analogy by showing that chemical combination, and other natural phenomena studied by physical science, is, according to the real Peirce's view, itself a vast scientific intelligence, is a debt for which I can only give a promissory note. It is important to note that in this situation it is scientific methodeutic as used by a semiotician that brings, through hypotheses and experimentation, an understanding of the laws and regularities of semeiosis. That this basis is the correct one for his semeiotic is reinforced by the latter part of the above quoted *MS* 798: "To speak summarily, and to use a symbol of abbreviation, rather than an analytical and iconical idea, we may say that the purpose of signs—which is the purpose of thought—is to bring truth to expression. The law under which a sign must be true is the law of inference; and the signs of a scientific intelligence must, above all other conditions, be such as to lend themselves to inference. Hence, the illative relation is the primary and paramount semiotic relation." From all this, I conclude that Peirce thought that in order to have a science of semeiotic, it would have to rely on a knowledge and use of logic (methodeutic), "the doctrine of truth, its nature, and the manner in which it is to be discovered"; and that this required reliance and use connects semeiotic with the entire Peircean effort in methodeutic, especially mathematical methodeutic, and all the ramifications of that.

Indeed, understanding Peirce's mathematics and his methodeutic is *essential* for understanding his entire philosophy. But most scholars, particularly philosophers, have neglected Peirce's mathematical work. Small wonder, then, that there is no mention of mathematics by most students of the mythical Peirce's semeiotic. That the key to understanding Peirce lies in his mathematical and scientific works is a principle that I have elsewhere called Eisele's Law, after Carolyn Eisele who first established it beyond reasonable doubt.

In brief, what conclusion did Peirce reach in his lifelong pursuit of methodeutic? It seems, in brief, that Peirce arrived at what I would call a unified theory of objective method, a theory that deals with all the sciences, with mathematics, with philosophy, and even religion by means of common principles and terminology. Yes, the real Peirce was deeply religious, unlike the mythical Peirce who got religion only when he became senile. Peirce's account of religion is unique, and one of the great untapped resources in his vast corpus of writing. It could be a means for accomplishing a rapprochement between religion and science in our own day.

Finally, the mythical Peirce is fragmentary, inconsistent, and unsystematic, a man who constantly changed his mind, who was able to get only a little published. The real Peirce published, in his lifetime, material that appeared on about 12,000 pages! The real Peirce was a master stylist of the English language and an indefatigable worker whose manuscripts run to some 80,000 sheets; all those of scientific relevance are published in microfilm and generally available for study. The real Peirce was as systematic and consistent a thinker as ever there has been, and his non-fragmentariness can be seen if one will read all of what he wrote, as he wrote it, instead of reading only the part that escaped some editor's knife. The real Peirce will also shine through if his mathematical and scientific works are consulted instead of being largely ignored as they have been. A convenient account of how to gain access to the massive writings of the real Peirce is now available.

Perhaps the foregoing can help us answer yet one other puzzling aspect about Peirce's career as a historical figure. Why has he, in view of his obvious greatness, been so neglected, misunderstood, and ill-treated as an object of study? That is, why has there been such a grotesque and popular mythical Peirce, so separated from the genuine one? Of course, all great historical figures have their mythical and their genuine personae, but there is a powerful difference in the two in this case. I surmise that it is because contemporary philosophy (and contemporary intellectual life) *is* sometimes hampered by what Peirce called "philodoxy" (love or pursuit of an orthodoxy). Contemporary students sometimes lament that Peirce changed his mind (only a philodoxer would complain about learning from experience), some complain that he is difficult (philodoxers make the same complaint about biology or chemistry), some say he speaks obscurely (scientific terminology will be opaque to anyone who reads it with ordinary language concepts only), and there are gripes about the length of his writings (philodoxers are usually lazy and even sometimes avoid original sources, preferring a convenient secondary description). If one couples the contemporary tendency toward philodoxy with our age's confirmed nominalism and relativism, and if one remembers that Peirce's inquiries *led* him to be a universalist, a scientist, and a realist, then we can be amazed and cheered that his work has received such attention it has gotten so far.

Perhaps we now have an outline of the question, "Who was Peirce?" Now what should be said about our homage to him? Surely his memory deserves it if for no other reason than the massive accomplishments of his life. But we can respect his work for another important reason—the Peircean corpus, because of the originality and foresight of his genius, can aid us in our own time with issues still unsolved, issues which he addressed and about which he wrote. Unfortunately his writings have, to a large extent, been as if buried in a time capsule. We are just now gaining full access to them, and they in effect add the input of a distinguished and talented older colleague to the problems that face us as a civilization today. Thus, let us respect him as a predecessor on whose shoulders we can sometimes stand, who is worthy of our accurate study, and let us praise him in the only terms he would have wanted: "Well done, thou good and faithful man of science."

Toward an Understanding of Peirce's Master Argument

Kenneth Laine Ketner

"Draw me a picture."
(Walker Percy to Kenneth L. Ketner,
May 9, 1987)

In working with Peirce's writings for several years, l believe I have detected an outline of what I shall identify as his master argument. By that phrase I mean the basic thrust of the way he would attempt to justify on a large scale the results of his decades of thinking about philosophy and science. I shall outline about half of it here. I present this as a hypothesis, and in outline form. Nor will I provide as many references as a full-scale study would require, but perhaps what I offer will be plausible. I conclude with a few remarks about some possible consequences.

First Peirce thought it was fruitless to wonder from what point we *must* begin our study of philosophy:

[We] cannot start from any other condition than that in which we actually are. To attempt such a solution of the problem as Hegel has done, seems like going to China by proceeding first due north to the pole and thence due south to China—a method which certainly has the merit of being highly systematic, and also has a pleasing paradoxical appearance, but which would present certain inconveniences in practice. We really *believe* many things, and, therefore, philosophic doubts upon such matters must be mere pretence and can result in nothing but a show of demonstration of things really taken for granted. Nothing can be gained by gratuitous and fictitious doubts, nor can any conclusions be reached without premisses. Now whatever is doubted by men whom there is reason to think competent judges is so far doubtful; and, therefore, a certain shade of doubt will hang over almost all psychological or very general propositions. It is, therefore, proper to rest philosophy—upon what every real science must rest—namely those ordinary facts of which (in a general way) we are actually assured and therefore *cannot*, if we would, mistrust. Moreover, to hold your own system to be certain when intelligent, candid, and well-informed persons cannot agree with you, is a thing to be ashamed of and to be eradicated, as a sin; and on that principle metaphysics must be held to be very uncertain. Thus, the strictly demonstrative style of argumentation usually adopted by philosophers has utterly failed of its purposes, and we might as well content ourselves with such probable inferences as support astronomy and chemistry, since if we can only reduce the uncertainty of metaphysics to a hundred times that appertaining to those sciences, we shall have much to congratulate ourselves upon. (*MS* 932)

From this we gain knowledge both of Peirce's base of operations, and of his first sortie. The base is simply the set of beliefs we find that we already have as we enter into philosophical duties. What are here called "ordinary facts" acquired the label of "Common Sense" in his later works.

The second moment arrives with doubt, a conflict in our present beliefs. On such an occasion, we are faced with the task of freely choosing a method which will take us out of doubt. This choice is an existential one (a person-creating choice); Peirce clearly understood that, and even expressed it in language that would please both French and Danish existentialists. The method Peirce chose for all the doubts that might arise in science and philosophy (a subclass of science, according to him) is generally known today as the hypothetico-deductive method. He referred to this as the method of science, and he regarded it as the general method for all science, from mathematics to medicine to metaphysics. I shall refer to it as the objective method. In effect, that choice set the tone for all of Peirce's work, especially in philosophy where his efforts can be seen as a lifelong search for an understanding of the nature of objective method and its consequences. Peirce thought that the alternative to the method of objective inquiry was some form of egocentric arbitrariness. An elementary concomitant of objective inquiry is the will to learn that which one does not now know. This is a factor that has important consequences, reaching even into religious questions. Peirce's initial methodological efforts produced an early set of now famous results, recorded in *The Journal of Speculative Philosophy* series of 1868–69.

As Peirce applied the methods of "astronomy and chemistry" to questions in philosophy, he soon discovered that there we possess no intuitive power of finding ultimate premises. The likely hypothesis recommended by that discovery is that no cognition is absolute—one can always ask for (and get) a cognition prior to the one under consideration. From such thoughts came Peirce's dictum that there is no premiss that could not be considered as a conclusion from other premisses in a later interpretation of the matter. In other words, there is no logically first cognition, and there is no cognition that cannot be additionally interpreted. Upon what, then, does one rely? One depends upon the self-corrective nature of objective method, and upon all those beliefs that are not now in doubt, being careful to remember that one is fallible. Eugene Rochberg-Halton has given an eloquent account of this and related matters in *Meaning and Modernity: Social Theory in the Pragmatic Attitude*.

The next crucial moment in Peirce's approach is often unnoticed, perhaps because it usually is implicit and seldom openly mentioned. Here are two examples I have found:

> Whatever we know, we know only by its relations, and in so far as we know its relations. (*MSS* 931, 396)

> In reality, every fact is a relation. Thus, that an object is blue consists of the peculiar regular action of that object on human eyes. This is what should be understood by the "relativity of knowledge." Not only is every fact really a relation, but your thought of the fact *implicitly* represents it as such. Thus, when you think "this is blue," the demonstrative "this" shows you are thinking of something just brought up to your notice; while the adjective shows that you recognize a familiar idea as applicable to it. Thus, your thought, when explicated, develops into the thought of a fact concerning this thing and concerning the character of blueness. (*CP* 3.416)

The thesis coming at this juncture is: What we can know are relations—all knowledge is of relations. The second citation above shows that this probably arose in Peirce's mind as a hypothesis suggested by thought or language, and through reflection upon those ordinary facts not now in doubt. If we can call the primacy of the objective method Peirce's fundamental methodological hypothesis, his proposal that relations are what there is for us to know could be identified as his fundamental notion of the content of knowledge (or perhaps as his primary thesis about the basis of intelligibility since Peirce urged that relations are really "out there," not just in our minds or in our language). At this point, he had a method and a subject matter (relations) upon which to focus it.

His next step involved use of a technique he learned from biology and chemistry. (In one sense, Peirce's career can be described as that of an adaptive methodologist: one who specializes in applying methods from one science into likely areas in other sciences, particularly philosophy.) This was a way of classifying, which he had learned while studying biology with Louis Agassiz at Harvard. He referred to this as "Cenopythagoreanism" and described it this way: "In classification generally, it may fairly be said to be established, if it ever was doubted, that Form, in the sense of structure, is of far higher significance than Material. Valency is the basis of all external structure; and where indecomposibility precludes internal structure, as in the classification of elementary concepts—valency ought to be made the first consideration. I term [this] the doctrine of Cenopythagoreanism" (*MS* 292.34ff.; compare *MS* 292.98).

"Valency" is also borrowed from chemistry—recall how a molecule with one free ion is said to have Valency One or is a monad, how those with two loose ions are dyads, with three triads, and so on.

Peirce, in effect, generalized the notion of chemical valency to encompass the valency of all relations. That can be illustrated in this fashion. Consider that the black dots below are some molecules, while the lines emerging from them stand for free ions, in effect points of possible connections with other loose ions:

FIGURE I. Diagrams for monads, dyads, and triads.

Now, instead of molecules, let the dots represent any relation content whatever (of the internal working of which we assume no knowledge), while the lines show places in the relation's external form where appropriate kinds of connections with other relational loose ends might connect. In sentences about relations, for instance, we note that "_____ is a Bolivian" is a monad, "_____ caused _____" is a dyad, and "_____ represents _____ to _____" is a triad. If we further generalize these sentence forms by letting the words that remain turn into place markers for any content appropriate to relations of that valency, we get diagrams in the fashion of those of Figure 1.

These diagrams Peirce called "valental graphs," or just graphs. With some clues from topology, he drew the following conclusions about how they could combine: "Every graph has a definite valency. . . . A number of dyads can only make a chain, and the compound will still be a dyad . . . unless the two ends are joined making it a medad [zero valent]. . . . But a number of triads can be joined so as to make a compound of any valency not exceeding the number of triads by more than two, and any odd number giving any odd valency under the same restriction. This shows that there are five natural classes of forms of graphs, namely medads, monads, dyads, triads, and higher perissids [odd valents], tetrads and higher artiads [even valents]" (*MS* 292.33ff.). This remark is but one of many in which we see Peirce applying mathematical method to philosophy or logic. He thought mathematics was the first science, and he regarded it as essential in his entire system of science, especially so in semeiotic. If we recall that relations are what there is to be known, and add on these findings from valency studies, we find Peirce concluding that there are but three natural classes of irreducible forms of relations: the forms for monadic relations, dyadic relations, and triadic relations. That is to say, with the graphical system Peirce considered, he found that: (1) monads cannot be combined to construct relations with dyadic form; (2) dyads cannot be combined to construct relations with triadic form; (3) but with triads we can construct the forms of medads, monads, or dyads; (4) moreover, relations having the form of tetrads or greater can be constructed using only triads.

Peirce thought this (and other considerations) lent strength to the hypothesis that all relations can be classified according to three natural kinds, parallel to the *external forms* of monadic, dyadic, and triadic relations. (Remember, he was practicing philosophy as a hypothetical science, so he did not offer proofs in any strong sense of that word.) Hence, he concluded that all relations (which is all that there is to know) fall into natural categories, which he called by the quite abstract names of Firstness, Secondness, and Thirdness (or First, Seconds, and Thirds). My proposal is that the vexed question of the nature of Peirce's categories can be answered in the way sketched above. A tempting, but I think erroneous, understanding is that his categories are kinds based upon content of some type—for instance, Firsts as all the qualities or feelings or properties in the cosmos. If I am correct, a First is not the feeling in its content, but a First is the external form of a feeling or any item that has but one means of connecting to a "free ion" in the external form (valency) of some other relation.

The next step in the master argument is to notice that thought is dialogic, or sign-like in nature, and that if one classifies it according to the external form of the kind of relation it is, it falls into the Third category. Peirce noticed early in his career that it seems likely that all thought is in signs. At this point, we add the result from above, that relations which are Thirds cannot be reduced to combinations of Seconds exclusively. In more traditional philosophical language, that would mean that thought (or mind) cannot be reduced to any number or combination of efficient causes (mechanical causes). From these considerations, it follows (among other important things) that all attempts to analyze or explain thought (the valency of which is triadic) *exclusively* in terms of factors that exhibit only dyadic valency—items such as materials, or finite algorithms, or efficient causes (chemical reactions, mechanical interactions, electrical discharges)—will fail.

Peirce's methodological pursuits culminated in his semeiotic, which is a grand hypothesis about the nature of signs and Thirds. Using his tentative findings in semeiotic about the nature of relations and methods for studying the same, he probed further into metaphysics, the traditional areas of philosophy. It is noteworthy that Peirce did not enter metaphysical study until he had first assured himself, to the extent possible, of a sound method in the form of semeiotic. This is a large subject in Peirce's writing, and many important passages are still not published.

The thesis about the irreducibility of Thirds is basic to Peirce's approach and is one of his most distinctive results. Probably some readers question it, so it might be wise to devote some additional space to it here.

The fundamental distinction of semeiotic is that between sign action (intelligent action, triadic action) and dynamic action (brute action, mechanical action), which is only a slightly altered form of the way we have been discussing the matter (in terms of valency). The account that follows is adapted from *MS* 318 and *MS* L327.5, Peirce's letter to Signor Papini, dated April 10, 1907.

Consider dyadic action between three events, A, B, and C. A may produce B, and, in turn, at a later time B may produce C. But the fact that C is about to be produced by B has no effect upon the production of B by A. Of course, an intelligent agent, for instance a physician, could intervene to have such an effect, but that would spoil the assumption that this is an example of dyadic action only. On the other hand, if we assume an intelligent or triadic relationship among these three events, we have A producing B as a means for production of C. Suppose an infantry officer (A) who wants a squad to place their rifles on the ground (C) gives the command (B) "Ground arms!" The action of the officer's will is not strictly dyadic, for if he thought the soldiers to be deaf, or recruits, or Chinese, he would not utter this command as a means likely to produce rifle-butts-placed-on-the-ground. The grounding of arms (C) in this example is an interpretant. Interpretants are the kinds of effects peculiar or proper to triadic action (intelligent action, sign action).

Another way to see the difference between dyadic and triadic relation forms is to consider the meaning of denying a triadic relational form. It would be sufficient to deny [consider the following lower-case letters in subscript, as commonly used in mathematical formulas] S_{abc} (a sold b to c) if one could show that there was only a chain of dyadic causes here, for instance that c forced a at rifle point to sign a deed for b, after which point c presented the deed in a courthouse as proof of ownership of b. If we subsequently came to know these underhanded events, we would say, "It is not the case that S_{abc}." Notice also that this pattern seems to be preserved in the case of dyads, for it is sufficient to establish the negation of the dyad "A causes B" if we can show that A and B are independent or monadic events (A happens and B does not, or A does not happen and B does). So, we seem to have found but another difference between the forms for dyads and triads: positing some relevant independent monads is sufficient to deny a dyad, positing some relevant dyads is sufficient to deny a triad. Yet another difference occurs to me, but I only conjecture it. It is well known that dyadic relations can be symmetric, or reflexive, or transitive (or all of the above, as in the case of "_____ is identical with _____"). I am unable to see how any triadic relation could be either symmetric, or reflexive, or transitive (but that may simply be a personal inadequacy). The reason that this seems to be the case lies in the appearance that these three properties require an even valency in the relation to which they are to be applied.

Now if we try to represent sign (triadic) action in the way that has become virtually traditional in some circles (Figure 2), we will fly in the face of all of Peirce's considerations.

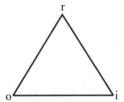

FIGURE 2. Sign action pictured as triangle.

This drawing amounts to stating that the relation between object, represent-amen, and interpretant is exclusively constituted by the conjunction of three dyadic relations, *or*, *ri*, and *oi*. That is but another way of attempting to analyze sign action (triadic sign relations) exclusively in terms of dyads.

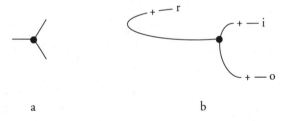

a   b

FIGURE 3. An abstract and a concrete sign relation.

Figure 3a shows the irreducible external form of a triadic relation in Peirce's pictorial manner. Figure 3b shows how three entities (whether they be things, ideas, habits, persons) can come to be related in an irreducibly triadic manner. Moreover, how we use a sign relation may in part be dependent upon how we "look into" it, our perspective we might say. For instance, if I am the receiver of a sign, I ask "To which of my habits of interpretation is this sign intended to appeal?" If I am the sender, I ask "How shall I constitute the nature of this representamen so that it will activate the one habit of interpretation in the receiver that I want to be activated?" If I am a representamen (as, for example, the Queen of England could be seen to be, on some occasions), I might worry about the proper use of my capacity to bring two persons or two social movements together. In all these cases, however, the secret of success, it seems to me, is to realize that there is an irreducibly triadic element, and that such a factor is logically primitive.

How then can we analyze thought, or signs, or mind, or communication? In this era, we seem to have an urge to analyze. That seems innocent enough. But if "analyze" always means "reduce to dyadic forms," then a hidden (and perhaps false) assumption accompanies the use of the word. If "analyze" means "come to have a better understanding of x," then the answer seems to be that we must analyze signs (triadic relations) by means of other signs or triadic relations. In particular, if there is a matter about which we lack understanding, we can use a set of relations we comprehend reasonably well to model the relations in the area of relative ignorance (a relative pun). Stated in a very abstract fashion, this is Peirce's method of diagrammatic thought, a technique he originally developed out of mathematical considerations, but adapted for other problem areas.

We might pause to ask at this point (following the lead of Walker Percy in his The Message in the Bottle), by way of some possibly useful speculation, why do we know relatively little about phenomena such as language and mind (if I can shock contemporary psychologists by using one of their unpopular but founding concepts)? The answer consistent with Peirce's approach would be that we lack progress in these areas because, by and large, scholars are (so to speak) trying to write poems by firing ink-loaded howitzers at stacks of newsprint. We are using the wrong methods, in other words. This is not to deny that we learn many useful and relevant things by studying the physiology and chemistry of the brain. But we will lack the whole story about the mind unless we study it according to diagrammatic thought—for a Third, about which we are relatively ignorant can only be fully understood in terms of Thirds we already partially understand. Where are any to be found that we already partially understand? They are among those "ordinary facts" or "common sense beliefs" that we do not now doubt, and which have evolved with our species over millennia. Peirce, by the way, saw the evolution of these beliefs as itself an extended kind of cosmic objective inquiry (but this is a deep pothole in the road of inquiry).

In diagrammatic method, Peirce preferred visual diagrams (pictures), probably because they appealed to sight, which is our most evolved sense. He also recognized diagrams based on auditory or other sensory channels, for example, speech as an auditory diagram (see *CP* 3.418). But he thought sight was probably best adapted for detecting new features of relational patterns in diagrams that model Thirds, which are presently not well understood and which are under study. To "draw a picture," then, is to proceed in the way that Peirce would recommend in response to the question "How then can we study Thirds if dyadic considerations alone cannot exclusively handle the load?" If we add here that Peirce recognized algebras or other arrays of symbols as also being visual diagrams, then we can state that mathematics, as the science that models relations in areas under study, would be among the finer tools for "drawing pictures" that mankind has yet developed. Peirce said as much in regard to semeiotic (*CP* 2.227).

But Peirce did not limit the concept of visual diagram to sketches or marks. He clearly allowed for mental diagrams, in a way that would make a behaviorist blush, as being important intellectual tools (for example, see *MS* 798). Some contemporary psychologists, such as Ned Block in his book *Imagery*, in a way quite consistent with Peirce's ideas, have made good empirical progress on the notion of mental diagrams. But I think there are even further consequences which we can extract here. The principles of diagrammatic thought extend even into art. An exploration of this notion for visual art may be found in Frances Scott's dissertation *C.S. Peirce's System of Science and an Application to the Visual Arts* (Texas Tech University).

But it seems to me that we could easily and profitably extend these insights to nonvisual art; for instance, we could think of a novel as a tool for producing mental diagrams on the part of readers. These are then available to readers who can perhaps learn something about an area of relative ignorance (perhaps within their person) by exploring the relations that are partially understood within the world (the diagram, the relational patterns) of a novel. So perhaps we could say that a novel is a large sign (a Third on a large scale) that can be a tool in diagrammatic thought, the technique whereby one Third that is relatively well understood is used to model, by means of mental diagrams, some relations (often personal ones) that are not as well understood. If so, novels might be outstanding tools of "analysis."

The Importance of Religion for Peirce

Kenneth Laine Ketner

This essay is a sketch of a proposed answer to these questions: What is the place of religion in Peirce's works, and what was its importance for him?

First, to find its place, we might well begin by considering his classification of the sciences, for as he stated in 1904, as cited in "A Brief Intellectual Autobiography by Charles Sanders Peirce" (*American Journal of Semiotics*, 1983): "In order to understand [my] doctrine, which has little in common with those of modern schools, it is necessary to know, first of all, how [I classify] the sciences." The classification has three broad divisions: science of research, science of review, and practical science. Religion is not found in the last two categories. So we turn to the first one.

Here is an outline of the sciences of research:

    I. Mathematics
    II. Philosophy
       1. Phaneroscopy
       2. Normative Science
          A. Esthetics
          B. Ethics

C. Semeiotic (Logic)
    a. Speculative
       Grammar
    b. Critic
    c. Methodeutic
  3. Metaphysics
III. Idioscopy or Special Science
    (Physics and Psychics)

This classification, and related discussions, show that Peirce did indeed have a system, but of science, not of philosophy, as that is now usually understood. In other words, trying to look at Peirce just with the attitudes of contemporary philosophy is an outstanding way to misunderstand him, for (among other considerations) his word "philosophy" stands for but one of many sciences, contrary to our contemporary meaning for that word, which for most persons, calls to mind nonscience.

Do we find religion situated within the sciences of research? Paul Weiss (*CP* 6, editorial note, p. v) has answered "Yes": "Metaphysics, as the third of the philosophic disciplines, has, according to Peirce, three branches—ontology, religion, and cosmology (see *CP* 1.192)." If we look at the paragraph Weiss cited, we don't find the word "religion" there at all. We do find that there is a place for religious metaphysics: "Metaphysics may be divided into, i, General Metaphysics, or Ontology; ii, Psychical, or Religious, Metaphysics, concerned chiefly with the questions of 1, God, 2, Freedom, 3, Immortality; and iii, Physical Metaphysics, which discusses the real nature of time, space, laws of nature, matter, etc." (*CP* 1.192). However, within Peirce's system, equating "religious metaphysics" with "religion" as Weiss did, is a misidentification. That is true because religious metaphysics is metaphysics, and is thereby a science and not religion. The place of religion, in Peirce's work, is outside of science, a point he mentioned on several occasions. Something that is not a science could not be a part of metaphysics, which for Peirce is a science.

So, now we have some information about the place of religion for Peirce—it is outside of science. That is a large area: Exactly where in logical space outside of science is religion to be found, according to Peirce? It is a presupposition of science (which we must remember is basically a method). This is clearly implicit in a draft of his proposed Adirondack Summer School Lectures (*MS* 1334): "The men of the third group who are comparatively few cannot conceive at all a life for enjoyment and look down upon a life of action. Their purpose is to worship God in the development of ideas and of truth. These are the men of science." Peirce gave a reason why religion is presupposed by science in one of his letters to Lady Welby published in *Semiotic and Significs*:

> Every true man of science, i.e., every man belonging to a social group all the members of which sacrifice all the ordinary motives of life to their desire to make their beliefs concerning one subject conform to verified judgments of perception together with sound reasoning, and who therefore really believes the universe to be governed by reason, or in other words by God—but who does not explicitly recognize that he believes in God—has Faith in God, according to my use of the term Faith. For example I knew a scientific man who devoted his last years to reading theology in hopes of coming to a belief in God, but who never could in the least degree come to a consciousness of having the least belief of the sort, yet passionately pursued that very mistaken means of attaining his heart's supreme desire. He, according to me, was a shining example of Faith in God. For to believe in reasoning about phenomena is to believe that they are governed by reason, that is, by God. That to my mind is a high and wholesome belief. (p. 75)

To be a bit more specific, religion is a part of that set of beliefs Peirce described as common sense. This whole collection of beliefs he described as "original" in the sense that all human beings have them, and that they have been developed in the species through long evolution. Such beliefs we cannot discard through false or "paper" doubts. All attempts to doubt them fail—we find that we simply believe them. The collection of common sensical beliefs, while not itself science, stands under the method of science which Peirce described in detail as he elaborated his system. And, as philosophy of religion (or religious metaphysics) is the theory of that of which religion is the living instance, so critical common sense (under critic in Peirce's system) is the theory of the living set of beliefs Peirce called common sense.

But, besides being nonscience, what is religion like, on his account? He gives rather detailed remarks about that, and from all periods of his career. According to his writings, religion seems to have at least these properties:

(1) In an individual, it is a sort of sentiment, which is

(2) an obscure perception of something in the All, with which the individual acknowledges a relationship, to that Absolute, of the individual's self, as a relative being.

(3) It is not only an individual matter—like every species of reality, it is essentially a social and public affair.

(4) It is the idea of a whole church welding its members together into one organic whole, an idea that grows across generations.

(5) This idea claims a supremacy in the determination of all private and public conduct.

(6) Only individuals who have had religious experience(s) can fully appreciate the nature of religion.

(7) Religion intensely true to itself, particularly in view of No. 6, will become animated by the scientific spirit, not as a servant or subservient of science, but as a religion with a bolder confidence in itself.

(8) Theory is *not* religion; orthodoxy (following formulae) is *not* religion.

(9) Religion is a way of life, motivated by fundamental beliefs, strengthened by religious experience.

(10) The Way of Life of Religion is based upon the law of love, which is "love God and love your neighbor."

(11) Following this supreme commandment of the "Buddhisto-Christian" religion, generalize, complete the whole system of religion, until continuity results, and distinct individuals weld together.

(12) In fulfilling this command, man prepares himself for transmutation into a new form of life, the joyful Nirvana in which the discontinuities of his will shall have all but disappeared.

Was Peirce a Christian? Because of his strong antipathy to theology (see *CP* 6.105, for instance), and because of his disregard for orthodoxy, surely he was not. He did make this self-description late in life (*MS* 318):

"[Pragmatism] must honestly acknowledge the uncertainty of metaphysical doctrine, while religion calls for an entire belief of the whole soul. . . . I beg leave to say, by the way, that I am myself a miserably unworthy follower of Jesus. . . ." Christians are a subset of followers of Jesus. Jesus was a notorious enemy of religious orthodoxy, and in this respect, very similar to Buddha. I find Peirce's religious practice to resemble closely that of some of the early (second-century) followers of Jesus known as Gnostics, especially the disciples of Valentinus (c. A.D. 140), Heracleon (c. A.D. 160) in particular. So perhaps he could be described as a Valentinian Gnostic.

Was Peirce a theist in his religious metaphysics? Vincent Potter, S.J., and Donna Orange think he was. It is clear that he was a mystic (see Orange's *Peirce's Conception of God: A Developmental Study*, pp. 45–46), and he often referred to Buddha, perhaps never with more admiration than in a letter of March 1897 to his close friend William James as found in the James Papers at Harvard University: "[In the last few years] a new world of which I knew nothing . . . has been disclosed to me, the world of misery. . . . Much have I learned of life and the world, throwing strong lights upon philosophy in these years. Undoubtedly, its tendency is to make one value the spiritual more, but not an abstract spirituality. . . . [It] increases the sense of awe with which one regards Gautama Booda." My own hypothesis is that Peirce may be better understood as a pantheist and a Buddhist (or Valentinian, which comes to about the same thing). This is a vexed question, which cannot be decided here.

What is the importance of religion for Peirce? I advance the hypothesis that it is extremely important, not simply in a personal sense, but as a key for understanding his whole career. Consider this comment found in the essays of Max H. Fisch in *Peirce, Semeiotic, and Pragmatism*: "I must count it as one of the most fortunate circumstances of life which the study of scientific philosophy in a religious spirit has steeped in its joy, that I was able to know something of the inwardness of the early growth of several of the great ideas of the nineteenth century" (p. 101). This seems to suggest that he regarded right religion as even more important than science. Other evidence for its importance is that Peirce was always mentioning some aspect of religion in almost all contexts. This was a consistent trend throughout his career. One of the noteworthy instances came early when Peirce announced his "new theory of immortality" in 1866 (*CP* 1.502).

Does Peirce's practice of religion, and his account of it, have any importance for us? Probably so. His life and work seem to suggest a universalizable approach to religion which, if it were more widely known, might be in the avant garde of contemporary practice. It seems to show that religion is consistent with general scientific attitudes, or the scientific spirit, as Peirce phrased it. That is, Peirce may have worked out, at least in outline form, the nature of the proper relation between science and religion, a problem that vexes us yet. Perhaps one of the principal features of that relationship would be that the spirit of science-in-the-best-sense and the spirit of religion-in-the-best-sense are one and the same spirit.

Another important contribution implicit in this matter is to force us who seek a deeper understanding of Peirce's works to consider that we have not fully understood him if we only grasp his system of science, including as it does mathematics and philosophy and all the other sciences. Since religion is not a science, and Peirce's work includes religion, we must also comprehend that nonscience. When we have finally understood all of Peirce's work, what will we call his total output? Not science, for it includes more than science—not philosophy, for that is but one of many sciences, and not even the most basic science, a place that was reserved for mathematics. Certainly we could not call his work religion, for science would thereby be excluded. Perhaps we should refer to his whole output as being a way of wisdom, and refer to Peirce's life not only as an intellectual one or a religious one, but as a kind of spiritual odyssey that includes all of the above, an odyssey that brought Peirce, for about the last third of his life, a more restful maturity, something like the joyful Nirvana of minimum discontinuities mentioned earlier.

Novel Science: or, How contemporary social science is not well and why literature and semeiotic provide a cure

Kenneth Laine Ketner

The social and human sciences are in a sorry state today. You don't have to take my word for it. Consider some others who have reached the same conclusion.

Walker Percy's Antinomy

For instance, consider Walker Percy's antinomy, stated in its most general form in his "Culture: The Antinomy of the Scientific Method" in *The Message in the Bottle*: "The functional method of the sciences is a nonradical method of knowing because, while it recognizes only functional linkages, it presupposes other kinds of reality, the intersubjectivity of scientists and their assertions, neither of which are space-time linkages and neither of which can be grasped by the functional method. Therefore, when the functional method is elevated to a total organon of reality and other cognitive claims denied, the consequence must be an antinomy, for a nonradical instrument is being required to construe the more radical reality which it presupposes but does not understand" (p. 240). I'm fallibly certain that I understand what Percy (the first hero of this story) meant by the distinction between radical and nonradical methods of knowing. It goes something like this. A radical science is one in which no limits are placed upon the kinds of knowledge sought by scientific intelligences. Thus, chemistry would be a nonradical science; for chemists seek only chemical knowledge and, as professional chemists, have no interest in knowledge about art, religion, psychiatry, or literature. Thus, in a nonradical science such as chemistry, when a question about human intersubjectivity arises, chemists using the functional method can only say, "We don't study that." But, human and social sciences would be radical, at least in regard to the inclusion of human intersubjectivity or other issues involving human nature, for that is precisely something they *must* study.

The phrase "functional method" here means the technique of conceiving "dependent variables" E as a function f of "independent variables" C. We could express that as:

E is a function of C, or
$E = f(C)$,
or in plain American,
C causes E to be the way it is.

It should be clear that the functional method is one that presupposes that all explanations of phenomena being considered will be given exclusively in terms of functional or causal statements or facts. Moreover, a practitioner of such a method does not ask whether there are other kinds of facts or data in the phenomena to be studied.

Culture, Percy argued, is largely a tissue of assertions. That appears to be obvious if one conceives an assertion as a kind of communication event, and even more evident if one is considering scientific culture, the community of persons capable of learning from experience. This brings us to an interesting and shocking fact. *Assertions and other intersubjective communication events, including those among scientists, are inexplicable if one's explanatory resources are self-limited solely to information about causal or functional linkages.* Naturally, you want the evidence for this claim. I promise you will have it, but for the moment, let us be clear about the antinomy.

It occurs when in science a strictly causal method is focused upon cultural realities such as assertions or communication events. We should carefully note that it is not a difficulty of science as such, but of science conducted exclusively according to a particular methodological conception; for reasons which will become clear, let us refer to a science, *limited by its practitioners* to strictly functional or causal resources, under the name of Dyadic Science. Such a science would only find functional data, for it would have *limited itself* to seeking only such phenomena. Percy's antinomy, a fundamental but heretofore hidden internal contradiction, becomes apparent as the habit (widespread in the physical sciences) of limiting one's explanatory resources to those of dyadic science is carried into the social or human sciences where it becomes self-defeating. For cultural realities are inexplicable solely in terms of functional or causal information. The antinomy arises equally whether the social realities studied are those of scientific culture itself or of some other culture conceived as alien.

Here is another way to grasp the point. Imagine there is a particular society of scientists who have a formal initiation requirement for every scientific intelligence wanting to join their community. Suppose you have just been initiated and, like all beginners, you have signed an oath that you will always use only the causal, functional methodological conceptions of dyadic science in studying any real phenomenon. Soon after taking the oath, at a beer-and-pizza reception in your honor, a senior member whose hobby is repairing antique radios remarks, "Some of those old dual-function AC-battery sets from the 1940's were amazing; when run from AC, a 35Z5 was on line in series with a large dropping resistor, and the I-square R through it was unbelievable." That comment, we must carefully note, is a real phenomenon, and for certain kinds of activities it would be important to have a full understanding of it. But as a beginner, you don't understand it. What is a 35Z5? What is I-square R, and why does it seem to be so important? However, if intersubjective communication were a strictly causal matter, you should now understand the remark upon being exposed to it as a causal factor. You don't understand it. Therefore, intersubjective communication is not a strictly causal matter. Topics (such as the understanding of a fellow scientist's remark) that involve more than causal considerations cannot be fully studied by a method that is self-limited to causal processes.

That is, one might say that the life of scientists working together is a cultural or community life, which has a reality in addition to that of the phenomena these scientists are studying. So, if in our method of studying culture we limit our explanatory resources strictly to causal relations, then the culture which is essential for that very scientific community, and the general nature of science itself, would always remain a mystery. This is the unhappy result because the culture of science, its assertions and communication events, involve social phenomena other than just causal linkages. While the focus of science was nonradical, was upon nonsocial realities such as chemistry or physics or astronomy, the antinomy would probably remain unnoticed. And in such situations, it is easy for one tempted by the false doctrines of dyadic science to follow its principles. But the moment one turns the gaze of science upon human and social realities, either within science itself or within subject matters such as psychology or anthropology in which intersubjectivity and community life are obviously fundamental, Percy's antinomy must eventually work its way to the surface, like a putrid ancient winter bubble of swamp gas rising in a hot April thaw.

Alan Turing's Machine

Alan Turing's machine constitutes another testimonial about the sorry state of the social and human sciences. At the turn of the century, David Hilbert, the eminent Göttingen mathematician, expressed in his essay "Mathematical Problems" his faith that it was but a matter of time before procedures would be found in mathematics that would enable most if not all the outstanding problems of that field to be solved by means of algorithms. An algorithm is a definite procedure such that, from explicitly defined starting conditions, a clearly stated result may be obtained using a known method requiring a finite number of steps. For instance, an algorithm for obtaining ten percent of any positive number is: "Write down the number including its decimal point, then move the decimal point one place to the left; the resulting second number will be ten percent of the original number." Of course, Hilbert's dream of a general algorithmic method is precisely an example of the mechanistic functional method of dyadic science applied to mathematics.

Turing made a number of clear definitions for such algorithmic or machine methods and, through a series of insightful observations of the consequences of his definitions, showed that there are some mathematical results that cannot be obtained algorithmically, that is, by means of a deterministic machine. One might summarize it this way. Finding algorithms, or finding new computer programs, is an important task in mathematics. But Turing's results suggest that the process of finding new algorithms or of developing new theorems cannot itself be an algorithmic or automatic technique. On the contrary, it seems likely to be a procedure that requires human creativity, serendipity, experimentation, and inventiveness. In other words, mathematics is not a dyadic science.

If that is the case in mathematics, the clearest and simplest of sciences, it is likely to be the case in any science, including the social and human sciences. That is, it seems likely that there is no set of algorithms for doing all that is to be done in the social and human sciences. But how many social scientists automatically start their work by assuming a kind of algorithm or noncreative recipe, often one that involves statistical research design procedures? If social science is based upon the notion (as it is frequently assumed to be) that you got to have an algorithm to do science, social science will shoot itself in the foot, because it will begin its efforts by throwing away human creativity, experimentation, and inventiveness, both as resources used by social scientists and as factors inherent in the realities such sciences propose to study.

Dean Jonathan Swift was a great wit whose humorous sentences often penetrated to the heart of an issue better than a long theoretical essay. He described in *Gulliver's Travels* a crank-powered thinking machine he represented a Laputan professor as trying to make, then remarked: "Every one knew how laborious the usual Method is of attaining to Arts and Sciences; whereas by his Contrivance, the most ignorant Person at a reasonable Charge, and with a little bodily Labour, may write Books in Philosophy, Poetry, Politicks, Law, Mathematicks, and Theology without the least Assistance from Genius or Study." The science of Artificial Intelligence has been occupied by partisans of dyadic science. However, it now shows signs of realizing that it cannot accomplish its goals with such a self-imposed limitation which omits important non-dyadic phenomena from study. This is the principal upshot of Turing's results. It seems to me that Alan Turing and Gulliver's father came face to face with one and the same reality.

Some Problems With Statistical Social Science

Social scientists often use statistics, so if there are problems in the way such operations are carried out, that might be another reason for the sad state of affairs in social and human science. I can detect a few such general problems. Perhaps you can think of others.

First, ask yourself this: What do weather forecasters mean when they say there is an 80 percent chance of rain tomorrow? Do they mean drops four-fifths the usual size, or that we ought to carry four-fifths of an umbrella? One meteorologist commented that it meant that there were five forecasters working at the local National Weather Service office.

Here is what I think it means. From the billions of years of past history of weather events at some particular location, the weather folks have a microcosmically small sample running from, in the United States, certainly no earlier than 1492. Of all the days in the sample in which weather conditions here were like they are now, in 80 percent of them it rained the next day. Notice an important thing about that sentence: the phrase "in 80 percent of them it rained the next day" describes a property of a *sample* from the standpoint of its *collective* properties; it is not a property of any one single day from the days sampled. First one forms the sample, then one notices that the sample as a collective has certain properties. That is, fleas are small, but if I had a metric ton of live fleas in my back yard, you would say that Ketner's *collection* of fleas is large. Suppose someone argued that Ketner's fleas weigh a ton, and this is one of them, therefore this one weighs a ton. Someone uttering such an argument pattern perpetrates an equivocation known among logicians as the fallacy of division. This involves an argument process that moves from premises that mention a property possessed by a collective as such to a conclusion that mentions a similar-sounding property possessed by an individual. This is a fallacy, for although the phrases presenting a collective property and an individual property often use the same words, they are very different in meaning. For example, a critic might assert that a play is good, and conclude that a particular actor in the play was therefore good. But we all know that a play as a collective thing can be good even though some individual actors in it are bad. I remember seeing a fine production of *Hamlet* that included one actor who had not overcome his native southern Oklahoma dialect (a noble language, to be sure, full of fine Choctaw and Chickasaw and Elizabethan resonances), so he uttered lines like: "*Git* Thee tew aiy *Nun*-ner-ree!" That, of course, is music for an Okie like me, but it tended to disturb the performance for some folks in the audience.

Sometimes when a statistical social scientist makes a prediction, something like the weatherman's technique is used. And if it is, a division fallacy occurs. Thus we have the result that the collective statistical features of a sample of some social phenomenon logically cannot be used to guide a concrete individual issue, such as some person's decision. A political scientist's prediction that 53 percent of the voters sampled would vote for a third term for Ronald Reagan is of no use to any one of us in making a personal decision about how to vote on such a matter.

An obliging objector or an objecting obliger might say, "But such statistical information about collective properties of samples could be useful for someone attempting to manage a large social organization which is itself a collective." Such a line of thinking might be represented by an imaginary manager of an imaginary corporation who has been ordered to lay off 40 percent of the workforce of a particular division. He has read of a recent statistical study that says that only 3.5 percent of workers sampled who were laid off by a female executive become verbally violent, whereas if the executive bearing the bad news were male, 68 percent of the affected workers become violently rude during the exit interview. This manager probably is thinking that here is some good and useful scientific information. I ask, "Useful to what end?" Surely the answer is: "To control the situation according to the Big Picture that a manager has in mind." And when this purpose is made explicit, do we not see clearly what image of individual humankind it presupposes?

Here is a second kind of difficulty that can happen when one uses statistics. Imagine that I want to conduct something like an opinion poll about some topic I am researching, so I prepare a questionnaire according to standard and accepted techniques. Next I select a random sample from the target population. Let's not quibble about whether the original sample is sufficiently large or sufficiently random. Let's agree that it is large and as perfectly random as you wish, through any technique you wish. So I now mail the questionnaire to persons in the selected sample. I'm told by those who do this sort of thing that something like a 30 percent return rate is typical and quite acceptable. At this point should I go on to assume that my sample, 70 percent smaller than before, is still random? Many researchers appear to assume that. But how can the remainder still be considered random? Surely it has been de-randomized by any number of relevant factors, an obvious one being that many of those nonreturners don't care for questionnaires. The reason samples are made random in the first place is to avoid bias; but now our reduced sample is exactly biased, in that it has an insufficient representation of questionnaire-haters. And if we note that persons who dislike questionnaires might plausibly be busy and intelligent persons, that could be a significant bias.

Here is a third difficulty, again with questionnaires. Often these documents ask us what we think about some issue, or ask us to describe our feelings. If you are a researcher and you ask me what I think about something, you might be assuming the doctrine of privileged access, namely that whatever description I give about my thoughts is automatically correct. After all, you might say, they are *his* thoughts. The difficulty with that kind of procedure is a simple one: I might be suffering from the peculiarly human and non-mechanistic malady of self-deception, which is to say that I might be systematically misdescribing my own thoughts. I once had a friend who described himself as a neat person, but every time I visited his apartment it was a mess. It always looked like Sam Spade's apartment after the crooks had searched it for the missing Maltese falcon. On every visit he had some excuse why it was not clean, and I am sure he would have answered a questionnaire about neatness to the effect that he believed in it and practiced it. We might put it this way: If it is so damned easy to describe one's thoughts correctly, why have great persons in every age, from Pythagoras to Percy, repeatedly urged, in every imaginable way, that in spite of the difficulties, we should struggle to know ourselves?

But these considerations do not get at the principal problem of statistical social science; that is, they illustrate the problem, which is more general than any one of the difficulties mentioned. Each of these matters is either a retreat from achieving an understanding of persons or assumes erroneously that persons are only complex machines, discountable as individuals and collectively quite suitable to be controlled or manipulated by a statistical social scientist who has, or who has been hired to have, the Big Picture in mind. This last option, of course, returns us to the unyielding grip of Percy's antinomy.

We could summarize this by saying that many of the practitioners of contemporary statistical social or human sciences (as well as other persons attracted by the false lure of dyadic science) appear to take for granted an erroneous philosophical anthropology, the theory of what it is to be a human being.

Peter Manicas's History

We can get another extended testimonial from Peter Manicas's book *A History and Philosophy of the Social Sciences*. I regard this work as extremely important. I believe Manicas has convincingly shown that the methods and assumptions of typical contemporary social science, what he calls "mainstream social science," are based upon an uncritical, almost historically accidental, acceptance of some rather questionable assumptions of technology and 20th-century logical empiricism. In other words, I think he has shown that contemporary mainstream social science is a methodological dead end. This is ironical, for positivism is a philosophical approach that is one of the most reductive in history, one with a philosophical anthropology than which there is no weaker. And its assumptions about the nature of science itself are a model for constructing a dyadic science. The historical component of the Manicas thesis is extremely important, but I have space to put forward only a few aspects of the philosophical part of his fine essay.

A central feature of his book is the claim, a correct one I think, that the logical empiricist account of the logic of explanation, the so-called covering law thesis (the "standard view" of explanation), remains culturally engrained in social science at a time when all the central points of that thesis have been disconfirmed and rejected by philosophers of science. Or, in words well chosen by Manicas: "Einstein, often ahead of most people, began his 1933 Herbert Spencer Lecture at Oxford with a significant prescription: 'If you want to find out anything from the theoretical physicists about the methods they use, I advise you to stick closely to one principle: Don't listen to their words, fix your attention on their deeds.' But if the practices of physical scientists bear little resemblance to the dominant philosophy of science, it is no exaggeration to say that, in consequence of their relatively late beginnings as 'sciences,' *the practices of mainstream social science have long since been constituted by it.* Yet in the last several decades, every key tenet in this 'standard view' [the covering law thesis] has either been abandoned, liberalized to the point of triviality, or thoroughly undermined" (p. 242).

One of the features of the covering law account of science is that explanation (the process of achieving understanding) and prediction are logically parallel. Accordingly, an explanation (an occasion of having achieved understanding) occurs when from a law plus some "instantial" conditions we deduce the event to be explained. Moreover, once we know the law, and can bring the instantial conditions to pass, we can predict that a given result will be present. This would mean that if one could explain, one could predict, and vice versa. But as Manicas indicates, we often predict lacking an explanation, or explain without being able to predict. Humans could predict rain in the Middle Ages by viewing certain kinds of ominous clouds nearby without having any correct understanding or explanation of the truth of how rain occurs (condensation, or dew point, or the like). Or we can understand or explain very well the process of combustion, yet fail to predict a terrible hotel fire. In other words, prediction and explanation on the covering law thesis presuppose a highly controlled, well-isolated environment.

Manicas argues that devotion to this standard view of science by mainstream social scientists (who have been socialized in it, and who continue to socialize their students in it) is intimately connected with the historical accident that saw social science in its formative years aping technology. For on the covering law approach, understanding and explanation collapse into control. It is true that control is the purpose of technology. Thus the technological dyadic social sciences of today have as their ultimate purpose the control of something or someone/or, perhaps better expressed, the control of collectives of someones.

At this point I add that a person who assumes that such widespread control is possible and desirable will most likely be someone who also is committed to a kind of general determinism. In such a cultural atmosphere, the person as free agent is lost, discarded, factored out, made into a ghost in the social/industrial/economic machine. It should be clear that this tendency in contemporary thought is starkly opposed to what has been called the fundamental principle of Western democratic society: the absolutely basic worth of each individual free person. I suggest that anyone who wants to meditate upon this point should read Percy's novel, *Lancelot*. There one finds a world in which there is no evil, only illness brought about through due cause. If you take up the book, be sure to select a chair with a good seat belt; the volume has been certified by the Logician General as an established hazard to current assumptions.

My theme now is that we stand on the edge of a new era in the social and human sciences. We may escape the difficulties noted above and find a new way to conduct social science by rethinking some rather basic points. My proposal is that the culprit is not the general idea of science, but the narrow and self-confining conception that science, any science, is equivalent to dyadic science. Whatever knowledge we have gained of causal or functional processes retains its value and reality, but (as we shall see) we now have strong reasons for concluding that such knowledge alone can never be fully sufficient for a complete social science. However, it is unscientific to reinvent the wheel; the process of rethinking began some time ago in the work of Peirce, the second hero of this story.

Charles Peirce's Triads

Charles Peirce made a number of interesting and original claims, but the first appearance in his thought of the one I shall focus upon here can be traced at least to 1866, when he was 27 years old, sitting at his desk in Cambridge, Massachusetts, thinking about the glaring gaps he had just discovered in the logic of Kant, which is how Kant became Peirce's fallen hero. He duly published a defense of this claim in 1868 (first read publicly in 1867: see *P* 3–4), then elaborated and defended it in many publications and manuscripts over the years, almost until the day of his death in 1914.

This notion was rediscovered by Walker Percy in this century, when he was in his mid-30's in the 1950's, while sitting at his desk one summer day in Louisiana thinking about an event in the life of Helen Keller on another summer day in Alabama in 1887 as recounted in his essay "The Delta Factor." As the 18th Jefferson Lecturer for the National Endowment for the Humanities, Percy focused this particular notion with deadly accuracy upon the contemporary social sciences (this lecture was published in *Signposts in a Strange Land*, pp. 271–91). In proper scientific lingo, this proposal ought to be known as the Peirce-Percy Conjecture. By the way, this Conjecture is a way of providing a defense of Percy's observation, noted earlier, that assertions are not something one can study with a method that admits only functional or causal explanations. If we express Peirce's claim in terms appropriate to our present discussion, it would read like this: "It is logically illegitimate, as many contemporary social and human scientists attempt to do, to construct triadic relations from collections of relations containing only dyads."

To aid in appreciating the strength of this, a little explanation is in order. We can grasp the sense of relation that Peirce meant by means of a generalizing technique he used. Here are two sentences, the first one describing a dyadic relation, and the second describing a triadic relation:

George pushed Mary.   John sold his car to Howard.

If we generalize the noun locations in these sentences by replacing them with blanks (which he also called "loose ends"), we get:

_____ pushed _____   _____ sold _____ to _____

If we convert the blanks to lines and call the remaining words the verb parts of the sentences, and generalize those verbs by replacing those words with big black dots, we get Figure 1. These diagrams, which Peirce called "valental graphs," have the following meanings:

Some two unspecified entities (ordinary things, concepts, any objects of discourse) are in some kind of as yet unspecified dyadic relation with each other.

Some three unspecified entities are in some kind of as yet unspecified triadic relation with one another.

FIGURE I

In other words, these two diagrams are highly generalized *models* of the *forms* of dyadic and triadic relation.

Peirce defined connections between relations represented by diagrams such as these in terms of what he called "relative product," which is a way of showing how relations combine. For instance, if we wanted to represent the sentence "John pushed George who sold his car to Howard," it would look something like Figure 2:

John—[pushed]—George—[sold]—car
└ to— Howard

FIGURE 2

The relative product identifies the recipient of John's push as the same person that sold a car to Howard. In the most general graphical form, that is represented in Figure 3, where "+" indicates relative product (which Peirce also called composition or bonding). Basically, bonding is a way of showing that two objects (in the sense of objects of discourse) previously thought to be separate are now to be considered as equal, and so treated as one:

FIGURE 3

Peirce considered two graphs equivalent in valency if, no matter what other properties they might have, each had exactly as many loose ends as the other.

With this as a background, we can state Peirce's claim as the following: "No genuine nondegenerate triadic relation forms can ever be constructed from combinations of only dyadic relation forms." This sentence can be demonstrated informally, within the body of assumptions Peirce made, in the following way. The valency of any unbonded valental graph is equal to the number of blanks (also known as loose ends) in the graphical form. If a new graph is constructed from some old graphs plus one or more new acts of bonding two blanks together, the valency of the new graph will be given by this rule:

Valency of new graph
equals
Sum of valencies of the old graphs
minus two times the number of new bonds.

In this context, constructing a triadic relation from a collection of dyadic relations would require that the triadic relation could be made up from bonding a number of dyadic relations. But the above rule, through a simple *reductio*, shows that this cannot be done. In such a case, the valency of the new graph would be three or any other higher odd positive whole number. The old graphs would all be dyadic, which means that their valency sum would be an even number. The number of new bonds multiplied by two will always be an even number. An even number subtracted from an even number is always an even number. An odd number is never equal to an even number. These considerations show that a triadic relation cannot be constructed from a collection containing only dyadic relations.

"But it could be done," says a careful objector. "If we have three dyadic relations like this [see Figure 4], we could join them like this [see Figure 5]." But notice that Figure 5 violates the provision that a triad be made from dyads only, for there is a bootleg triad, namely the trivalent graph to the right of the three plus signs. Or, if the figure to the right of the plus signs is disallowed as a triad, the proposed maneuver violates one of the basics of Peirce's set of assumptions: that each bonding involves joining exactly two loose ends, never three:

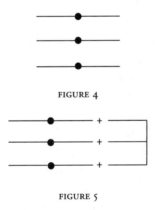

FIGURE 4

FIGURE 5

These results obtained by Peirce are extremely important, for they show that the preference of contemporary dyadic social scientists for explanations based exclusively upon dyadic relations is logically illegitimate. This is true because communicative and social phenomena involve genuine triadic relations, so any decision to allow only dyadic relations in the explaining material is *ipso facto* an attempt (bound logically to fail by the Peirce-

Percy Conjecture) to reduce such triads to dyads only. It might be said that I am not supporting my claim that communicative or social phenomena involve triadic relations. It is true that I don't provide a supporting argument. It seems obvious that in communication we essentially have triadic relations such as "John gave a note to Susie," or "Howard made a photograph of the Louvre," or "Watson understood Holmes's wave as a gesture of urgency." The same would apply to social phenomena, since communication is presupposed in society, and the same would apply in any science, social or otherwise, because every science presupposes and makes essential scientific use of social phenomena, even the so-called "hard sciences," such as physics and chemistry. One of the conclusions here, then, is that the social sciences are "the logically-first sciences." The typical reductionist claim by dyadic scientists that physics (or some other hard science viewed dyadically) is the first or basic science is exactly upside down, 180 degrees out of phase, precisely backwards.

"But," the objector persists, "Willard Van Orman Quine in his essay 'Reduction to a Dyadic Predicate' in *The Journal of Symbolic Logic* (1954), has shown, within contemporary formal logic, that an interpreted theory having triadic (or higher adicity) predicates can be reduced to (constructed from) a theory containing only dyadic predicates." This is a crucial article, because logicians inevitably refer to it in the course of saying that the Peirce-Percy Conjecture is simply false.

First, it is important to notice the broad structure of Quine's reduction. There are three general elements in it. First, there is the target of reduction: a body of relations that are triadic or higher in valency. Second, there is a group of tools for performing the reduction of the target (call these his resources). Third, there is a group of relations exclusively dyadic, which under the procedures of the resources rewrite the target. Quine has successfully and correctly used his resources to rewrite the target relations as strictly dyadic. Logicians have widely assumed that this is a wholesale reduction of any triadic relation to dyadic relations only (call this Claim Two). Quine himself, as far as I know, has not made such a claim; as far as I know, Quine has only claimed (and quite correctly) that with his resources he can reduce relations of valency three or higher to expressions containing just dyadic relations (call this Claim One). It is obvious that Claim One is not equivalent to Claim Two. And, for Claim Two to be true, Quine's resources must also be exclusively dyadic. It can be shown that Quine's resources are not completely dyadic, and that in at least two ways.

First, a careful examination of Quine's presentation shows that among the resources he assumes in executing the reduction is the notion of an ordered pair. A pair is a set containing two entities, for instance (b,z). An ordered pair is a set of two entities with a specified order, for example $(c;m)$, where c is first and m is second. In other words $(c;m)$ and $(m;c)$ are not identical, for while the members of each are the same, the order of each is different.

The interesting point here is that the concept of an ordered pair incorporates a genuine triadic relation. One can appreciate that by considering two entities not currently joined together in a set, but which by means of an act of imagination, are placed together in a set. Notice that without such an act of imagination on someone's part, there will be no set before us for consideration, not to mention an ordered set. That is to say, no matter whether a set is a natural being or a created being, a set imaginer is essential; if natural, the set imaginer is needed to direct our attention to *that* set, and if created, then the set imaginer creates it through an act of imagination. Imagining sets is second nature for mathematicians, for they begin their most formal discussions of them with phrases like: "Let H be the set (o,s)," which is clearly an act of imagination, or an invitation for one. In any case, if neither the mathematical writer of such a sentence nor any reader of it undertook such an act of imagination, there simply would be no set present for study. Suppose I say, "Imagine a set composed of George Washington's toothbrush and Andrew Jackson's wooden comb." As yet the set is an unordered pair, and I must engage in an additional speech act before it becomes an ordered pair. I do that by saying something like, "Imagine Washington's brush as the first item in an ordered pair in which Jackson's comb is the second item." If we describe that speech act of mine in terms of Peirce's generalization technique for relations, we get: "Ketner ordered Washington's brush as first and Jackson's comb as second," or "_____ ordered _____ as first and _____ as second." This is obviously a triadic relation. Actually, we don't even need to consider the case of ordered pairs, for just the very notion of a set that is an unordered pair involves a triadic relation: "_____ imagined _____ and _____ as a set." Additional features of set theory relevant to these points, as well as responses to other objections to the position here taken, are discussed in my essay "Hartshorne and the Basis of Peirce's Categories." Probably the most tempting additional objection involves invoking a property of ordered pairs: namely, that $(x;y) = (u;v)$ implies $(x = u \ \& \ y = v)$. But I believe I have shown in "Hartshorne and the Basis of Peirce's Categories" that this objection does not succeed, because this implication states a necessary condition or consequence of that which is already an ordered pair, not a sufficient condition which *makes* something an ordered pair. My point is that a triadic relation is indispensable to create an ordered pair in the first place.

My objecting obliger at this point says, "But you are mixing psychological issues with mathematical matters; mathematicians don't get involved in the psychic activity of imagination or of speech acts." If this is true of mathematics, then it seems to me that mathematics is simply impossible, which is a kind of reduction to absurdity of this objection. If no mathematician ever imagined anything nor ever communicated with anyone else about imaginary concepts, then mathematics as a practice and a science would simply cease. Actually, here we are face to face with what is probably the most abstract form of Percy's antinomy (we might call this its mathematical form): to wit, as long as mathematicians are discussing some other subjects using mathematics, no antinomy arises, but when the discussion is about the nature of mathematics or the foundations of mathematics, topics such as acts of imagination by individual mathematicians or social phenomena such as intersubjective communication between mathematicians are unavoidable. And if a mathematician refuses to discuss such topics, then mathematics as a human activity becomes inexplicable or full of contradictions. This situation is parallel to the predicament of the behaviorist psychologist who discusses stimulus and response all day at work, but goes home in the evening to the same old behavioristically inexplicable love/hate relationship with her own false true love.

Robert W. Burch in *A Peircean Reduction Thesis* (and also in his presentation to the Peirce Sesquicentennial International Congress, September 1989), in inventing a powerful formal system based upon Peirce's work, has achieved a major result with broad consequences; he has provided strong support at a high level of confidence to the Peirce-Percy Conjecture about the nonreduction of genuine triads, and in a manner corresponding to the highest standards of mathematical rigor. He has also provided convincing evidence (at an equally rigorous level) for Burch's thesis, an important new proposal, which states that Peirce's logic of relations, with its irreducible genuine triadic relations, is adequate to express all relations. Furthermore, he has shown, at the same level of rigor, that while Quine's reduction proof is correct, it does indeed assume at least one genuine triadic relation among its resources, quantification for example. Therefore Quine's work is not a disproof of the Peirce-Percy Conjecture, as proponents of Claim Two above have thought (this is the promised second way of discarding Claim Two). And by the way, in view of Burch's breakthrough, we must adopt the correct mathematical terminology for this matter and henceforth refer to it as the Peirce-Percy *Principle,* for it has been mathematically *established.* Burch's work is a major new finding of sweeping importance.

It is possible to confuse my way and Burch's way of freeing the Peirce-Percy Principle from the claim that Quine's reduction refutes it, so it would be wise to be quite clear about the differences in these two ways. Burch has proved, within standard assumptions about the nature of mathematics and mathematical signs, that the Principle is correct and that Quine's reduction to the dyadic is consistent with the Principle, because in achieving his results Quine makes use of constructive resources (quantification for instance) that are irreducibly triadic. In other words, Burch's contribution is sufficient to show that even on Quine's own assumptions about the nature of mathematics and mathematical signs, Quine's reduction does not contradict the Principle. On the other hand, I have gone slightly beyond (or perhaps behind) Burch and have made an additional point that is consistent with his results by showing that the formalistic assumptions made by Quine about the nature of mathematicians and mathematical signs amounts to a hand-waving attempt to bypass what is irreducibly a triadic relation: the relation between (1) the mathematical mind that assembles or orders two objects into a set or ordered pair and (2) those two objects. And my claim is that this relation between the mathematical mind and the objects it considers cannot, by a wave of the formalist wand, be excluded in this case, nor in mathematics in general. "There is no such thing as the silly notion of the mind of a mathematician," you say. Is my mathematician friend Tom then a formula, or equation, or an ordered pair, or a set? I do really talk with him and he with me, and sometimes we come to a meeting of our minds. Talking, agreeing, socializing are realities on the basis of which the edifice of science is erected; they are not scientifically dispensable "extras" that can be left aside. Am I doing philosophy of mathematics? Perhaps (and it is nothing to be ashamed of), but only in the sense that I am pointing out a truth without which mathematics, no matter how austere or pure, would be impossible.

Burch's book, together with the other considerations cited above, strongly imply the indefensibility of dyadic science approaches in another contemporary topic of considerable interest for students of human and social science. I refer to semiotics, a conglomeration of reductionist approaches that includes themes from such arch-dyadic-scientists as Ferdinand de Saussure and Charles Morris. The foundational role of dyadic relations in the work of both figures is well documented in recent books by Milton Singer and Eugene Rochberg-Halton. In Burch's thesis we now have a striking new mathematical result, one with consequences as important as those of Turing's thesis or Gödel's proof. One such consequence is that no theory of signs is possible that reduces all communication to a series of dyadic relations. That such a thing is possible is precisely the claim *and* the aim of Saussure and Morris and disciples. Their principal hypothesis, that all communication is fundamentally and basically and exclusively composed of dyadic relations, has now received a strong disconfirmation. This is, on the other hand, a strong confirmation for Peirce's semeiotic, the principal hypothesis of which is that all communication is fundamentally constituted of genuine triadic relations. These considerations also show that scholars who would like to mix dyadic semiotics with semeiotic are attempting to mix oil and water. This state of affairs will also serve as a means for discovering whether contemporary semiotics is really a science or a mere worldview. For the test of a genuine science is whether its practitioners can acknowledge when a previously valued hypothesis is disconfirmed and change their procedures accordingly.

But I digress. Back to social science proper.

Here is a list of events usually described as dyadic relations. *A* bumped into B; A reacted chemically with B; A flowed into B; A is connected to B; A stimulated B; B responded to A; A caused B.

Here is a list of events typically described as real triadic relations. A understood B to mean C; A interpreted C as B's message; A promised C to B; A bought C from B; C inherited B from A.

In terms of the Peirce-Percy Principle, no item in the second list is constructible from combinations of items in the previous list. Triadic relations cannot be reduced to (constructed or composed from) sets comprised exclusively of dyadic relations. It now follows that each member of a third list, containing explanatory strategies that have been popular in dyadic human and social science, is logically inadequate: materialism, behaviorism, the social physics of Comte and others, or any program such as that of Saussure-Morris semiotics or behavioral psychology which relies exclusively upon efficient causal connections or other such strictly dyadic explanatory schemata.

Then what explanatory strategies are available to social science, given that the Peirce-Percy Principle is correct? How can we analyze thought, or mind, or communication, or society, or culture, or literature, if these are essentially triadic? For one thing, we know how *not* to proceed: it is a non-option to explain triadic activities such as understanding, interpreting, promising, buying, narrating, or inheriting exclusively in terms of dyads. That is, there might be some dyads in a successful social scientific explanation, but there must be at least one triad. Consider it this way. Socrates might have committed suicide with an Ivers Johnson gun. If so, any dyadic causes that could be given by physics and chemistry, of the pistol's action and effect, would be relevant. But a social scientist would *necessarily* have to take up other topics, such as the reasons for the act, its significance in the culture, or whether it represented a social trend.

Thus, we stand at a bold juncture. Having disestablished an old explanatory habit, a new one must be found to replace it. No bandaid will suffice. We require a conversion experience, a fundamental change in basic practices.

How then shall we analyze thought, or mind, or communication, or literature, or society, or culture if these are essentially triadic? In this era we seem to have an urge to analyze. That seems innocent enough. But if *analyze* always means "reduce to dyadic forms," then a hidden (and false) assumption accompanies this use of the word. On the other hand, if *analyze x* means "come to have a better understanding of *x*," then the answer seems to be in this principle: "*We must analyze triadic relations by means of other triadic relations.*" In particular, if there is a matter about which we lack understanding, we can use a set of triadic relations we already comprehend reasonably well to model the relations in the area of relative ignorance. Once such a model is constructed, we can study or manipulate it to discover new things about the relations within it, hoping that the newly discovered relations there will be analogous to undetected relations in the area modeled. If they are analogous, then we will have increased our understanding of the area modeled. Stated in a very abstract fashion, that is Peirce's general method of diagrammatic thought, to which we now turn.

I hope this account doesn't contain too many loose ends.

Diagrammatic Thought

In one of the most remarkable theoretical paragraphs ever written, Peirce brought together the concepts we need to make sense of diagrammatic thought as a nonreductive technique for modeling, and for thereby gaining an understanding of triadic phenomena. It is from a draft of his article, "The Logic of Relatives" which appeared in *The Monist* in 1896 (see *CP* 2.227). Semeiotic, of course, is the study of semeiosis or sign action (triadic action) as opposed to the study of dynamic action. Where in this extract Peirce mentioned *signs*, read "genuinely triadic phenomena," and for *diagram* read "model":

> Logic, in its general sense, is, as I believe I have shown, only another name for *semiotic* . . . the quasi-necessary, or formal, doctrine of signs. By describing the doctrine as quasi-necessary or formal, I mean that we observe the characters of such signs as we know, and from such an observation, by a process which I will not object to naming Abstraction, we are led to statements, eminently fallible, and therefore in one sense by no means necessary, as to what *must be* the characters of all signs used by a "scientific" intelligence, that is to say, by an intelligence capable of learning by experience. As to that process of

abstraction, it is itself a sort of observation. The faculty which I call abstractive observation is one which ordinary people perfectly recognize, but for which the theories of philosophers sometimes hardly leave room. It is a familiar experience to every human being to wish for something quite beyond his present means, and to follow that wish by the question, "Should I wish for that thing just the same, if I had ample means to gratify it?" To answer that question, he searches his heart, and in doing so makes what I call an abstractive observation. He makes in his imagination a sort of skeletal diagram, or outline sketch, of himself, considers what modifications the hypothetical state of things would require to be made in that picture, and then examines it, that is, *observes* what he has imagined, to see whether the same ardent desire is there to be discerned. By such a process, which is at bottom very much like mathematical reasoning, we can reach conclusions as to what *would be* true of signs in all cases, so long as the intelligence using them was scientific. The modes of thought of a God, who should possess an intuitive omniscience superseding reason, are put out of the question. Now the whole process of development among the community of students of those formulations by abstractive observation and reasoning of the truths which *must* hold good of all signs used by a scientific intelligence is an observational science, like any other positive science, notwithstanding its strong contrast to all the special sciences which arises from its aiming to find out what *must be* and not merely what *is* in the actual world.

I ask you to note carefully several things about this remarkable paragraph. First of all the sheer power of it will grow on you, so please give it a chance to serenade you. One instance of its power is the connection it makes between mathematics and novels! Second, by reading *sign* as "triad," we get the result that semeiotic is the study of triadic action, a study accomplished by constructing and observing models! Abstractive observation is of course observation of relations in models. Also, a sign or representation, this paragraph encourages one to infer, is itself some kind of model of that which it represents (its object) to that which interprets it (its interpretant). Notice that Peirce called to mind a common-sense example of something we are constantly and routinely doing, making mental models of our life situations (often miniature narratives) and experimenting upon those as a way of planning our affairs. (He might just as easily have used examples such as *Märchen*, or folktales, or proverbs, which in effect often say to interpreters thereof, "life is like this.") For future reference, let us refer to one of these as a—here I was going to make up a new word, but a perfectly accurate one already exists—*self-image*.

In diagrammatic method, Peirce preferred visual diagrams, probably because they appealed to sight, which is our most evolved sense. But he also recognized diagrams based upon auditory or other sensory channels, for instance speech as an auditory diagram (see *CP* 3.418). By the way, old radio dramas are outstanding examples of auditory diagrams—remember how Molly would say, "Don't open that closet!" but Fibber did anyway, followed by a memorable sound effect?

But Peirce thought sight was probably best adapted for detecting new features of relational patterns in diagrams that model triadic relations presently under study. People sometimes say, when they want an explanation, "Draw me a picture." To "Draw a picture," then, would be to proceed in the way that Peirce would have recommended in response to the question, "How can we study phenomena rich in triadic relations if dyadic considerations alone cannot exclusively do the explanatory job?" If we add that Peirce recognized algebras and other arrays of symbols as visual diagrams, then we can state that mathematics, not in the narrow sense in which it is usually understood today, but as the science that models (diagrams) relations in areas under study, would be among the finer tools for "drawing pictures" that humankind has yet developed. Peirce said as much in the paragraph above.

But he did not limit the concept of visual diagram to sketches or marks. He clearly allowed for mental diagrams, in a way that would make a behaviorist blush, as being important intellectual resources. Some contemporary psychologists, such as Ned Block in his book entitled *Imagery*, in a way quite consistent with Peirce's ideas, have made good empirical progress concerning the notion of mental diagrams.

But I think there are even further consequences we can extract here. The principles of diagrammatic thought extend even into art. An exploration of this notion for visual art may be found in Frances Scott's dissertation

C. S. Peirce's System of Science and an Application to the Visual Arts (Texas Tech University).

And we could easily and profitably extend these insights to nonvisual art: novels, for instance. Percy has observed the following in "The State of the Novel: Dying Art or New Science?," in *Signposts in a Strange Land*, concerning novels: "So my main assumption is that art is cognitive, that is, it discovers and knows and tells, tells the reader how things are, how we are, in a way that the reader can confirm with as much certitude as a scientist taking a pointer-reading. A corollary to the proposition that art in general and the novel in particular is cognitive is that the stance of the novelist in the late twentieth century is also diagnostic. The implication is that something has gone wrong, which it certainly has, and that the usual experts cannot tell us what it is—and indeed that they may be part of the problem" (pp. 140–41).

Suppose we answer our question about how to proceed as scientists in the essentially triadic world studied by social and human sciences by taking this insightful suggestion in only a slightly different way than Percy intended. Suppose that "novel science" is one of the secrets of further progress in social and human sciences. What is novel science? I'm saying that we now have in our hands all the necessary elements for what may be a new and very fruitful way of conceiving the method of social science. I'm trying to connect those basic parts.

For instance, we could think of a novel as a tool for aiding readers to construct mental (or nonmental) diagrams. These models would then be available to readers who can perhaps learn something about (have an insight about—an IN-sight!) an area of relative ignorance within their persons (within their personal self-knowledge, in the Socratic or gnostic sense) by exploring the relations that are partially understood within the world (the diagram, the relational patterns) of a novel. Perhaps we could say that a novel is a large sign, a triadic relational pattern on a large scale, that can be a tool in diagrammatic thought (which is to say diagrammatic inquiry), the technique whereby one triadic relation that is relatively well understood is used to model, by mental diagrams, some other relations (often personal) that are not as well understood. If so, within the social and human sciences, novels might be outstanding tools for *analysis*, the process of achieving deeper understanding.

Alternatively, we could say that a good novelist provides materials with which readers construct artificial self-images. Once these are constructed, the novel scientist tries to offer ways a self-imager can manipulate such images to discover new relations in them. And if artificial self-image manipulation is successful, the self-imager's understanding of whatever is being addressed is thereby increased.

There could be many variations on this general theme, many subtechniques within it. A more detailed pursuit of the problem, which cannot be undertaken now, would include consideration of Peirce's three kinds of iconic representation. There is space only for a brief outline.

Peirce's idea was that a quality an icon has as thing renders it fit to represent. He distinguished three kinds of iconic representation: images, diagrams, and metaphors. Images represent through having the same qualities as their objects. A diagram represents the mainly dyadic relations of parts of its object by analogous relations in its own parts. Metaphors represent the representative character (triadic character) of a representation by representing a parallelism in something else. I take it that Peirce meant that the object of a metaphor is the representative character of some sign presently not as well understood as one might wish. By showing that this representative character, probably a law or symbol, is parallel to the representative character of some better known sign (another law or symbol), the target or object representative character is interpreted, explained, better understood. Probably there is no example of a single pure image, pure diagram, or pure metaphor, but some experiences have one of the three factors more strongly, hence such cases are useful examples.

Obviously my description of Peirce's much fuller discussion of these matters is only a sketch, but perhaps by its fruits we will know it.

Given all the difficulties of social science, one is tempted to ask some fundamental questions, such as: What is the aim or object of social science? What would it look like if it succeeded? At this point we can provide a few negative answers and propose some positive hypotheses.

I think we can safely propose that a sound social science would not have control or prediction as its aim, and that its object should be to increase our understanding of social realities. Such a notion arises directly from Peirce's conception of science in general. Stated negatively, no one who desires dictatorial control over other persons can be a scientist (see, for instance, *CP* 2.318ff.; see also *CP* 2.653–55).

Previously I have often thought that the social sciences might be secure if only one could arrive at a dramatic breakthrough, a convincing new crucial experiment or observation based upon some technique derived from a lightning-flash of insight by some genius. Mired in that rut, I would often mutter to myself, "Be patient, a Newton of the social sciences will arrive some day." I now think this way of thinking is a mirage. For if such a new technique were based upon dyadic considerations, as this thought seems to presuppose, it would fail for the reasons already noted.

Then what is to be done? In fact, that which is to be done is in kind already being done. Every day each of us accomplishes multiple acts of understanding. The requisite breakthrough occurred many thousands of years ago when one of our ancestors, instead of merely reacting to the course of events, somehow first understood something. The Newton of the social sciences is that unknown ancestor who first understood and conveyed that ability to descendants.

This seems to imply that what has been called "common sense psychology" or routine experience is a likely starting point in social science. However, beginning should not include reducing these phenomena to dyadic patterns, a tendency which has been dominant among social scientists in our age. That will fail. Instead, operating out of everyday and routine experience, in a spirit of fallibilism, let us begin to use novel science and other nonreductive procedures that will improve and correct common sense and routine experience. Although it cannot be argued here, I suspect that unanalyzed common sense abilities, which are rich in triadic relations, lurk in the background everywhere in contemporary science of all kinds, and that these factors constitute irreplaceable contributions and indeed make the otherwise unintelligible dyadic science approach (which doesn't recognize these factors) semi-palatable and serviceable in a jury-rigged sense.

If we do that, what end or object might we envision? We might understand understanding better. At the very least we could avoid destructive reductionism. The brightest hope is that we might understand ourselves and others better. That is to say, the aim or object of social science would be seen not as prediction, or control, or reduction, or statistics of the collective properties of samples, but as the kind of improved self-understanding that necessarily includes a better understanding of other selves and of community.

My colleague Shelby Hunt has suggested that I am proposing to discard all causal knowledge. To say the least, that is an inaccurate description of my hypothesis, which is a way of countering the chief underpinning of dyadic science—the strange identification of all knowledge with knowledge of causes. By all means, let us retain and employ all causal knowledge, and let us seek to obtain new knowledge of that kind. But in the Peirce-Percy Principle, as supported by Burch's results, we now have the strongest scientific evidence to support the claim that social science is not possible with *only* dyadic or causal knowledge. It is our duty *as scientists* to take notice of this result and to adjust accordingly in our future work. It would not be good science if persons who are tenaciously in love with the fundamental hypothesis of dyadic science were to refuse to consider these new findings. After all, the basic requirement for life as a scientist is the will to learn, which presupposes a capacity to change one's mind in the face of new evidence. And these results for social science have serious implications for the "hard" sciences, for as Percy's antinomy shows, the practice of hard science is inescapably social, so the practice of hard science presupposes social science.

An insistent voice intones, "But your proposal isn't science—it's philosophy or literature at best and obscurantism at worst."

I suppose that for a dyad addict, notions like those advanced here are unpleasant, even repugnant (which in itself is a phenomenon worth serious study. Why should many of our best and brightest have a serious phobia about stepping outside the house of causation?). But they certainly don't amount to obscurantism, although I would be the first to admit that I am treating understanding as primitive, as basic, as underived. And it seems to me that literature and other fine arts, plus our friends from the art and science of nursing, have preserved that chunk of wisdom through the ages, sometimes against rather serious attack. Every explanatory hypothesis requires a primitive component, an unjustified starting point in terms of which everything else is discussed. My suggestion is that we make the primitive element of social science equal to those irreducibly triadic abilities that are unique to human social life. And I don't say that understanding must be permanently a mystery. Nonreducibility does not equal unintelligibility. Perhaps through diagrammatic thought we will deepen our familiarity with understanding. That sort of thing has begun, as represented in some of the topics mentioned in the story I have been telling.

Ironically, it seems clear that dyad addicts are the obscurantists here, for they refuse to investigate any noncausal phenomena. Moreover, on a closely related matter, they also adopt a certain eschatology: when confronted with a problem, their usual move is to say that further research into causation will eventually produce the desired solution; in the Peirce-Percy Principle, we now have solid reason for regarding this particular eschatology within social science as simply false. To borrow a distinction from Peirce, the real is everything having properties that are independent of any individual's whim or wish or desire as to the nature of such properties. Causal knowledge then is one species of reality. But phenomena such as communication, rich in triadic relation, what Percy described as nonlinear, nonenergic, natural phenomena, or what Peirce identified as semeioses, are also real in the same sense. If I really convey ownership of my ancestral farm to my son, something more than a series of causes has occurred, and this something more is also real. (This, by the way, is the principal logical point that Patricia Poteat in her book *Walker Percy and the Old Modern Age* seriously misapprehended in a way that brought her to propose a radically distorted and inaccurate interpretation of Percy.) Along about here someone usually charges me with resurrecting vitalism, the old notion that there are ghosts which biologists study. Nothing could be further off the mark. Nothing!

I will accept the accusation that what I conceive for the social sciences is philosophy, but not in the sense of some pleasant line of bull, which is unfortunately what some folks today think it amounts to being. I accept "philosophy" in the sense that it is derived from the Greek word for that phenomenon for which *scientia* is the Latin word—one's devotion to the goal of increasing one's understanding of human beings and their relation to the cosmos. If we understand those two concepts in that sense, philosophy is not just pleasant talk; and literature or other art forms are disclosed as its intimate friends.

Letter of Charles Sanders Peirce to Signor Papini (*MS* L327.5)

22 Prescott St. Cambridge, Mass
1907 April 10

My dear Signor Papini:

Nothing could have been more flattering to me than your note which I received this instant, where I am sojourning for a time. My admiration for the Italian intellect of our day is most intense. Gen'l Ferrero was a personal friend of mine. Cremona's presentation of projective geometry and his celebrated transformation have helped me greatly. Fra Bruno's early exposition of invariantive algebra was my *vade mecum* for a long time. Only two days ago I sent to the editor of a popular Magazine, the "Atlantic Monthly," an attempt to explain pragmatism to the peculiar public of Boston—still somewhat, wisely, provincial, without special training, but loving intellectual things, the progeny of Emerson—in which I spoke of your article in the February Leonardo as a work of high intelligence, genius, and literary skill. I doubt very much whether the editor will accept my article; though perhaps he may so, provided I deviscerate it, as I am willing to do; and if not, the Editor of the Nation will take a shorter article. I cannot write Italian, I am sorry to say. For it is as beautiful a language for the expression of exact conceptions as for the purposes of poetry (including unrhymed fiction.) Some decade[s] ago, I surrounded myself as well as I could with Italian. I took only an Italian newspaper; and endeavored in that way to enter into the speech. But speech is not the kind of representation of forms in which I naturally think; and therefore my efforts did not come to as much as I hoped they might. Besides, one cannot escape reading German, however much one may detest the language, the rhetoric, and the style of expression.

Naturally, therefore, nothing in the world could be more gratifying, to me, than your kind suggestion of translating those thirty year old articles into Italian, and of course I give my heartiest consent. Only I feel that they should be accompanied by some corrections from my pen of their errors. In the first article there are two or three places where the logic is dubious, owing to my desire to be decided and clear to all the world. To represent, as I did, that we only desire to settle our beliefs is not quite correct, unless it be meant that the settlement should be final for all possible future time; and my third state, or method, of settling opinion is open to dispute. As for my second article, it was first entirely written (in French, substantially as it appeared in the Revue Philosophique, Vol. VII, p. 39?) on an ocean steamer which was carrying me in September 1877 to a meeting of the Association Géodesique in Stuttgart, where I had an important controversy to sustain; and I am not a particularly good sailor. I do not think it surprising therefore that I erred on some of the subtle points; and at any rate, I desire to correct those slips, in remarks to be appended to your translation. The worst error I made was when I declared that if a crystal of carbon were to be formed upon a tuft of cotton wool and were never to be touched by any hard body until it was finally consumed, then it would be merely a question of the convenience of phraseology, whether that were said to be hard or soft. Perhaps, I said, it was *chiefly* that and if so, the error would not be so great. But it seems to imply that an unrealized possibility is nothing—to make Existence the only mode of being, which that nominalism that has dominated all modern philosophy, on account of the accidental circumstance that, at the revival of philosophy, at the time of Gassendi and Descartes, it was the realists who happened to be in power in the universities and who therefore appeared as the prominent obscurantists. As a matter of fact, all "scientific" men, i.e., physicists, unless they have been sophisticated by reading metaphysics, are Realists. They regard law as quite as real as any event, and mathematicians regard $\sqrt{-1}$ as quite as independent of vagaries of opinion as any "real" quantity. In all that, I was quite wrong and the error is of momentous importance. However, I care comparatively little whether my explanation of the meanings of concepts, or James's, or Royce's, is the correct one. The vital thing is that every man should anxiously put the question to himself "What do I really mean?"; and if it be true that it was I who (after Berkeley) first drew living attention to the supreme importance of this question in philosophy, I shall tell myself that I had done enough for one man. For my own part, I have been brought to the conviction that while there is no real general which could not *conceivably* have practical, or existential, results, yet there are real habits (both in minds and in what we are in the habit of regarding as quite inanimate objects); and furthermore that there are real *possibilities*, or capacities, which *may* never come into existential being. Having considered these questions for many years, with their practical results before my mind, I hold to my opinions about them very warily. Yet I am open to conviction. James, on the hand, or Royce, on the other, may be right, and I wrong. That the question what we do mean should be rationally thrashed out, *that* is what I most of all desire. At present I am a *conditional idealist*, meaning that I think "would be" to be a great element of reality. I do not now think, as I seemed to think in 1877, that what the race of intelligent beings *shall* come to think is necessarily the reality, but only what they *would* come to think, if inquiry came to its delimitive result. These ideas I should be glad to press, in an appendix to your translation of my papers.

Hoping that you will pardon the extreme length of my letter, I will outline to you the principal argument in favor of the truth of pragmatism in that MS which I have sent to the "Atlantic Monthly," but which I fear will rightly be deemed too difficult for a popular magazine. I begin by arguing that a concept is a mental sign, that all our deliberations within ourselves take a dialogic form, the ego of one instant appealing to the ego of the next instant for reasonable assent. That granted, I say that a sign is essentially a medium between two correlates which it brings into connection with each other. The one correlate of the sign is the Object which is supposed to determine it. The other is the meaning, or Interpretant, which the sign is intended to determine, and to represent as the outcome of the Object. Of the two words "Meaning" and "Interpretant," I prefer the latter, as not being embarrassed by other significations; but in this paper I mostly use "Meaning" as a familiar word which nearly expresses to the popular mind what I wish to suggest. I did so use it in my papers for the Popular Science Monthly of November 1877 (in a French redaction in Vol VI of the Revue Philosophique) and of January 1878. I regret that I have no copies of these publications to send you. I go on to remark that logicians distinguish the Immediate Object of a sign from its Real Object. I look for an analogous distinction as to the Interpretant; but I find there are *not* two, but *three* Interpretants; namely, 1st, the immediate, or as I call it, the emotional interpretant, involving (at least) in every case a sense of comprehending the sign, as something familiar in some sense; 2nd, the Existential Interpretant, or the actual events which the sign, *as sign*, may bring about, by however indirect a process; and 3rd, the Logical Interpretant, which is imperfectly represented in the definition of the sign. Imperfectly, I say, because the *ultimate* interpretant cannot itself be a sign, since every sign has an interpretant. What then is the Logical Interpretant? I show that the Emotional Interpretant corresponds to the Immediate Object, and the Existential Interpretant to the Real Object. Why should there be a *third* Interpretant, though there are but *two* Objects? It must be because of the difference in the natures of the Object and the Interpretant. But that difference is that the Object is the cause, the Interpretant the effect of the sign. As effect it extends into futurity and therefore the logical interpretant must be, in some sense, in the *future tense*. But not all signs have any logical interpretant. Just as all signs necessarily have Immediate Objects, but not all have Real Objects, so every sign has an emotional interpretant; but a piece of concerted music, for example, has no other. The infantry officer's word of command, "Ground arms!" must of course be comprehended; and therein is its emotional interpretant. But the infantryman does not reason, he forthwith slams down the butt of his musket, and there is the existential interpretant of the sign, which goes no further. It is only intellectual concepts that have logical interpretants; and these signs are either themselves general, or refer to something general. The logical interpretant is, no doubt, something psychical; and therefore I ask "What constituents of our psychical life are general?" For the adequate interpretant of a general must itself be general. Such constituents are only Concepts, Desires, and Habits, all of which are always general. Concepts, however, being signs cannot be ultimate interpretants. Desires cannot be so, either. For desires are antecedent to the fact, not consequent upon it. So the logical interpretant can only be a Habit, which consists in a conditional future; namely that, with a given motive, a man, under given circumstances, *would rationally* behave in a certain way. That is the proof of pragmatism which I selected as being among all scientific proofs with which I am acquainted the one that seems to me to come nearest to popular apprehension. As I have said, I fear even this is too difficult; but I was unwilling to descend to rhetorical arguments.

I wish I had space left on this sheet to tell you the story of that voyage on which I wrote that article, beside preparing myself for a discussion in the meetings of the Association; because you would not only find it entertaining, but would learn from it some of the difficulties with which such a student as I had to contend with in my time in America. But I have already encroached by far too much of your kind attention, and can only close with a reiterated expression of the gratification that your note has given me. Believe me then

dear Colleague,
Your admiring friend,
C. S. Peirce

I will send to my home for a photograph suitable to you, though I detest these disguises that usage compels us to assume. Oh, I must not forget my warmest thanks for the valuable numbers of "Leonardo," which I treasure.

Pragmaticism is an Existentialism?

Kenneth Laine Ketner

"You misspelled part of your title," said a loyal and diligent proofreader. "It's pragmatism."

So one day when I was doing nothing in particular in the library I looked for the word in the 1958 edition of *Webster's Unabridged Dictionary*.

Here is what I found on p. 1938: "Pragmaticism. The philosophic doctrine of C. S. Peirce; adopted by Peirce to distinguish his philosophy from other forms of pragmatism." Where and when did he adopt the strange word? It happened in 1905, in an article for *The Monist* entitled "What Pragmatism Is." There Peirce recalled his introduction of pragmatism in the Metaphysical Club at Cambridge, Massachusetts, in the 1870's. Peirce had virtually lived in a laboratory since age six. So, it was an experimentalist's theory, "that a *conception*, that is, the rational purport of a word or other expression, lies exclusively in its conceivable bearing upon the conduct of life; so that, since obviously nothing that might not result from experiment can have any direct bearing upon conduct, if one can define accurately all the conceivable experimental phenomena which the affirmation or denial of a concept could imply, one will have therein a complete definition of the concept, and *there is absolutely nothing more in it*" (CP 5.411ff.).

That, of course, is a version of the pragmatic maxim—excuse me, the pragmaticistic maxim—one of the jewels of American technical philosophy, a way of finding the meanings of concepts. A common erroneous tendency is to regard this maxim as an early form of logical empiricism, erroneous because logical empiricism is inconsistent with Peircean realism and his notion of open inquiry, not to mention being inconsistent with semeiotic. Moreover, Peirce explicitly denied that it was a kind of positivism (*CP* 1.545ff.). Perhaps that is why, if our eyes are lifted toward the more human elements of those remarks, we can detect a statement by a man struggling through the cosmos as we all must do, to the effect that life is an experiment, with nothing guaranteed in advance, and no sure path except to continue experimenting, correcting our past errors as well as we can, as we push toward future interpretations. That is hardly the stance of a foundationalist, whether of the Cartesian or sense-datum variety.

Peirce is often understood only as a technician in philosophy. But consider that passage from a wider perspective. Doesn't the phrase "finding the intellectual purport of conceptions," which is the utility of Peirce's maxim, begin to bring to mind the possibility that alongside words like "argument" or "reality," he is also thinking of the intellectual purport of "happiness" or "community" or "person"?

Why did he adopt the strange term? In the interval since the public announcement of the philosophical conception of "pragmatism" in a lecture by William James in 1898, until Peirce's article in 1905, multiple versions of "What Pragmatism Is" had appeared in the United States and elsewhere. The situation was about as varied then as it is now. Now, as then, it is difficult to keep track of all the pragmatists, especially when the list contains persons as diverse as Henry Kissinger, Richard Rorty, or Lee Iacocca. One is tempted to observe that pragmatism has become too successful. Peirce reflected (*CP* 5.411ff.) that the situation had become so bad that his brat "pragmatism" was even beginning to appear in literary journals, "where it gets abused in the merciless way that words have to expect when they fall into literary clutches." Peirce then made a radical decision: "The writer, finding his bantling 'pragmatism' so promoted, feels that it is time to kiss his child good-by and relinquish it to its higher destiny; while to serve the precise purpose of expressing the original definition, he begs to announce the birth of the word 'pragmaticism,' which is ugly enough to be safe from kidnappers." This result appeased my proofreader. But in the course of sifting the foregoing material, certain other questions came to me. Why, more than eighty years later, is this name for Peirce's work still so little used? Surely not because it is ugly, or that Edwardian kidnappers have a stronger stomach than their contemporary comrades—which is to say that many more ugly bastards have been kidnapped since 1905. Moreover, why is Peirce's work, by any name, still less well known today and less used now, even by those among us who are identified as pragmatists? Why are philosophers and academicians today, similar to those of 1905, likely to know nothing of pragmaticism, the overall philosophical doctrine of C. S. Peirce, the founder of pragmatism as a philosophic movement?

I can't give complete answers in this short compass. Some evidence relevant to these issues is already generally available. But I can offer a hypothesis, which if correct, will be relevant.

Abruptly expressed, it has occurred to me that pragmaticism is an existentialism. If that were true, because existentialism is rather out of fashion among the majority of philosophically inclined intellectuals in North America, it would tend to answer my questions about pragmaticism and its relative nonabsorption into American and English intellectual life. It would also tend to explain the rather curious fact that Peirce is more generally appreciated in Europe than in his native Massachusetts. Behold, the fate of prophets!

If pragmaticism is an existentialism, there should be some recognizable consequences of that claim. At least we ought to be able to find some parallels with some of the existentialist thinkers. But the first problem encountered there is that the existentialists are about as varied as the pragmatists! Probably the best I can do here is to select some writers who are generally acknowledged as good representatives of existentialist tendencies. I will use an inductive sample of two: Walker Percy and Jean-Paul Sartre. And I limit the sampling to just a few points.

One general character in common between the existentialists and Peirce is the recognition of the reality of persons: acting, choosing, suffering, living, searching, interpreting, dying beings. This factor in Peirce's thought sometimes is obscured by his proper emphasis upon community and his disgust with Cartesian subjectivism *in science*. But there is a strong, not well-known, personalist strain in Peirce's general system (which is wider than his account of science and philosophy). You will have to accept my promissory note for a defense of that claim on another occasion.

To descend to more particular similarities, we might first notice that when we initially come to realize our personhood, we find that we are in a *world*, as Percy in *Lost in the Cosmos* (p. 96) phrases it, as opposed to just an *environment*. An environment, in his sense, is a setting in which only efficient causal relations are to be found. A world, on the other hand, along with environmental factors, also includes significance, meaning, interpretation, understanding, and selves. These additional factors Percy places under the heading of triadic behavior, or sign-use. Percy's discovery was that such triadic relations cannot be reduced to conglomerates of dyadic relations. Or, worlds are not reducible to environments. In this point Percy is actually an independent rediscoverer (see Percy's "The Delta Factor") of the almost identical principle noticed by Peirce about 1866. I have traced aspects of these two parallel discoveries elsewhere ("Peirce's 'Most Lucid and Interesting Paper': An Introduction to Cenopythagoreanism") in considerable detail.

It is a major confirmation of my thesis that Percy, after a period of intense immersion in the literature of existentialism, rediscovered this point independently. Only later did he come to realize that Peirce had worked it out almost a century earlier. That the two thinkers are so close on this fundamental point is a major confirmation, and hence perhaps the principal point of comparison that tends to support pragmaticism really being an existentialism.

This world of triadic phenomena, in which we first come to recognize ourselves, has a fundamental place in Peirce's late work. I think that there is only a terminological difference between it and related topics in existentialism. He referred to it as "common sense." All of his mature philosophical elaborations arise from his belief that the world of common sense is a fundamental guide to all philosophizing, a process he understood as only a task of clarifying in a controlled way what in a vague form we already accept as residents of the common sense world. There is also much in Peirce's semeiotic that can be brought forth to bolster the notion of a world (but not today).

The very definition of existentialism can be seen as a way of claiming this same point. My favorite example of this is from Sartre's "Existentialism is a Humanism" as found in *Existentialism From Dostoevsky to Sartre*, edited by Walter Kaufmann: "What [the existentialists] have in common is simply the fact that *existence* comes before *essence*—or, if you will, that we must begin from the subjective. . . . There is at least one being whose existence comes before its essence, a being which exists before it can be defined by any conception of it. That being is man or, as Heidegger has it, the human reality. What do we mean by saying that existence precedes essence? We mean that man first of all exists, encounters himself, surges up in the world—and defines himself afterwards. If man as the existentialist sees him is not definable, it is because to begin with he is nothing. He will not be anything until later, and then he will be what he makes of himself. Thus there is no human nature . . ." (pp. 289–90). This passage provides the opportunity for an interesting experiment. Suppose we rewrote it using the terminology of pragmaticism? Would we get something that the existentialists would accept, at least those who savvy Peirce's lingo? ("What do we mean by saying that man's reality comes before man's nature or significance? We mean that first of all the human mind acquires the power of interpretation, then begins to engage in interpretation, including interpretation of self. Thus a person will be what his or her interpretation of self creates. There is no a priori human nature: yet there is an 'image of man' which is but the collective consequence of many individual instances of interpretive actions, or semeioses.") That is, a pragmaticist would urge that Sartre could have made his point more accurately by means of Peirce's existence/reality distinction. Instead of "existence precedes essence," it would have been more accurate to have explained that "the reality of the process of semeiosis precedes any actual interpretations." In other words, for Peirce, existentialists might be better identified as "Realistentialists." Peirce might have agreed with Sartre that man is nothing, in the sense of "no thing," but could have gone on to elaborate that not being a thing (not being a *res cogitans*, nor just a collection of banging, wiggling molecules), man is a process of semeiosis or system of relations, the central feature of which is the action of interpreting. This is the upshot of Peirce's essay "Man's Glassy Essence" (*CP* 6.238ff.), the title referring to our mirror-like essence. By this allegory of mirrors I take it that Peirce was imagining one of us looking in a mirror and thinking "That is me." That is to say that the essence of a self is that it interprets, and that the very reality of a self is as a continuing process of interpretation.

Existentialists of all varieties are widely known for their emphasis upon human freedom. There are few clear statements in Peirce about that topic. However, consider this one (*MS* 448.25): "My account of the facts you will observe leaves a man at full liberty, no matter if we grant all that the necessitarians ask." This infrequency of comment on the subject, is, I believe, somewhat misleading. Peirce is well known as an exponent of interpretation. I think this is but a somewhat logically oriented way of asserting the same point for which Sartre, for instance, is widely known—the claim that man is "condemned to be free." There are occasions in Sartre's prose when for him to continue to talk of choosing causes reader nonresonance, leading one to wish that he would switch over to interpretation-talk, for his point would make more sense that way. For example, his dictum that "In choosing for myself, I choose for all mankind" would on the face of it be more plausible if it were: "In making an interpretation I am aiding in forming the idea or general image of humanity."

In "Existentialism as a Humanism," we can catch Sartre making the switch himself, for there he virtually accepted "interpret" as an explication of his sense of "choose": "No rule of general morality can show you what you ought to do: No signs are vouchsafed in this world. The Catholics will reply, 'Oh, but they are!' Very well; still, it is I myself, in every case, who have to interpret the signs" (p. 298). A bit later on the same page, Sartre made it clear that each of us bears full responsibility for the "decipherment of signs," that each of us decides the meaning of our being through interpretation. Coming to knowledge of this brings with it the experience of one of those Sartrian emotions, "abandonment," the feeling that we are inevitably separated from any a priori source that will create our person. An accompanying feeling is anguish, brought about through the realization that each of us and no other is responsible for the interpretations we make. One familiar with semeiotic who reads these sentences in Sartre will find it difficult to escape the conclusion that Sartre's enlarged conception of "choice" is very much more than likely equivalent to Peirce's notion of "interpretation." Thus, the slogan widely associated with Sartre can be restated in equivalent Peircean language: "We are condemned to interpret."

For Peirce, the first move out of the world of common sense is a major person-forming choice—selection of a method of resolving doubt. In typical existentialist manner, he is aware that there is nothing guiding or forcing the choice of the objective or rational method versus any of the nonobjective or egocentric approaches (authority, tenacity, fashion). He described that choice, on which all his later intellectual work was based, in ringing prose that is reminiscent of the focus and tone of Sartre and Percy:

> Such are the advantages which the other methods of settling opinion have over scientific investigation. A man should consider well of them. . . . Upon such considerations he has to make his choice—a choice which is far more than the adoption of any intellectual opinion, which is one of the ruling decisions of his life, to which, when once made, he is bound to adhere. . . . Yes the other methods do have their merits: a clear logical conscience does cost something—just as any virtue, just as all that we cherish, costs us dear. But we should not desire it to be otherwise. The genius of a man's logical method should be loved and reverenced as his bride, whom he has chosen from all the world. He need not condemn the others; on the contrary, he may

honor them deeply, and in doing so he only honors her the more. But she is the one he has chosen, and he knows he was right in making that choice. (*CP* 5.358ff.)

Which of the two concepts, "choice" and "interpret," is more encompassing? I can but guess now that the answer is "neither"; that a more complete study would show that they are equivalent notions.

Let us end this exercise as we began it, by thinking of the maxim of pragmaticism. Instead of being some vague precursor of the verification principle, Peirce stated on a number of occasions that it was but a corollary of the theory of signs, a corollary of semeiotic, which is in effect a theory of interpretation. Presented in the semeiotic mode, the pragmaticistic maxim might read in general that the meaning of a concept lies in future interpretations, in particular those interpretations on which we will be prepared to act. That suggests that it might be plausible for us to summarize our results by modifying a well-known philosophical graffito:

To be is to interpret.
[Peirce]

To be is to do.
[Sartre]

Do be do be dooo.
[Sinatra]

Hartshorne and the Basis of Peirce's Categories

Kenneth Laine Ketner

Peirce's categories have not received a warm general welcome, either in his day or in ours. However, Charles Hartshorne is one master philosopher who has taken them seriously, and with revisions, used them in his own work.

I don't intend here to look into the categories as Peirce proposed them (initially in 1867) or as Hartshorne has revised them (1983 and 1984). Instead I want to consider the basis for them to be found elsewhere in Peirce's work. This distinction between the categories and the basis for them is one that some students of Peirce have missed, but which Hartshorne knows accurately: the categories are hypotheses within Peirce's metaphysics which are based upon certain suggestive results Peirce obtained in mathematics and the logic of relatives. (These results are hereafter mentioned simply as "basis" or "the basis.") I believe it can be shown that this basis has been misinterpreted by a number of students of the topic who also happen to be persons who may have influenced Hartshorne's understanding of this matter. After presenting and defending my interpretation of the basis, I hope Hartshorne can be induced to comment upon it, and whether it would change the way in which he understands and deploys Peirce's categories.

After becoming aware a few years ago that Peirce's existential graph system of logic was a key for gaining an understanding of many basic points within his work, I began to seek for its roots. I believe I discovered them, in both the intellectual sense (reported in "Peirce's 'Most Lucid and Interesting Paper': An Introduction to Cenopythagoreanism") and textual sense ("Identifying Peirce's 'Most Lucid and Interesting Paper' "). Textually, the beginning of his existential graphs is found in *MS* 482, wherein Peirce developed it out of graph theory within topology. Under the heading of "valency analysis," I have isolated one aspect of the means for that development. This is a convenient name which I have coined; "valency analysis" is not a phrase Peirce used, but it is consistent with his intent and practice. For some time scholars have complained about being unable to find Peirce's proof for two distinctive theorems, which are (in uninterpreted form) as follows:

Nonreduction Theorem:

No triad can be composed exclusively from dyads.

Sufficiency Theorem:

Tetrads or higher *n*-ads can be composed exclusively from combinations of monads, dyads, or triads.

In *MS* 482, these two theorems are established within valency analysis, which consists of a formal system of uninterpreted graphs. An entity with one "loose end" is a monad, with two loose ends a dyad, with three loose ends a triad, with *n* loose ends a *n*-ad. The number of loose ends is a property that can also be described as the adicity of the graph. It is convenient to represent such entities with drawings like these.

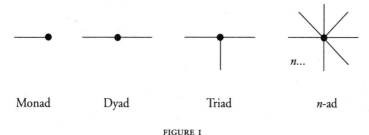

| Monad | Dyad | Triad | *n*-ad |

FIGURE I

Loose ends are places in which any connection that is possible or permissible *may* occur. Connection of loose ends is by the process of bonding exactly two of them at a time. Within valency analysis, one ignores material reasons for joining two loose ends to focus upon formal patterns of composition or rules associated with bonding. Two graphical entities are said to be "valency equivalent" if, no matter what other properties they possess, they have exactly the same number of loose ends. Thus all of the following four graphs are valency equivalent (valency of each is two).

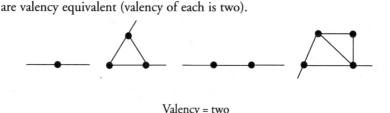

Valency = two

FIGURE 2

With these understandings, it is easy to prove that Nonreduction and Sufficiency are theorems of *valency analysis* (proofs are in "Peirce's 'Most Interesting and Lucid Paper': An Introduction to Cenopythagoreanism"). It is important to note at this point that these are not theorems about categories, because so far we are working with just an uninterpreted formal system.

Peirce's next step was to interpret valency analysis over relations. He did it in this manner. He conceived relations rhematically, meaning that he first considered a relation sentence, then conceptually subtracted ("precided") all noun-like aspects to produce what he called a rheme (a kind of partial sentence form). In that manner,

"George is a Bolivian"
becomes
"_____ is a Bolivian";

"Excess current caused the resistor to melt"
becomes
"_____caused _____";

"Smoke represents fire to the priest in the tower"
becomes
"_____ represents _____ to _____."

Peirce referred to the kinds of sentence forms (exemplified by the second of each pair above) as "relatives," from whence is derived his phrase "logic of relatives." I will avoid that phrase for now, because in his later philosophy, it became virtually a general name for his entire effort. Let us use a terminology similar to that Peirce employed before "relative" became such a general term for him. We may call these "partially precided relation sentences," for only the noun-like elements have been "precided" away. A fully-precided relation sentence is one in which the relating aspect is also generalized. That is accomplished by replacing the remaining words, the verb-like elements, with a big black dot. At this level of precision we find that monadic, dyadic, triadic, and n-adic relation sentences look just like corresponding graphs in valency analysis. That is, the graphical entities of Figure 1 now mean respectively:

"Some object has some property."

"Some one object is in some dyadic relation to some second object."

"Some first object is in some triadic relation with some second object and some third object."

(Of course, "object" is understood to range over "objects of discourse.")

Now it is clear that Peirce regarded that which we can know as consisting of relations. He rarely mentioned this important aspect of his system, but here are two clear instances:

> Whatever we know, we know only by its relations, and in so far as we know its relations [*MS* 931, 396]. . . . In reality, every fact is a relation. Thus, that an object is blue consists of the peculiar regular action of that object on human eyes. This is what should be understood by the "relativity of knowledge." Not only is every fact really a relation, but your thought of the fact implicitly represents it as such [*CP* 3.416].

Once valency analysis is interpreted over relation sentences, it has another contribution to make, for valency analysis in conjunction with Peirce's long interest in the nature of scientific classification inspired the doctrine of Cenopythagoreanism:

> In classification generally, it may fairly be said to be established, if it ever was doubted, that Form, in the sense of structure, is of far higher significance than Material. Valency is the basis of all external structure; and where indecomposibility precludes internal structure—as in the classification of elementary concepts—valency ought to be made the first consideration. I term [this] the doctrine of Cenopythagoreanism. (*MS* 292.34, 98)

Looking with Cenopythagorean eyes, once valency analysis is interpreted over relations, Peirce found that all relations (and hence all knowables) divide into just three natural classes: monads, dyads, and triads. Dyadic relations so interpreted cannot be constructed from monadic relations; the nonreduction theorem shows that triadic relations cannot be constructed exclusively from dyadic relations; and the Sufficiency Theorem shows that relations of adicity n, where n is equal to or greater than four, are reducible to (are valency equivalent to) a combination of n-minus-two triadic relations. That is, a tetrad (adicity four) is reducible to two triads (four minus two is two), a pentad is reducible to three triads, a heptad is reducible to four triads, and so on. Furthermore, existential graphs can be generated out of valency analysis. Don D. Roberts has shown in *The Existential Graphs of C. S. Peirce* that the existential graph system is consistent and complete for predicate logic with relations. From this point to the categories is but a short step, but one which will not be taken now, for I want to stay within the basis to see if it can be sustained.

When I had what I thought was a good understanding of the topological foundations of Peirce's natural classification of kinds of relations via the Nonreduction and Sufficiency Theorems, it immediately occurred to me that these are important results. For instance, if the interpreted Nonreduction Theorem is correct, then all kinds of reductive explanatory strategies could be shown to fail. For instance, behaviorism or materialism in psychology, which are basically ways of reducing triadic relational phenomena to dyadic causal chains, would collapse. Here I am inspired by Walker Percy's "The Delta Factor"; Percy is an independent re-discoverer of many of the conceptions about relations I have sketched above. Or, for another example, attempts to develop artificial intelligence only from deterministic resources would be doomed from the start. I also quickly found that I was not alone in my research, for two fine Canadian scholars were active in the same general area: Hans Herzberger and Jacqueline Brunning, of whom more later.

The first thing I wanted to know was what had happened in the logic of relations since Peirce's day. In talking with colleagues specializing in mathematics and logic, a number of persons mentioned that it was well known that Peirce was wrong about Nonreduction, and that triadic predicates could be reduced to dyadic ones. Inevitably I was referred to a 1954 paper by Willard Van Orman Quine where reduction was said to have been achieved. That paper is a formal investigation, but it is clear Quine intended to interpret his formal results over relations. That point is further reinforced by some of later comments in his *Mathematical Logic* (p. 201). It will be convenient to have the first two paragraphs of Quine's reduction before us:

> Consider any interpreted theory θ formulated in the notation of quantification theory (or lower predicate calculus) with interpreted predicate letters. It will be proved that θ is translatable into a theory, likewise formulated in the notation of quantification theory, in which there is only one predicate letter, and it a dyadic one. . . . Let us assume a fragment of set theory, adequate to assure the existence, for all x and y without regard to logical type, of the set (x,y) whose members are x and y, and to assure the distinctness of x from (x,y)

and ($\{x\}$). ($\{x\}$ is explained as $\{x,x\}$.) Let us construe the ordered pair $x;y$ in Kuratowski's fashion, namely, as ($\{x\},\{x,y\}$), and then construe x,y,z as $x;(y;z)$, and x,y,z,w as $x;(y,z,w)$, and so on.

To show that Peirce's Nonreduction Theorem is incorrect, and that reduction is possible, it would be sufficient to show that there is at least one triadic relation that can be reduced to some collection composed exclusively of dyadic relations. It seems clear that Quine proposes to do that, not only for one triadic relation, but for all relations of adicity three or greater. And one of the essential tools he employed in the proof is the notion of an ordered pair. Let us take a careful look at "ordered pair."

The definition for ordered pair was given by Kuratowski in 1921, inspired by Norbert Wiener. Pairs sound quite dyadic. However, I shall argue that the concept of an ordered pair is indeed a triadic relation. Therefore, use of it in a proof that many understand as breaking Peirce's Nonreduction Theorem would be a violation of the rules of the game. That is so because a proper reduction would have to constitute a triad from a collection of dyads only, not from a collection constituted by a bunch of dyads plus one triad. If ordered pairs are really triadic relations, then Peirce's Nonreduction Theorem, construed in terms of his definitions, is still standing in view of Quine's results. That is not to say that Quine's results are wrong; but it would mean that Quine's correct results do not break Peirce's Nonreduction Theorem.

Let us begin at a common sense level, and start with the notion of a set that is an unordered pair. I take that step, because a triadic relation seems to be buried even in the idea of a set that is an "unordered pair." I am trying to think of two widely disparate items such that nobody now considers them as a set or collection. Suppose that in the Arbuckle Historical Society Museum in Murray County, Oklahoma, there exists an object known locally as Mazeppa Turner's pocket knife, and that in Saint Tammany Parish, Louisiana, exists what people there call General Earl Van Dorn's battle flag. A set is some number of objects of discourse brought together in our conception or imagination. I can say, "Collect or bring together in your imagination those two objects, Turner's knife and Van Dorn's flag; when you have done that, call the result of that process the set

H." Since the process of bringing these two extremely disparate items together in imagination is an action of a person, a collector who puts a collection together, we can see that even the notion of a set that is an unordered pair presupposes a triadic relation. Based on our example, that relation would be represented in this sentence: "Robert Earl imagined a set composed of Turner's knife and Van Dorn's flag." That can be written rhematically as "_____ imagined a set composed of _____ and _____," which is clearly trivalent.

Now let us consider the concept of "ordered pair." Suppose there are two particular rocks on a table in front of us. One of us notes their presence, then imagines them as a set. But suppose further that we wanted to designate one of these as the *first* rock *a* and another as the *second* rock *b*. That is, we want to move from an unordered set to an ordered set. To bring that about, I state, "I order *a* as first and *b* as second." That statement, considered as a partially precided rheme, becomes "_____ ordered _____ as first and _____ as second." In other words, it is a triadic relation involving a giver of order to two objects which are thereby ordered. Its fully precided form is that of a valency analysis triad (where *O* is the above triadic relation):

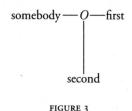

FIGURE 3

Here is an often-used way of defining an ordered pair. We can define the ordered pair *a;b* as the set composed of the set *a* and the set *a,b*, where (*a*) is simply the set one obtains at or before the first location in the order intended in *a;b*, and (*a,b*) is the set obtained at or before the second location in the order intended in *a;b*. This, however, is no better, for a triadic relation is evident in the definition of ordered pair, almost in the common sense way. Furthermore, the set (*a;b*) presupposed in the definition itself presupposes a triad as in the case of Robert Earl's unordered pair.

Some set theoreticians take a more simplified approach. For example

Jean E. Rubin writes in *Set Theory for the Mathematician*: "The actual technique used to define an ordered pair is unimportant. . . . What is important, however, is that it is a set and it has the one property that an ordered pair must have to deserve its name. That is $(x;y) = (u;v)$ implies that $(x = u$ & $y = v)$" (p. 47). This definition also presupposes Robert Earl's triad. But let us hold that card in reserve, and consider the definition from another aspect. The definition could be understood as a way in which the equality relation can be used to produce the notion of order.

I take this definition to mean that if two ordered pairs are equal, then it follows that the first element of the first pair must be equal to the first element of the second pair (and ditto for the second elements of the two pairs), and that if this condition holds, we therefore have an ordered pair. But one cannot produce order in this way without implicitly introducing the above mentioned triadic relation. Consider two unordered pairs p,q and r,s. And suppose that we are talking about a universe of discourse that does not include the predicate of serial order. We now assert that $p = r$ and $q = s$. In so saying we have not introduced a concept of serial order into this serially orderless universe. However, if we now allow the predicate of serial order to enter our universe, for p to be equal to r, the two must be equal in all predicates, including the serial order predicate. And for a pair to be ordered, someone must combine them according to some principle of order. Therefore, it seems to me that this method of defining an ordered pair cannot smuggle in the requisite conception of order using the notion of equality, so it is no different from the first common sense case.

Some set theoreticians simply avoid verbiage and get right to the point by unflinchingly biting the bullet in (it seems to me) an unavoidable manner, for example Samuel Selby and Leonard Sweet in *Sets, Relations, Functions: An Introduction*: "A pair of objects, one of which is designated as the first component and the other as the second component, is called an ordered pair" (p. 73). Here clearly we are asked to consider a designator, a combiner, an orderer—whether a person, an intelligent algorithm, or a Martian—as being the agency which brings two components together and designates one as first and another as second. And if we imagine such a thing, what we are imagining is a triadic relation.

The process of producing a set, whether ordered or unordered, is in-

303 *Appendix II*

deed just that: a process. The process begins with no set present. A set-maker comes on the scene and puts two things together in imagination. At the end of that process we have something new, a set. This set is what Peirce would have called a "hypostatic abstraction." By that he meant that it is often profitable within inquiry to give the result of a predictable and already known process a noun or substantive name, and to thereby refer to it as a fact. And to refer to such substantives routinely sometimes leads researchers to forget the original process. Perhaps that has happened in the case of set theory. I believe that one could add a small footnote to Peirce's notion of a hypostatic abstraction by saying that when science is intimately involved in studying a problem for the first time, the language of research is typically full of process phrases. Once a piece of research is complete, known, de-pendable, often the language of research becomes noun-like in regard to those items just recently mastered, so one can handily refer to the previously established results in the context of the new problems at hand.

One paragraph in Paul Halmos's *Naïve Set Theory* strikes me as pro-phetic: "However important set theory may be now, when it began some scholars considered it a disease from which, it was to be hoped, mathematics would soon recover. For this reason many set-theoretic considerations were called pathological, and the word lives on in mathematical usage; It often refers to something the speaker does not like. The explicit definition of an ordered pair $[(a;b) = (a),(a,b)]$ is frequently relegated to pathological set theory" (pp. 24–25). I would not use the term "pathological." There is nothing wrong from my point of view about the concept of ordered pair; however, there is good reason to think that there is something inappropriate about conceiving it as being a dyadic relation. Therefore, someone who uses the notion to reduce triadic relations is really reducing a triad to a collection composed of dyads plus one triad (ordered pair)—or plus two if one adds Robert Earl's triad. Obviously I have not advanced anything like a formal proof that ordered pairs are triadic. I have tried instead to appeal to the level of reasonable considerations.

Abraham Fraenkel ended his article on set theory for *The Encyclopedia of Philosophy* (Vol. 7) by stating that "the modern development of set theory seems to shatter mathematics altogether, at least in its analytical parts. New axioms apparently need to be introduced, corresponding to a deeper understanding of the primitive concepts underlying logic and mathematics. Yet nobody has so far succeeded in discovering even a direction in which such axioms might be sought" (p. 426). One wonders if Peirce's logic of relatives, which accepts triadic relation as a primitive, might be a direction that Fraenkel has considered. In any case, these words seem to suggest that set theory is at a revolutionary phase of its development. Perhaps one of the reasons it has reached a dead end is its almost studious elimination of triadic relations in its explicit fundamentals—one hardly finds overt discussions of triadic relations anywhere in treatises on set theory, and never as far as I can see, as a primitive element. It is as if they were not real. This means that set theory as it is now constituted harbors a serious implicit metaphysical bias, which might be some part of the cause of its apparent self-limitation.

The first case to be considered now may have provided Hartshorne with a false lead in his dealings with Peirce's categories. In 1934, Eugene Freeman published *The Categories of Charles Peirce*, still a solid treatise on the subject. Hartshorne wrote its preface. There are a number of prescient insights in this work, an important one being Freeman's recognition that Peirce was a mathematical empiricist. Freeman realized that valency was important in the basis of Peirce's categories, and he proceeded to give an outline of the matter. After a good start, however, he made some mistakes. After introducing the graphical forms of monads, dyads, and triads, he forgot to mention that all bonding occurs two at a time. And when he began to present diagrams of actual compositions (bondings) of graphs and relation sentences, he made additional mistakes. For instance (on p. 16), composition of two monads is represented as:

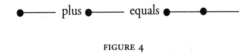

FIGURE 4

This shows a bond at a place Peirce did not allow, and because of that, a result with the wrong valency is produced. Freeman's bonding of two monads produced another monad. Bonding of two monads in Peirce's system actually produces a medad, a zero-valent graph in which every loose end is bonded, thus:

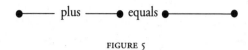

FIGURE 5

A similar mistake was made in Freeman's next example, which I draw here first in its erroneous form, followed by the correct form:

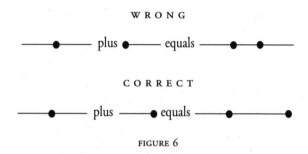

WRONG

CORRECT

FIGURE 6

Three other graphs he drew are correct.

In Peirce's system, a monad bonded to a monad always produces a medad; a dyad bonded with a monad always produces a monad; a dyad bonded with a dyad always produces another dyad; a dyad bonded with a triad always produces another triad; a triad bonded with a triad produces a tetrad, and so on.

When Freeman turned from graphs to parallel English sentences, he again made some serious errors. I list below his first such form, followed by the correct form:

WRONG

The monad "there is whiteness" plus the monad "there is hardness" gives the more complex monad "there is whiteness and there is hardness."

CORRECT

The monad "something is white" plus the monad "something is hard" gives the medad "some white thing is a thing that is hard," or "Some white thing is hard," the Aristotelian *I* proposition, in other words (see "Peirce's 'Most Lucid and Interesting Paper': An Introduction to Cenopythagoreanism").

He gave three additional examples like this one, incorporating relations of higher adicity. But in the additional three cases provided, bonding cannot occur in the way Freeman described, principally because most sentences in his examples are already medads—sentences with no "loose ends"—and hence not further bondable on Peirce's approach.

Freeman was aware that Peirce moved from this basis to a set of hypotheses about metaphysical categories, Firstness, Secondness, and Thirdness. But with this seriously erroneous grasp of the basis, his description of the transition from basis to categories must be suspect.

The next instance to be considered does involve more than a suspicion. Arthur Skidmore, another student of Charles Hartshorne, has argued for the incorrectness of Peirce's Nonreduction Theorem. His argument, illustrated below in graphical form, is that three dyads *can* be combined to form a triad:

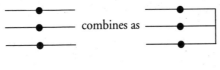

FIGURE 7

That this is wrong from Peirce's point of view can be seen from either one of two standpoints. From one, the move is incorrect because it allows three loose ends to be bonded in one step. Peirce allowed two and only two loose ends to be joined in any single act of bonding. So this move would simply not be licensed by Peirce's valency analysis system. From another standpoint, the diagram in the right side of Figure 7 *can* be construed in Peirce's system as the composition of three dyads and one triad, thus:

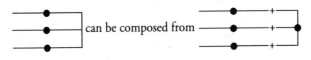

FIGURE 8

This, of course, does not break Peirce's Nonreduction Theorem, for here one has composed a triad from three dyads and a triad. The point of triple junction was something Peirce allowed (which he called "teridentity"), but he clearly recognized it as a triadic relation. Herzberger has given additional reasons for rejecting Skidmore's account as inconsistent with that of Peirce.

Rosemarie Christopherson and Henry Johnstone are two additional persons with suspicions about the Nonreduction Theorem. The reason they give is by now familiar: Set-theorists know that all relations can be treated as sets of ordered pairs, and that as a consequence n-place relations can be reduced to dyadic ones. This claim has been covered above. They go on to consider Thirdness with suspicion, but since this falls outside the basis, it is beyond my present scope.

In "A Revision of Peirce's Categories" in *Creativity in American Philosophy*, Hartshorne characterizes Peirce's approach in this way: "Peirce regards the single other as definitive of Secondness, and dependence upon two others [Thirdness] as essentially different, while dependence on more than two can, he holds, be reduced to cases of Thirdness. Thus he *counts the number of items* on which a phenomenon depends, defining Firstness as dependence on zero others, Secondness, on one other, Thirdness, on two others, and dismissing all higher numbers as reducible. My suggestion is that here Peirce misapplied the numerical model and thereby incurred needless trouble. . . . The number of items on which a phenomenon depends or does not depend is, I suggest, categorically irrelevant. What counts are the *kinds of relations* of dependence or independence" (pp. 77–78).

Let us display in tabular form the basis Hartshorne attributes to Peirce alongside the basis Peirce actually used (where Roman numerals represent Peirce's categories):

Hartshorne

I = depend on no others
II = depend on one other
III = depend on two others

Peirce

I = kind of relations with monovalent external form
II = kind of relations with bivalent external form
III = kind of relations with trivalent external form

Again, I don't want to focus upon the categories proper (keeping them mostly in our peripheral vision), but I do want to inquire what kind of understanding about Peirce's basis Hartshorne might have, as exemplified in the remarks above. It strikes me that the first two sentences of the above paragraph are not at all what Peirce had in mind as the basis of his hypotheses about the categories. It would be helpful to know which passages from Peirce Hartshorne regards as supporting that interpretation. Counting the number of items upon which a phenomenon depends is something that Hartshorne has introduced, and it seems particularly foreign to Peirce's basis. This topic is repeated later in Hartshorne's paper "A Revision of Peirce's Categories," where he recommends, "He should not have been so fascinated, almost hypnotized, by the idea of counting, 'One, two, three.' " That is not the point at all within Peirce's basis; instead it is a question of topology interpreted over forms of relation. Simple counting is not the mathematical basis of Peirce's categories. Indeed, had Peirce (with his meticulous concern for terminology) proceeded in the way Hartshorne suggests, Peirce would have named his categories Zeroness, Firstness, and Secondness.

In a somewhat related essay, "Peirce's Fresh Look at Philosophical Problems," Hartshorne seems to accept the dismissal, supplied by his student Skidmore, of Peirce's Nonreduction Theorem. But he went on to say that his revision of Peirce's categories need not accept the Nonreduction Theorem, for he does not distinguish the categories by counting the number of terms in the dependence or independence relations. Now that seems strange, for the Nonreduction Theorem is at the heart of the basis of Peirce's categories. If one rejected that principle, which is so fundamental for Peirce, I don't see how Hartshorne can speak of a "revision"—it seems much more like a wholesale renovation, of the basis, at any rate. Perhaps in view of the previous discussion Hartshorne would not now accept Skidmore's proposed refutation of the Nonreduction Theorem.

I have the impression that Hartshorne wishes to have a categorial set in which each category is separable from the others. That is to say that on his account there would be a clear and pure instance of Firstness (and of each of the other categories). But this was not Peirce's way, for he asserted in many places that his categories were universal: each one and all of them are to be found in any experience in some degree; there is no pure example of any one of them. Indeed, some experiences exhibit more strongly one or another of the categories. For instance, surprise is a favorite example of

Secondness, but no experience of surprise on Peirce's view is lacking either in Firsts or Thirds. That is why Peirce called them the Universal Categories: each of them is in every experience. The phrase "Universal Categories" does not mean that "some category is to be found everywhere." The only way to gain some understanding of an individual category is to abstract each of them out of any given experience through clues such as valency. This means that to some extent Peirce was a rationalist—not an unexpected result, since his work incorporated a little bit of many things, usually combined in a brilliant new way.

Finally, Hartshorne tells us that what "really" counts are kinds of relations. That is precisely Peirce's point too. But the kinds Peirce had in mind were kinds of forms of relations; Hartshorne seems to have in mind material kinds of relations.

Would the above explorations in Peirce's basis make his approach more acceptable to Hartshorne, or influence Hartshorne to be less inclined to revise Peirce's categories, or perhaps bring him to accept them outright?

Notes

1. Professor Ketner sent Walker Percy the first draft of the lectures subsequently published in *Reasoning and the Logic of Things*, plus a draft of his essay entitled "Identifying Peirce's 'Most Lucid and Interesting Paper': An Introduction to Cenopythagoreanism," subsequently divided and published in two journals: *International Philosophical Quarterly*, 26 (December 1986), pp. 375–92, and *Transactions of the Charles S. Peirce Society*, 23 (Fall 1987), pp. 539–56.

2. See Appendix II for Ketner's "Peirce's 'Most Lucid and Interesting Paper': An Introduction to Cenopythagoreanism." The Ketner essays in Appendix II have been slightly modified, with the author's consent, so that the critical apparatus would not become burdensome. Those who wish to read the original versions should consult the bibliography at the end of this volume.

3. Professor Ketner sent Percy a number of Peirce's essays in xerox form.

4. See Appendix II for Ketner's "Charles Sanders Peirce: An Introduction" and Ketner's "Who Was Charles Sanders Peirce? And Does He Deserve Our Homage?."

5. The texts were subsequently published in *Classical American Philosophy: Essential Readings and Interpretative Essays*.

6. Published as Lecture 1 in *Reasoning and the Logic of Things*, pp. 105–22.

7. See Appendix II for Ketner's "Toward an Understanding of Peirce's Master Argument."

8. The essay, read originally at Texas A & M University, was an early draft of "Novel Science; or, How contemporary social science is not well and why literature and semeiotic provide a cure."

9. Professor Ketner sent Percy the first three volumes of *Charles Sanders Peirce: Contributions to "The Nation."*

10. Professor Ketner sent Percy a later draft of his essay "Toward an Understanding of Peirce's Master Argument."

11. Walker Percy is referring to Ketner's "Toward an Understanding of Peirce's Master Argument."

12. Professor Ketner circulated the following note to his colleagues in the social sciences at Texas Tech University, and the results were later forwarded to Percy: "I'm looking for books and articles that might discuss the theme that the social sciences nowadays are in a bad shape. To use the kind of language preferred by Thomas Kuhn, they are in paradigm crisis—the old one has worn out (or they never got their first one), and they haven't yet found another to take its place. For instance, a recent psychology commentator stated, 'Why is there just one accepted account of chemistry, but 400 brands of talk psychotherapy?' Similar comments could be made, it seems, about all of the social sciences. Can you provide any references on this or similar themes from within your discipline?"

13. Professor Ketner sent Percy an early draft of a book tentatively entitled *The Consequences of Mathematics*, which was later published as *Reasoning and the Logic of Things*. The quote that Percy refers to can be found on p. 151 of *Reasoning and the Logic of Things*.

14. These essays can be found in *CP* 5.213–357.

15. See *CP* 6.25.

16. See *CP* 7.583.

17. See *Semiotic and Significs: The Correspondence Between Charles S. Peirce and Victoria Lady Welby*, pp. 80–81.

18. Professors Hilary Putnam and Ketner asked Percy to be a principal speaker at the Charles Sanders Peirce Sesquicentennial International Congress, to be held September 5–10, 1989, at Harvard University.

19. In his letter of October 24, 1987, to Percy, Ketner recommended one book each by these two authors. When sending these two books, Ketner suggested that Percy read, in particular, Chapter 4 of Rochberg-Halton's *Meaning and Modernity*.

20. Professor Ketner had sent Percy a brief note asking whether or not he had *Peirce, Semeiotic, and Pragmaticism: Essays by Max H. Fisch*. He inclosed a postcard for easy reply.

21. See Appendix II for Ketner's "The Importance of Religion for Peirce."

22. Professor Ketner had sent Percy a copy of the prospectus of his current course (Spring 1988) on the semeiotic of Peirce and Percy, and asked if Percy would like to comment on some of the students' papers. In this prospectus, he noted that the class would be introduced to the subject of semeiotic through a consideration of *Lost in the Cosmos, Love in the Ruins*, the work of Peirce (in *Classical American Philosophy: Essential Readings and Interpretative Essays*), and the work of Josiah Royce (also in the Stuhr anthology).

23. See Appendix II for Ketner's "Novel Science; or, How contemporary social science is not well and why literature and semeiotic provide a cure." An early version of this essay was sent to Percy.

24. See Appendix II for Peirce's letter to Papini.

25. Walker Percy had this operation on March 10, 1988.

26. Professor Ketner informed Percy that the National Endowment for the Humanities had decided to support the Peirce Sesquicentennial International Congress at Harvard University.

27. Professor Ketner had written to Percy about James Gleick's book *Chaos: Making a New Science* (New York: Viking, 1987).

28. See Appendix II for Ketner's "Pragmaticism is an Existentialism?."

29. See Appendix II for Ketner's "Hartshorne and the Basis of Peirce's Categories."

30. The reference is to Jean Umiker-Sebeok's letter, dated November 1, 1988 (see Appendix I). Professor Ketner wrote this brief note to Percy at the end of Umiker-Sebeok's letter.

31. Professor Ketner subsequently sent Percy a hand-written note indicating that he planned on attending the Jefferson Lecture.

32. Professor Ketner inclosed a U.S. Geological Survey map with Covington on it, plus a map and photographs of Arisbe and environs.

33. A sketch done by Percy's daughter, Mrs. John (Ann Percy) Moores, was inclosed.

34. Professor Ketner later sent Percy a copy of Donna Orange's *Peirce's Conception of God*.

35. See *Reasoning and the Logic of Things*, p. 10.

36. See *Reasoning and the Logic of Things*, pp. 8–11.

37. Professor Ketner inclosed a cartoon by Ben Sargent, plus the program for

the Charles Sanders Peirce Sesquicentennial International Congress to be held at Harvard University.

38. Letter of recommendation written and signed by Percy on behalf of Kenneth Laine Ketner to the National Endowment for the Humanities. It was typed on a form provided by the N.E.H.

39. A letter from Professor Ketner published in bowdlerized form as "Commentary" in *The Wilson Quarterly*, 13 (Autumn 1989), 143. On p. 144 of this issue, *The Wilson Quarterly* published a "Correction": "The photograph that appeared on p. 80 of the Summer 1989 issue of *The Wilson Quarterly*, identified as a picture of Charles Sanders Peirce, was in fact a picture of Joseph Lovering, a professor of mathematics and natural philosophy at Harvard University (1838–83). We received his photograph from the Harvard archives, which had mislabeled it as Peirce. We regret the error. At right is a photograph of Dr. Peirce taken about 1909 (five years before his death) at Arisbe, Peirce's home in Milford, Pennsylvania."

40. Professor Ketner had written Percy inquiring about his understanding of the term "philosophical anthropology." In reply to Percy's question, "Did CSP have a philosophical anthropology?," Ketner replied: "Yes, and the anthropologist Milton Singer has laid it out in his article 'For a Semiotic Anthropology'," in his *Man's Glassy Essence: Explorations in Semiotic Anthropology*.

41. See Robert W. Burch's *A Peircean Reduction Thesis: The Foundations of Topological Logic*.

42. Professor Ketner sent Percy a photo of himself taken at the Charles Sanders Peirce Sesquicentennial International Congress at Harvard University, along with a finished version of his essay "Pragmaticism is an Existentialism?."

43. Dean Langford sent Percy an unpublished paper he read to the Texas Tech Christian Faculty Association entitled "Walker Percy's Jefferson Lecture."

Bibliography

Four Basic Reference Works on Peirce

Collected Papers of Charles Sanders Peirce, edited by Charles Hartshorne and Paul Weiss (Volumes 1–6) and Arthur Burks (Volumes 7–8) (Cambridge: Harvard University Press, 1931–58). References to Peirce's papers begin with *CP* and are followed by volume and paragraph numbers. Also available (MS-DOS version) in the Past Masters series, InteLex Corporation, P.O. Box 859, Charlottesville, Va., 22901.

A Comprehensive Bibliography of the Published Works of Charles Sanders Peirce With a Bibliography of Secondary Studies (second edition, revised), edited by Kenneth Laine Ketner with the assistance of Arthur Franklin Stewart and Claude V. Bridges (Bowling Green, Ohio: Philosophy Documentation Center, Bowling Green State University, 1986). A microfiche edition of Peirce's extensive lifetime publications is available from the same source. References to Peirce's publications begin with *P*, followed by a number from this bibliography.

Peirce manuscripts in Houghton Library at Harvard University, beginning with *MS*—or L for letter—and followed by a number, refer to the system of identification established by Richard R. Robin in *Annotated Catalogue of the Papers of Charles S. Peirce* (Amherst: University of Massachusetts Press, 1967), or in Richard R. Robin, "The Peirce Papers: A Supplementary Catalogue," *Transactions of the Charles S. Peirce Society*, 7 (Winter 1971), pp. 37–57.

Peirce, Charles Sanders. *The New Elements of Mathematics* (5 volumes), edited by Carolyn Eisele (The Hague: Mouton de Gruyter, 1976).

Brent, Joseph. *Charles Sanders Peirce: A Life* (Bloomington: University of Indiana Press, 1993).

Burch, Robert W. *A Peircean Reduction Thesis: The Foundations of Topological Logic* (Lubbock: Texas Tech University Press, 1991).

Colapietro, Vincent M. *Peirce's Approach to the Self: A Semiotic Perspective on Human Subjectivity* (Albany: State University of New York Press, 1989).

Fisch, Max H. *Peirce, Semeiotic, and Pragmaticism: Essays by Max H. Fisch*, edited by Kenneth Laine Ketner and Christian J. W. Kloesel (Bloomington: Indiana University Press, 1986).

Ketner, Kenneth Laine. "Charles Sanders Peirce: An Introduction," in *Classical American Philosophy: Essential Readings and Interpretative Essays*, edited by John J. Stuhr (New York: Oxford University Press, 1987), pp. 13–25.

———. "Commentary," *The Wilson Quarterly*, 13 (Autumn 1989), p. 143. On p. 144 of this issue, *The Wilson Quarterly* published a "Correction."

———. *Elements of Logic: An Introduction to Peirce's Existential Graphs* (Lubbock: Texas Tech University Press, 1990).

———. "Hartshorne and the Basis of Peirce's Categories," in *Hartshorne, Process Philosophy, and Theology*, edited by Robert Kane and Stephen H. Phillips (Albany: State University of New York Press, 1989), pp. 135–49.

———. "Identifying Peirce's 'Most Lucid and Interesting Paper'," *Transactions of the Charles S. Peirce Society*, 23 (Fall 1987), pp. 539–56.

———. "Novel Science; or, How contemporary social science is not well and why literature and semeiotic provide a cure," *Semiotica*, 93 (1993), pp. 33–59.

———. "Peirce and Turing: Comparisons and Conjectures," *Semiotica*, 68 (1988), pp. 33–61.

———. "Peirce's 'Most Lucid and Interesting Paper': An Introduction to Cenopythagoreanism," *International Philosophical Quarterly*, 26 (December 1986), pp. 375–92.

———. "Pragmaticism is an Existentialism?," in *Frontiers in American Philosophy* (Volume 2), edited by Robert W. Burch (College Station: Texas A & M University Press (forthcoming).

————. "The Importance of Religion for Peirce," in *Gedankenzeichen: Festschrift für Klaus Oehler*, edited by Regina Claussen and Roland Daube-Schackat (Tübingen: Stauffenburg Verlag, 1988), pp. 267–71.

————. "Toward an Understanding of Peirce's Master Argument," *Cruzeiro Semiotico* (Lisbon, Portugal), 8 (Janeiro 1988), pp. 57–66.

————. "Who Was Charles Sanders Peirce? And Does He Deserve Our Homage?," *Krisis*, 1 (Summer 1983), pp. 10–18.

Manicas, Peter T. *A History and Philosophy of the Social Sciences* (Oxford, England: Basil Blackwell, 1987).

Moore, Edward C., editor. *Charles S. Peirce and the Philosophy of Science: Papers From the Harvard Sesquicentennial Congress* (Tuscaloosa: University of Alabama Press, 1993).

Orange, Donna. *Peirce's Conception of God: A Developmental Study* (Lubbock: Institute for Studies in Pragmaticism at Texas Tech University, 1984).

Peirce, Charles Sanders. *Charles Sanders Peirce: Contributions to "The Nation": Part 1: 1869–1893*, edited by Kenneth Laine Ketner and James Edward Cook (Lubbock: Texas Tech University Press, 1975).

————. *Charles Sanders Peirce: Contributions to "The Nation": Part 2: 1894–1900*, edited by Kenneth Laine Ketner and James Edward Cook (Lubbock: Texas Tech University Press, 1978).

————. *Charles Sanders Peirce: Contributions to "The Nation": Part 3: 1900–1908*, edited by Kenneth Laine Ketner and James Edward Cook (Lubbock: Texas Tech University Press, 1979).

————. *Charles Sanders Peirce: Contributions to "The Nation": Part 4: Index*, edited by Kenneth Laine Ketner (Lubbock: Texas Tech University Press, 1987).

————. *Reasoning and the Logic of Things: The Cambridge Conferences Lectures of 1898 by Charles Sanders Peirce*, edited by Kenneth Laine Ketner with an introduction by Kenneth Laine Ketner and Hilary Putnam (Cambridge: Harvard University Press, 1991).

————. *Writings of Charles S. Peirce: A Chronological Edition*, edited by Max H. Fisch et al. (Bloomington: Indiana University Press, 1982-).

Poinsot, John. *Tractatus de Signis: The Semiotic of John Poinsot*, with interpretive arrangement by John Deely (Berkeley: University of California Press, 1985).

Potter, S. J., Vincent G. *Charles S. Peirce on Norms and Ideals* (Amherst: University of Massachusetts Press, 1967).

Proceedings of the C. S. Peirce Bicentennial International Congress, edited by Kenneth Laine Ketner, Joseph M. Ransdell, Carolyn Eisele, Max H. Fisch, and Charles S. Hardwick (Lubbock: Texas Tech University Press, 1981).

Rochberg-Halton, Eugene. *Meaning and Modernity* (Chicago: University of Chicago Press, 1986).

Sebeok, Thomas A. *American Signatures: Semiotic Inquiry and Method*, edited by Iris Smith (Norman: University of Oklahoma Press, 1991).

———. *The Play of Musement* (Bloomington: Indiana University Press, 1981).

Semiotic and Significs: The Correspondence Between Charles S. Peirce and Victoria Lady Welby, edited by Charles S. Hardwick (Bloomington: Indiana University Press, 1977).

The Semiotic Web, edited by Thomas A. Sebeok and Jean Umiker-Sebeok (Berlin: Mouton de Gruyter, 1989).

Singer, Milton. *Man's Glassy Essence: Explorations in Semiotic Anthropology* (Bloomington: Indiana University Press, 1984).

Transactions of the Charles Peirce Society: A Quarterly Journal in American Philosophy (Greenwood, Florida: Penkevill Publishing Company).

Index

Abbot, Francis, 223; *Scientific Theism*, 9, 217

Aelred of Rievaulx, Saint, 127; *De spiritali amicitia*, 136

Agassiz, Louis, 243

American Journal of Semiotics, The, 179, 250

American Men of Science, 232

Aristotle/Aristotelian philosophy, 36, 98, 119, 209, 210, 222

Ashworth, Earline J., 179

Atlantic Monthly, The, 284, 286

Augustine, Saint, 140

Austin, John, 107

Bacon, Francis, 222

Bakker, James, 139

Bakhtin, Mikhail, 69

Baldwin, James Mark, 34

Bannister, Bryan, 54, 55, 73; "Semeiotic, Valency Equivalence, and Cenopythagoreanism," 56

Barta, Peter, 69

Bellow, Saul, 123

Berkeley, Bishop George, 79, 285, 286

Block, Ned, *Imagery*, 249, 278

Boole, George/Boolean set theory, 210, 227

Bork, Judge Robert, 142

Brecht, Bertholt, 69, 176

Brock, Jarret, "An Introduction to Peirce's Theory of Speech Acts," 17

Brodmann 44 (area of brain), 24, 25

Brooks, Cleanth, 123

Brunning, Jacqueline, 300

Bruno, Fra, 284

Buber, Martin, 33, 122, 131

Buddha/Buddhism, 6, 8, 12, 57, 76, 79, 83, 93–94, 96, 130–31, 132,138, 225, 227, 253, 254

Burch, Robert W., 153, 155, 186–91; *A Peircean Reduction Thesis*, 160, 272–74, 282, 314 *n*41

Cambridge, Massachusetts, xii-xiii, 134, 145, 223, 232, 230, 266, 284, 289

Carlson, Neil R., 121; *Physiology of Behavior*, 73–74, 110